What a Long Strange Strip It's Been

What a Long Stra

Top Shelf
PRODUCTIONS

cartoons by
Keith Knight

nge Strip

It's Been

yet another
K CHRONICLES
compendium

Introduction by Keith's Evil Twin Sister

Dedicated

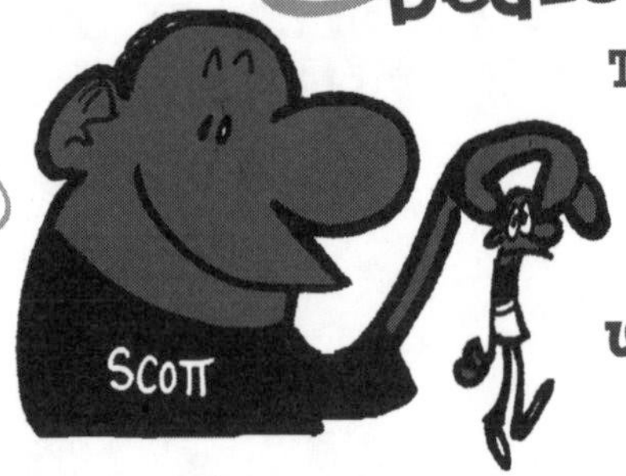
SCOTT

This book is dedicated to my "little" cousin, Scott Smith, who is showing the family what strength and courage really is... we love you.

Acknowledgments

Thanks to Pete and Lisa for their patience and most righteous skills: new publishers Chris and Brett for taking me on; Jennifer Joseph for starting the ball rolling; all the publications that run the strip; to my faithful readers (keep sending those tips and little victories!!); my friends; to Ms. Konietzka; and most of all, thanks and much, much love to my family (which is growing by leaps and bounds with every book!!)...I love you all.

The K Chronicles:
What a Long Strange Strip It's Been:
Yet another K Chronicles Compendium

For more information, please contact:
Top Shelf, P.O. Box 1282, Marietta, GA 30061-1282.
www.topshelfcomix.com
ISBN 1-891830-30-9 5 4 3 2 1
political cartoons / graphic novels
Printed in Canada.

Cover and book design: Pete Friedrich and Lisa Beres
at Charette Communication Design

Send tips and little victories to:

Keith Knight
P.O. Box 591794
San Francisco, Ca
94159-1794
keef@kchronicles.com
www.kchronicles.com

Also by Keith Knight:
Dances With Sheep: a K Chronicles Compendium (Manic D Press)
Fear of a Black marker: Another K Chronicles Compendium (Manic D Press)

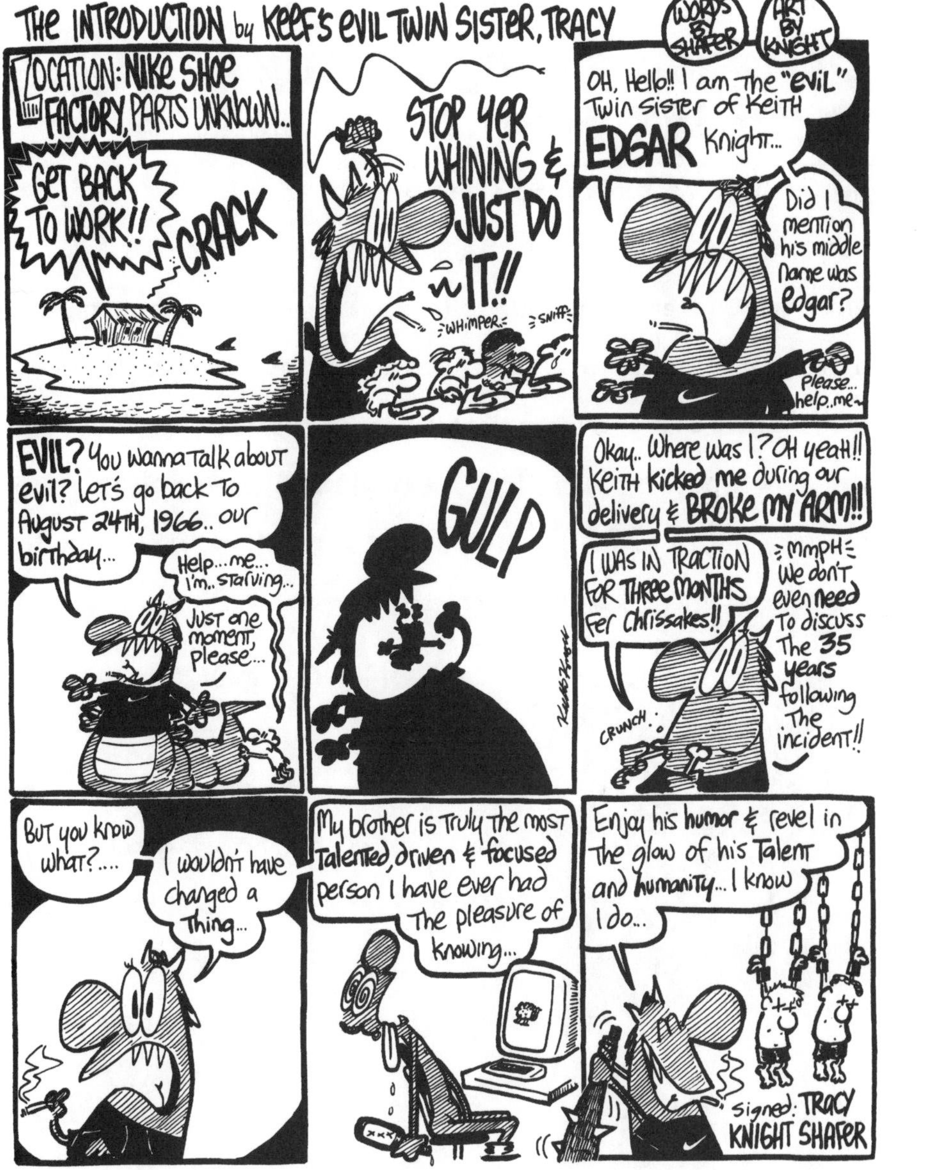
THE INTRODUCTION by KEEF'S EVIL TWIN SISTER, TRACY
WORDS BY SHAFER
ART BY KNIGHT
LOCATION: NIKE SHOE FACTORY, PARTS UNKNOWN...
GET BACK TO WORK!!
CRACK
STOP YER WHINING & JUST DO IT!!
WHIMPER
SNIFF
OH, Hello!! I am the "EVIL" Twin Sister of Keith EDGAR Knight...
Did I mention his middle name was Edgar?
Please... help..me...
EVIL? You wanna talk about evil? Let's go back to August 24th, 1966.. our birthday...
Help... me... I'm.. starving...
Just one moment, please...
GULP
Okay.. Where was I? OH yeah!! Keith kicked me during our delivery & BROKE MY ARM!!
I WAS IN TRACTION FOR THREE MONTHS Fer Chrissakes!!
MMPH
We don't even need to discuss the 35 years following the incident!!
CRUNCH
BUT you know what?....
I wouldn't have changed a thing...
My brother is truly the most talented, driven & focused person I have ever had the pleasure of knowing...
Enjoy his humor & revel in the glow of his talent and humanity... I know I do...
Signed: TRACY KNIGHT SHAFER

(**Note:** Tracy Knight Shafer is **NOT** a multi-armed, horned slug that smokes, eats children and works for NIke...)

Oh what a long strange strip it's been...

Sitting on my throne here in the corporate headquarters of K Chronicles Incorporated, located in a fortress-like castle perched atop the Swiss Alps, I sometimes wonder with amazement how it was only a mere ten years ago that I started this massive media empire in the tiny bedroom of a modest apartment in the heart of San Francisco. The K Chronicles is now a **multi-billion dollar** industry, with blimps, a **nude Las Vegas showgirl revue**, huge endorsement deals (in Japan), and its own

brand of bacon.

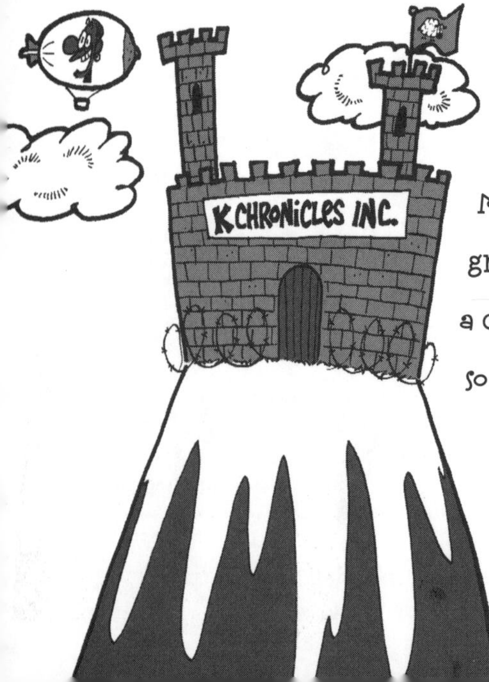
K CHRONICLES INC.

Many folks ask me, how do you stay grounded? How can you possibly create a comic strip that still resonates so strongly with the common people?

I will tell you:

INTERNS.

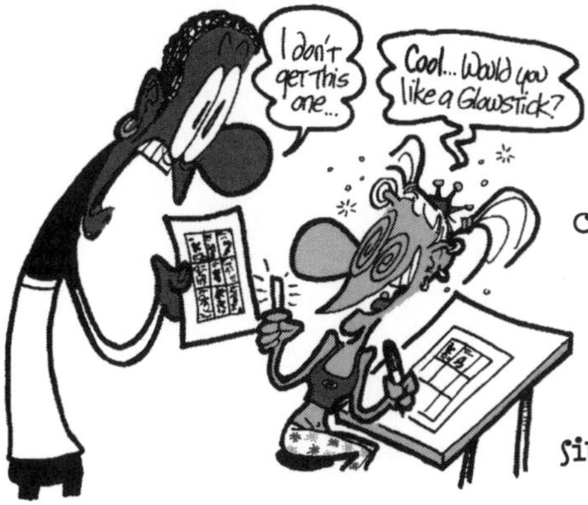
I don't get this one...
Cool... Would you like a Glowstick?

I stopped writing and drawing the comic strip YEARS ago when it was clearly evident that few people could relate to my honestly true, sincerely real-life adventures of cavorting with celebrities and royalty, high-priced call girls and the occasional gibbon. So I began taking on interns. Mostly ecstacy-addled art academy students with nothing better to do between raves. **Cheap labor for me and easy college credit for them.** K Chronicles Incorporated now employs several million people. Sewing t-shirts, stapling zines, stealing paper clips, and posing as me at comic book conventions. (Why do you think I have a different hair-do every time you see me?)

Oh, what a long strange strip it's been...

P.S.: And to all you **gawddamned patriotic hippies** who keep hassling me about sweatshop labor: K Chronicles Incorporated uses only **authentic American children** in its sweatshops. Ask them terrorists at Nike if they'd ever do that...

Cheers!

Keith Knight (C.E.O.)

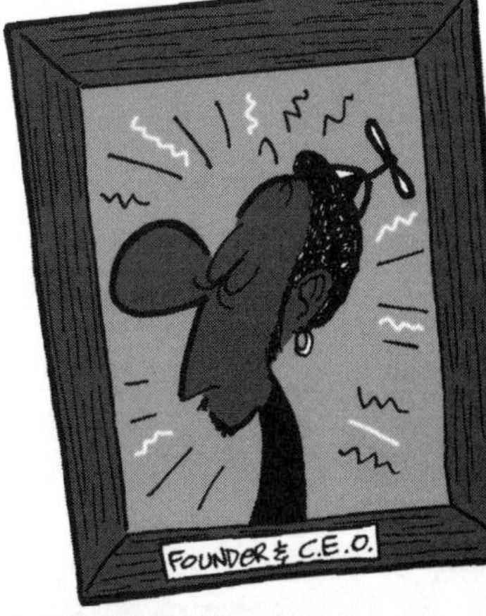
FOUNDER & C.E.O.

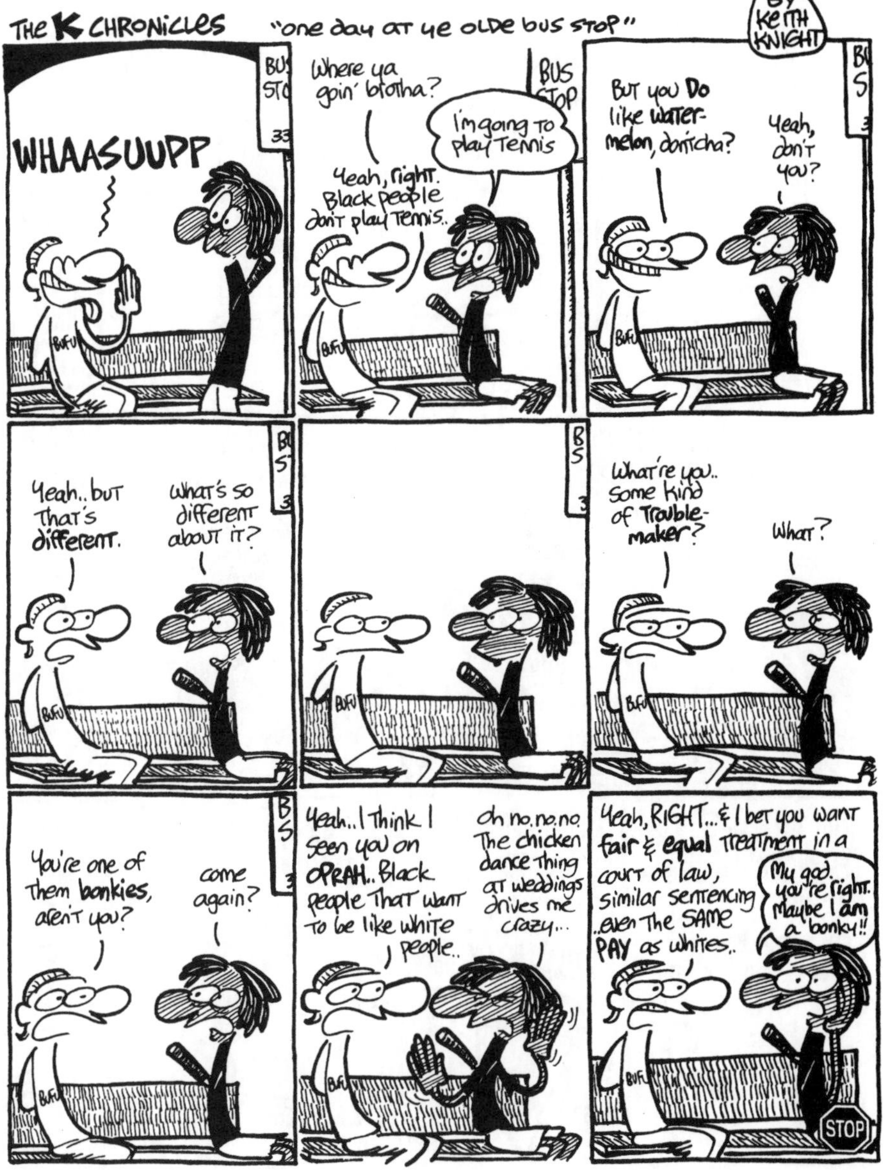
THE K CHRONICLES
"one day at ye olde bus stop"
BY KEITH KNIGHT
BUS STOP
WHAASUUPP
Where ya goin' brotha?
I'm going to play Tennis
Yeah, right. Black people don't play Tennis..
But you Do like water-melon, dontcha?
Yeah, don't you?
Yeah.. but That's different.
What's so different about it?
What're you.. Some kind of Trouble-maker?
What?
You're one of Them bonkies, aren't you?
come again?
Yeah.. I Think I seen you on OPRAH.. Black people That want to be like white people..
oh no. no. no. The chicken dance Thing at weddings drives me crazy...
Yeah, RIGHT... & I bet you want fair & equal Treatment in a court of law, similar sentencing ..even The SAME PAY as whites..
My god. you're right. Maybe I am a bonky!!
BUFU
STOP

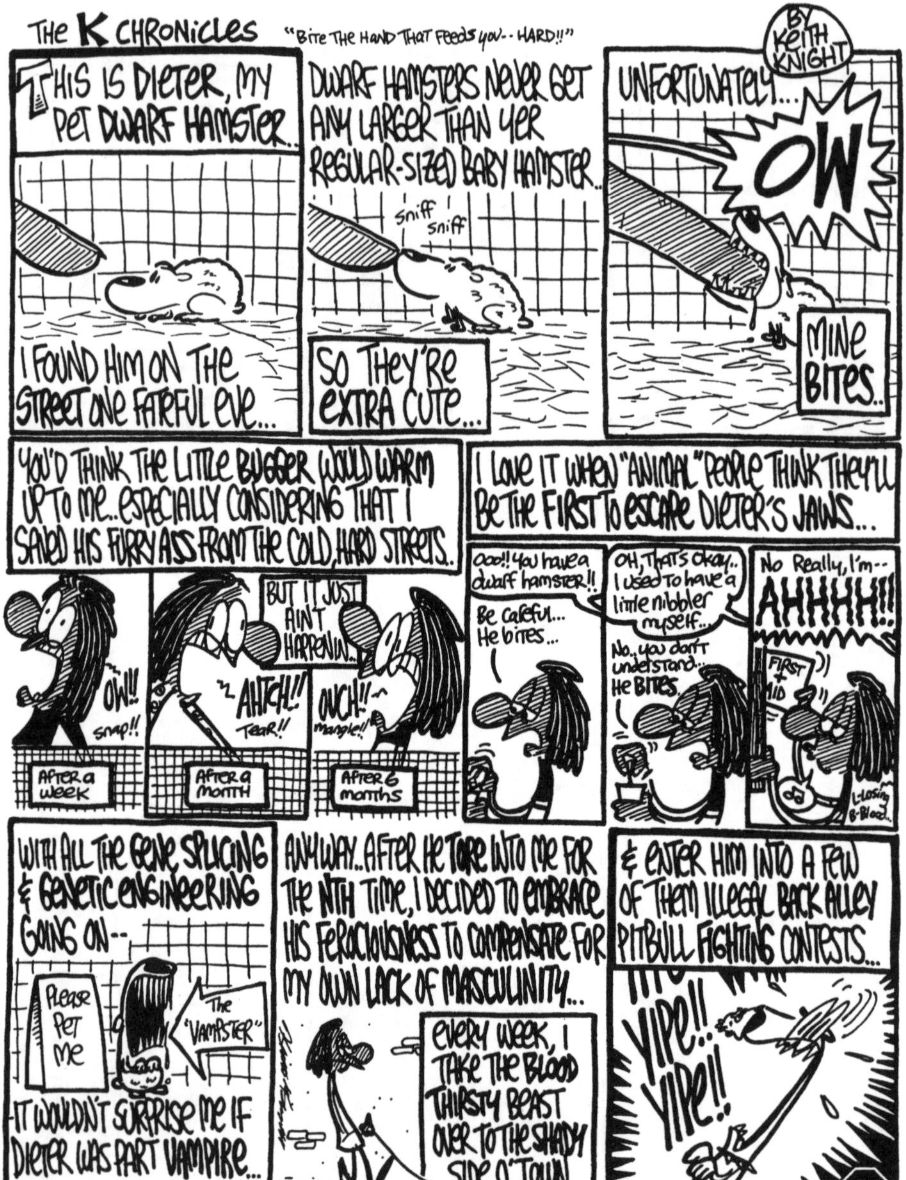
THE K CHRONICLES
"BITE THE HAND THAT FEEDS YOU-- HARD!!"
BY KEITH KNIGHT
THIS IS DIETER, MY PET DWARF HAMSTER..
I FOUND HIM ON THE STREET ONE FATEFUL EVE...
DWARF HAMSTERS NEVER GET ANY LARGER THAN YER REGULAR-SIZED BABY HAMSTER..
sniff sniff
SO THEY'RE EXTRA CUTE...
UNFORTUNATELY...
OW
MINE BITES..
YOU'D THINK THE LITTLE BUGGER WOULD WARM UP TO ME..ESPECIALLY CONSIDERING THAT I SAVED HIS FURRY ASS FROM THE COLD, HARD STREETS..
OW!!
snap!!
AFTER A WEEK
BUT IT JUST AIN'T HAPPENIN..
AHTCH!!
TEAR!!
AFTER A MONTH
OUCH!!
mangle!!
AFTER 6 MONTHS
I LOVE IT WHEN "ANIMAL" PEOPLE THINK THEY'LL BE THE FIRST TO ESCAPE DIETER'S JAWS...
Ooo!! You have a dwarf hamster!!
Be careful... He bites...
OH, THAT'S okay.. I used to have a little nibbler myself...
No.. you don't understand... He BITES.
No Really, I'm--
AHHHH!!
FIRST AID
L-Losing B-Blood..
WITH ALL THE GENE SPLICING & GENETIC ENGINEERING GOING ON--,
Please Pet Me
The "VAMPSTER"
IT WOULDN'T SURPRISE ME IF DIETER WAS PART VAMPIRE...
ANYWAY..AFTER HE TORE INTO ME FOR THE NTH TIME, I DECIDED TO EMBRACE HIS FEROCIOUSNESS TO COMPENSATE FOR MY OWN LACK OF MASCULINITY...
EVERY WEEK, I TAKE THE BLOOD THIRSTY BEAST OVER TO THE SHADY SIDE O' TOWN...
& ENTER HIM INTO A FEW OF THEM ILLEGAL BACK ALLEY PITBULL FIGHTING CONTESTS...
YIPE!!.. YIPE!!
STOP

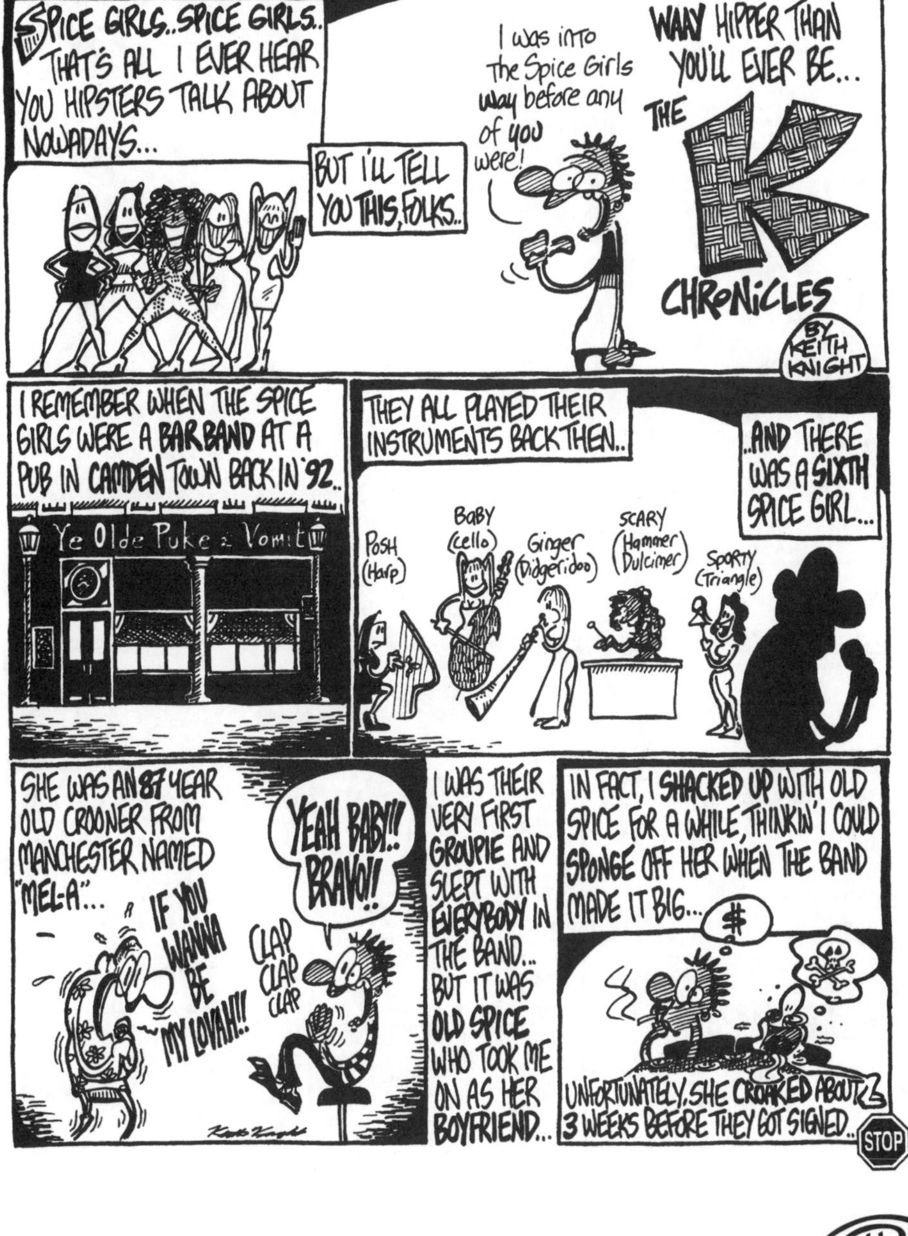

SPICE GIRLS..SPICE GIRLS.. THAT'S ALL I EVER HEAR YOU HIPSTERS TALK ABOUT NOWADAYS...
BUT I'LL TELL YOU THIS, FOLKS..
I was into The Spice Girls way before any of you were!
WAAY HIPPER THAN YOU'LL EVER BE... THE K CHRONICLES
BY KEITH KNIGHT
I REMEMBER WHEN THE SPICE GIRLS WERE A BAR BAND AT A PUB IN CAMDEN TOWN BACK IN '92..
Ye Olde Puke & Vomit
THEY ALL PLAYED THEIR INSTRUMENTS BACK THEN..
..AND THERE WAS A SIXTH SPICE GIRL...
POSH (Harp)
BABY (cello)
Ginger (Didgeridoo)
SCARY (Hammer Dulcimer)
SPORTY (Triangle)
SHE WAS AN 87 YEAR OLD CROONER FROM MANCHESTER NAMED "MEL-A"...
IF YOU WANNA BE MY LOVAH!!
YEAH BABY!!.. BRAVO!!
CLAP CLAP CLAP
I WAS THEIR VERY FIRST GROUPIE AND SLEPT WITH EVERYBODY IN THE BAND... BUT IT WAS OLD SPICE WHO TOOK ME ON AS HER BOYFRIEND...
IN FACT, I SHACKED UP WITH OLD SPICE FOR A WHILE, THINKIN' I COULD SPONGE OFF HER WHEN THE BAND MADE IT BIG...
$
UNFORTUNATELY, SHE CROAKED ABOUT 3 WEEKS BEFORE THEY GOT SIGNED...
STOP

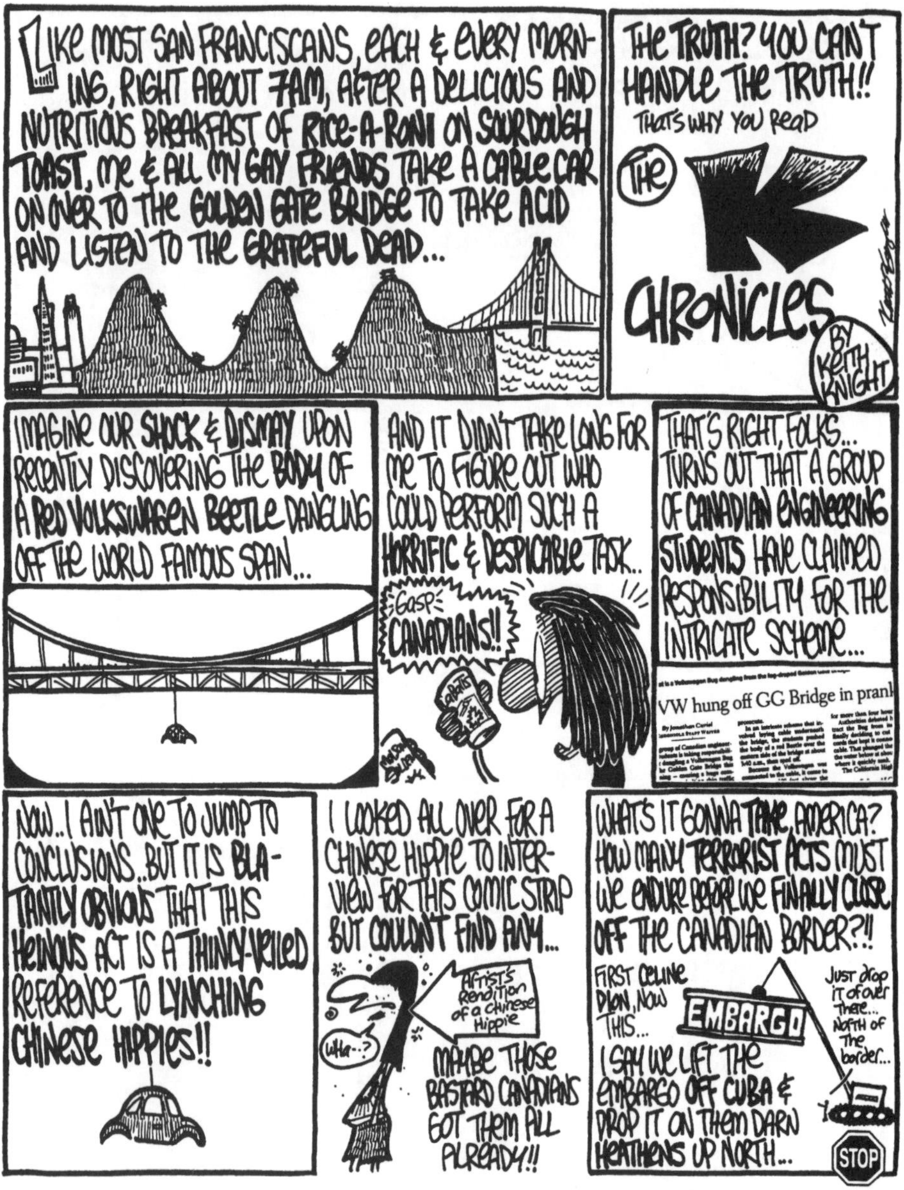
LIKE MOST SAN FRANCISCANS, EACH & EVERY MORNING, RIGHT ABOUT 7AM, AFTER A DELICIOUS AND NUTRITIOUS BREAKFAST OF RICE-A-RONI ON SOURDOUGH TOAST, ME & ALL MY GAY FRIENDS TAKE A CABLE CAR ON OVER TO THE GOLDEN GATE BRIDGE TO TAKE ACID AND LISTEN TO THE GRATEFUL DEAD...
THE TRUTH? YOU CAN'T HANDLE THE TRUTH!!
THAT'S WHY YOU READ
THE K CHRONICLES
BY KEITH KNIGHT
IMAGINE OUR SHOCK & DISMAY UPON RECENTLY DISCOVERING THE BODY OF A RED VOLKSWAGEN BEETLE DANGLING OFF THE WORLD FAMOUS SPAN...
AND IT DIDN'T TAKE LONG FOR ME TO FIGURE OUT WHO COULD PERFORM SUCH A HORRIFIC & DESPICABLE TASK...
GASP
CANADIANS!!
THAT'S RIGHT, FOLKS... TURNS OUT THAT A GROUP OF CANADIAN ENGINEERING STUDENTS HAVE CLAIMED RESPONSIBILITY FOR THE INTRICATE SCHEME...
VW hung off GG Bridge in prank
By Jonathan Curiel
NOW... I AIN'T ONE TO JUMP TO CONCLUSIONS... BUT IT IS BLATANTLY OBVIOUS THAT THIS HEINOUS ACT IS A THINLY-VEILED REFERENCE TO LYNCHING CHINESE HIPPIES!!
I LOOKED ALL OVER FOR A CHINESE HIPPIE TO INTERVIEW FOR THIS COMIC STRIP BUT COULDN'T FIND ANY...
Artist's Rendition of a Chinese Hippie
Wha-?
MAYBE THOSE BASTARD CANADIANS GOT THEM ALL ALREADY!!
WHAT'S IT GONNA TAKE, AMERICA? HOW MANY TERRORIST ACTS MUST WE ENDURE BEFORE WE FINALLY CLOSE OFF THE CANADIAN BORDER?!!
FIRST CELINE DION, NOW THIS...
EMBARGO
Just drop it off over there... North of the border...
I SAY WE LIFT THE EMBARGO OFF CUBA & DROP IT ON THEM DARN HEATHENS UP NORTH...
STOP

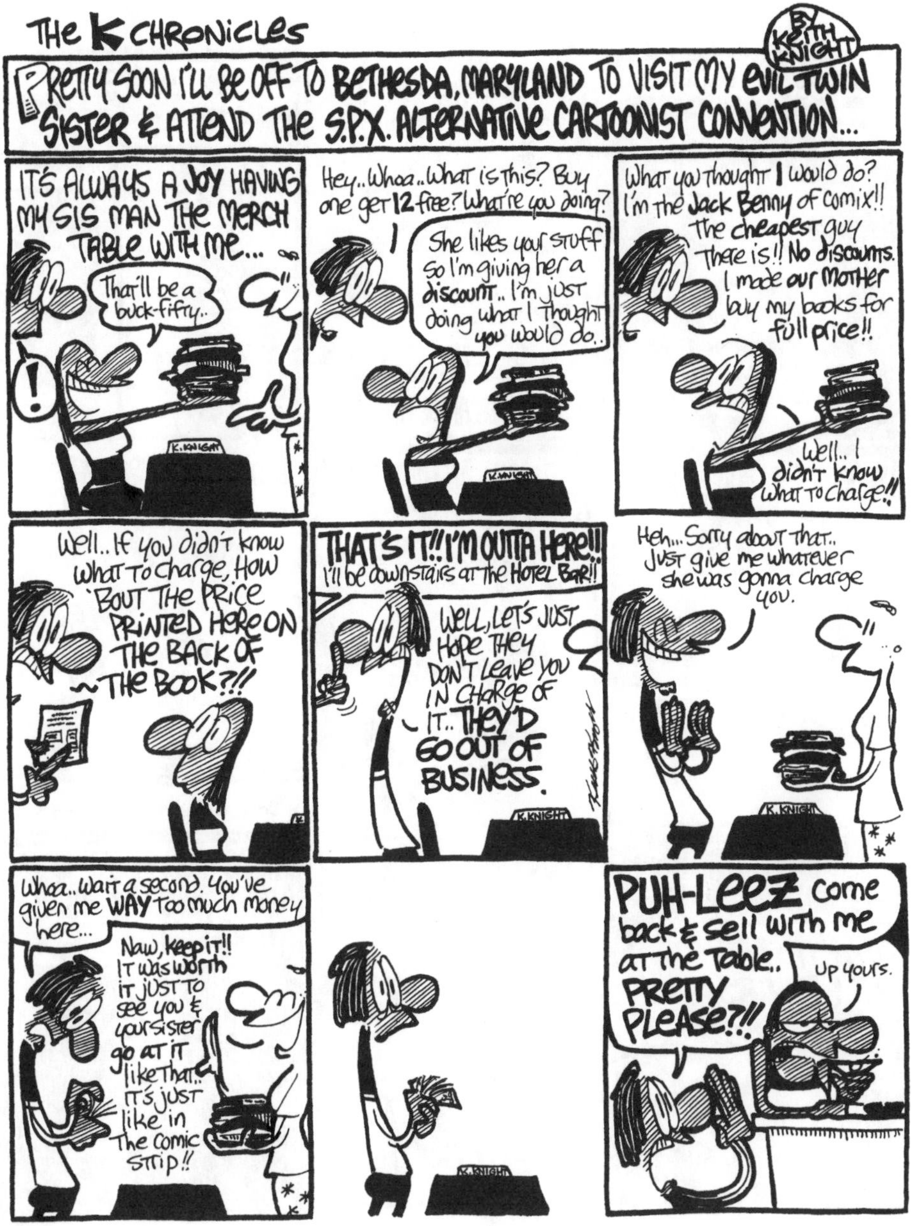
THE K CHRONICLES
BY KEITH KNIGHT
PRETTY SOON I'LL BE OFF TO BETHESDA, MARYLAND TO VISIT MY EVIL TWIN SISTER & ATTEND THE S.P.X. ALTERNATIVE CARTOONIST CONVENTION...
IT'S ALWAYS A JOY HAVING MY SIS MAN THE MERCH TABLE WITH ME...
That'll be a buck-fifty..
!
K. KNIGHT
Hey.. Whoa.. What is this? Buy one get 12 free? What're you doing?
She likes your stuff so I'm giving her a discount.. I'm just doing what I thought you would do..
K. KNIGHT
What you thought I would do? I'm the Jack Benny of comix!! The cheapest guy there is!! No discounts. I made our Mother buy my books for full price!!
Well.. I didn't know what to charge!!
Well.. If you didn't know what to charge, how 'bout the price printed here on the back of the book?!!
THAT'S IT!! I'M OUTTA HERE!! I'll be downstairs at the HOTEL BAR!!
WELL, LET'S JUST HOPE THEY DON'T LEAVE YOU IN CHARGE OF IT.. THEY'D GO OUT OF BUSINESS.
K. KNIGHT
Heh... Sorry about that.. Just give me whatever she was gonna charge you.
K. KNIGHT
Whoa.. Wait a second. You've given me WAY too much money here...
Naw, keep it!! It was worth it just to see you & your sister go at it like that.. It's just like in the comic strip!!
K. KNIGHT
PUH-LEEZ come back & sell with me at the table.. PRETTY PLEASE?!!
Up yours.

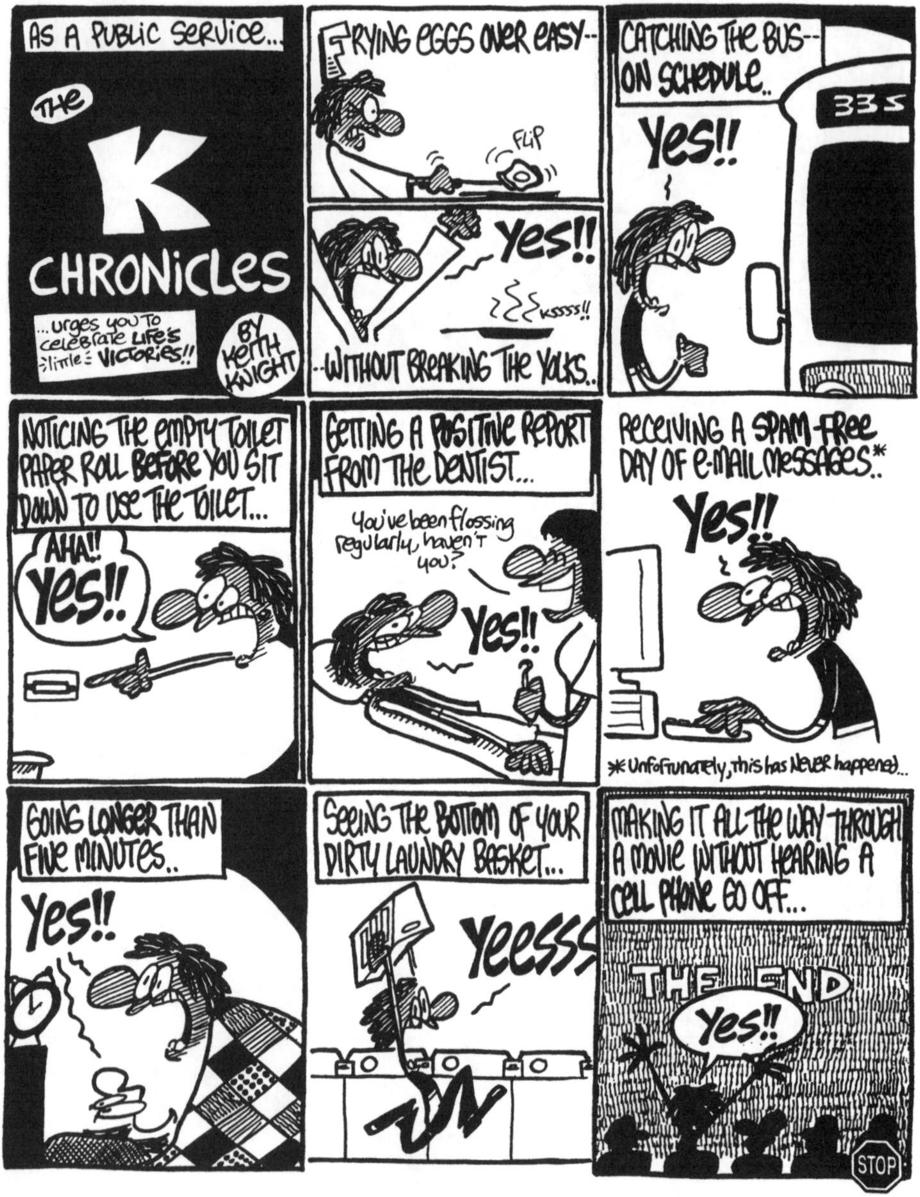

AS A PUBLIC SERVICE...
THE K CHRONICLES
...URGES YOU TO CELEBRATE LIFE'S LITTLE VICTORIES!!
BY KEITH KNIGHT
FRYING EGGS OVER EASY--
FLIP
YES!!
KSSSS!!
--WITHOUT BREAKING THE YOLKS..
CATCHING THE BUS--ON SCHEDULE..
33S
YES!!
NOTICING THE EMPTY TOILET PAPER ROLL BEFORE YOU SIT DOWN TO USE THE TOILET...
AHA!! YES!!
GETTING A POSITIVE REPORT FROM THE DENTIST...
You've been flossing regularly, haven't you?
YES!!
RECEIVING A SPAM-FREE DAY OF E-MAIL MESSAGES*..
YES!!
* Unfortunately, this has NEVER happened...
GOING LONGER THAN FIVE MINUTES..
YES!!
SEEING THE BOTTOM OF YOUR DIRTY LAUNDRY BASKET...
YEESSS
MAKING IT ALL THE WAY THROUGH A MOVIE WITHOUT HEARING A CELL PHONE GO OFF...
THE END
YES!!
STOP

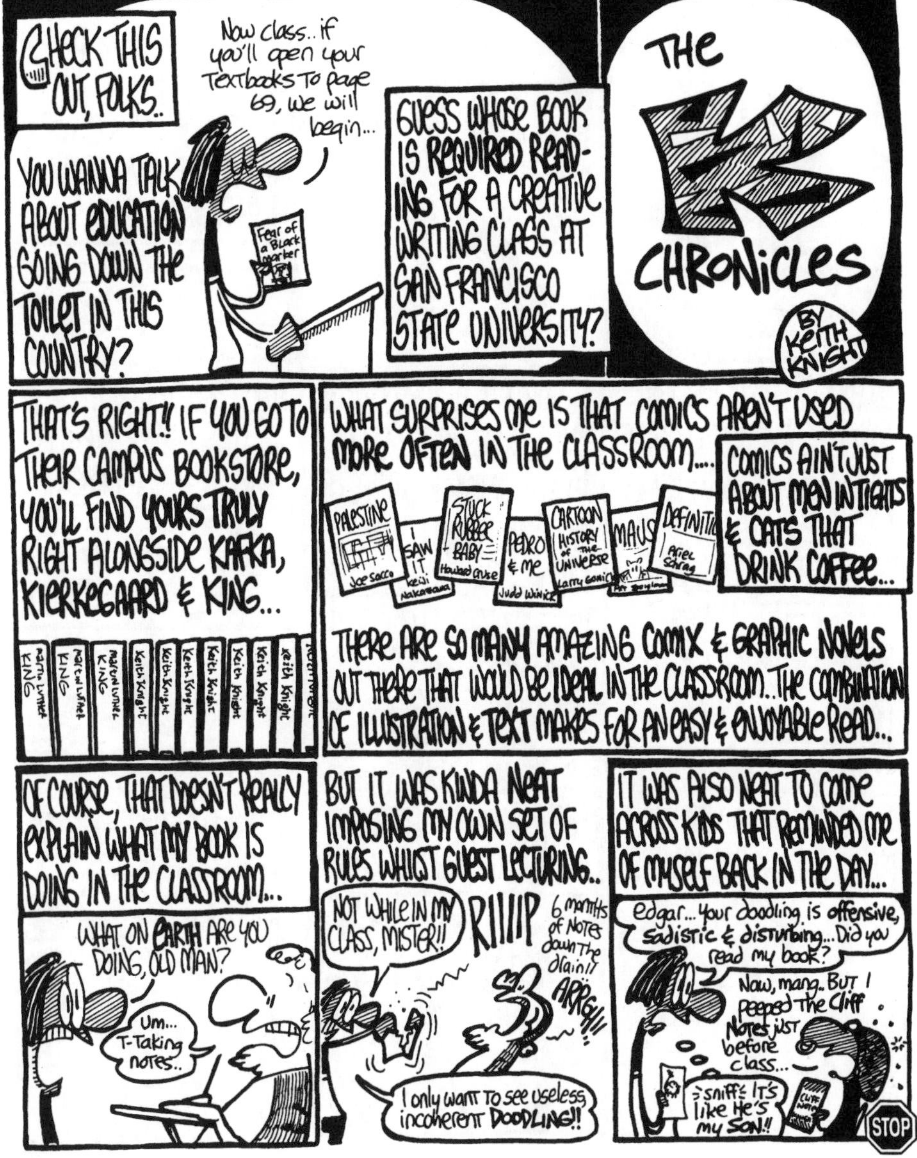

CHECK THIS OUT, FOLKS..
Now class.. if you'll open your Textbooks To page 69, we will begin...
YOU WANNA TALK ABOUT EDUCATION GOING DOWN THE TOILET IN THIS COUNTRY?
Fear of a Black marker
GUESS WHOSE BOOK IS REQUIRED READING FOR A CREATIVE WRITING CLASS AT SAN FRANCISCO STATE UNIVERSITY?
THE K CHRONICLES
BY KEITH KNIGHT
THAT'S RIGHT!! IF YOU GO TO THEIR CAMPUS BOOKSTORE, YOU'LL FIND YOURS TRULY RIGHT ALONGSIDE KAFKA, KIERKEGAARD & KING...
Martin Luther KING
Martin Luther KING
Martin Luther KING
Keith Knight
Keith Knight
Keith Knight
Keith Knight
Keith Knight
Keith Knight
Keith Knight
WHAT SURPRISES ME IS THAT COMICS AREN'T USED MORE OFTEN IN THE CLASSROOM....
COMICS AIN'T JUST ABOUT MEN IN TIGHTS & CATS THAT DRINK COFFEE...
PALESTINE Joe Sacco
I SAW IT Keiji Nakazawa
STUCK RUBBER BABY Howard Cruse
PEDRO & ME Judd Winick
CARTOON HISTORY OF THE UNIVERSE Larry Gonick
MAUS
DEFINITI Ariel Schrag
THERE ARE SO MANY AMAZING COMIX & GRAPHIC NOVELS OUT THERE THAT WOULD BE IDEAL IN THE CLASSROOM..THE COMBINATION OF ILLUSTRATION & TEXT MAKES FOR AN EASY & ENJOYABLE READ...
OF COURSE, THAT DOESN'T REALLY EXPLAIN WHAT MY BOOK IS DOING IN THE CLASSROOM...
WHAT ON EARTH ARE YOU DOING, OLD MAN?
Um... T-Taking notes..
BUT IT WAS KINDA NEAT IMPOSING MY OWN SET OF RULES WHILST GUEST LECTURING..
NOT WHILE IN MY CLASS, MISTER!!
RIIIIP
6 months of Notes down the drain!!
ARRGH!!
I only want to see useless, incoherent DOODLING!!
IT WAS ALSO NEAT TO COME ACROSS KIDS THAT REMINDED ME OF MYSELF BACK IN THE DAY...
edgar... your doodling is offensive, sadistic & disturbing... Did you read my book?
Naw, mang.. But I peeped the Cliff Notes just before class...
CLIFF NOTES
<sniff> IT'S like He's my SON!!
STOP

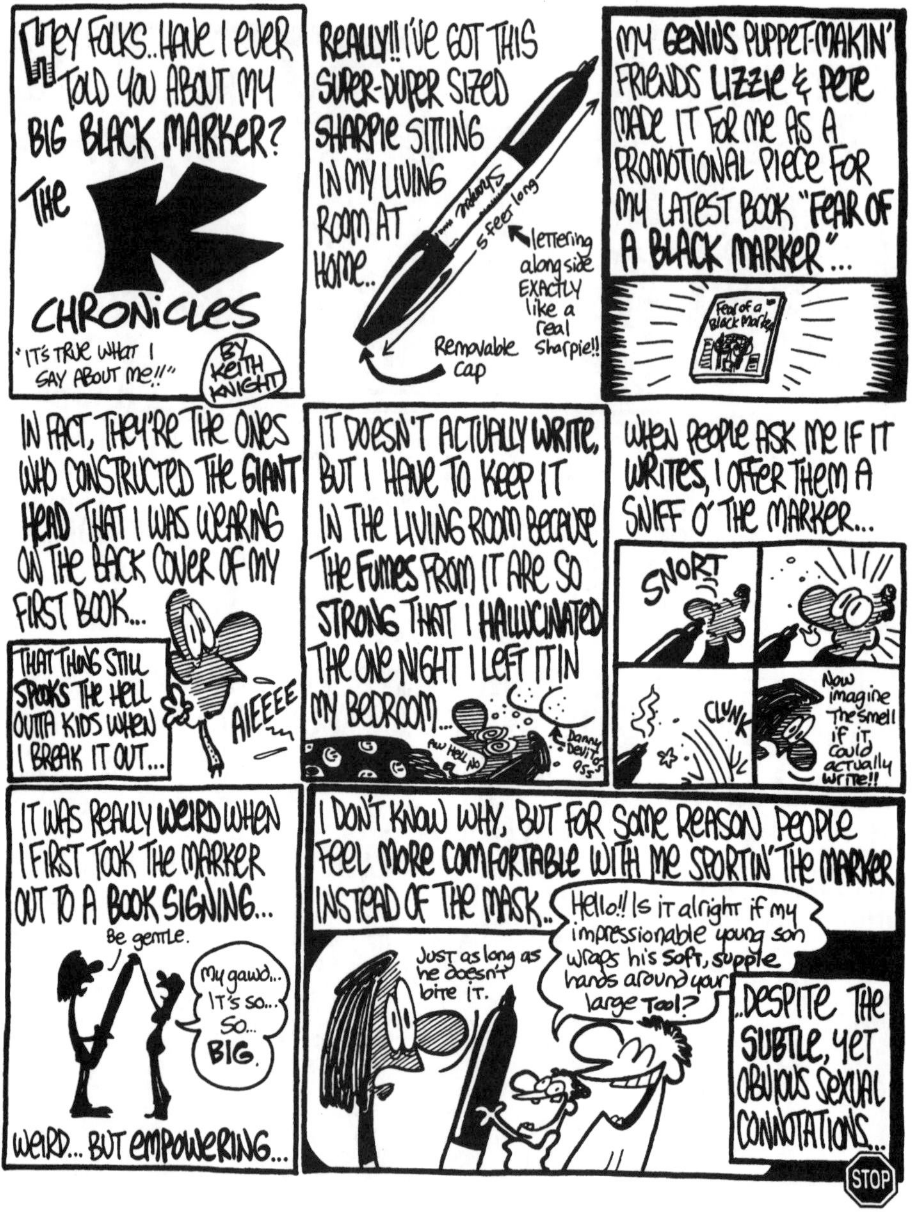
HEY FOLKS.. HAVE I EVER TOLD YOU ABOUT MY BIG BLACK MARKER?
THE K CHRONICLES
"IT'S TRUE WHAT I SAY ABOUT ME!!"
BY KEITH KNIGHT
REALLY!! I'VE GOT THIS SUPER-DUPER SIZED SHARPIE SITTING IN MY LIVING ROOM AT HOME...
Sharpie
5 feet long
lettering along side EXACTLY like a real Sharpie!!
Removable cap
MY GENIUS PUPPET-MAKIN' FRIENDS LIZZIE & PETE MADE IT FOR ME AS A PROMOTIONAL PIECE FOR MY LATEST BOOK "FEAR OF A BLACK MARKER"...
Fear of a Black Marker
IN FACT, THEY'RE THE ONES WHO CONSTRUCTED THE GIANT HEAD THAT I WAS WEARING ON THE BACK COVER OF MY FIRST BOOK...
THAT THING STILL SPOOKS THE HELL OUTTA KIDS WHEN I BREAK IT OUT...
AIEEEE
IT DOESN'T ACTUALLY WRITE, BUT I HAVE TO KEEP IT IN THE LIVING ROOM BECAUSE THE FUMES FROM IT ARE SO STRONG THAT I HALLUCINATED THE ONE NIGHT I LEFT IT IN MY BEDROOM...
AW HELL NO
Danny DeVito's ass
WHEN PEOPLE ASK ME IF IT WRITES, I OFFER THEM A SNIFF O' THE MARKER...
SNORT
CLUNK
Now imagine the smell if it could actually write!!
IT WAS REALLY WEIRD WHEN I FIRST TOOK THE MARKER OUT TO A BOOK SIGNING...
Be gentle.
My gawd... It's so... so... BIG.
WEIRD... BUT EMPOWERING...
I DON'T KNOW WHY, BUT FOR SOME REASON PEOPLE FEEL MORE COMFORTABLE WITH ME SPORTIN' THE MARKER INSTEAD OF THE MASK...
Hello!! Is it alright if my impressionable young son wraps his soft, supple hands around your large tool?
Just as long as he doesn't bite it.
...DESPITE THE SUBTLE, YET OBVIOUS SEXUAL CONNOTATIONS...
STOP

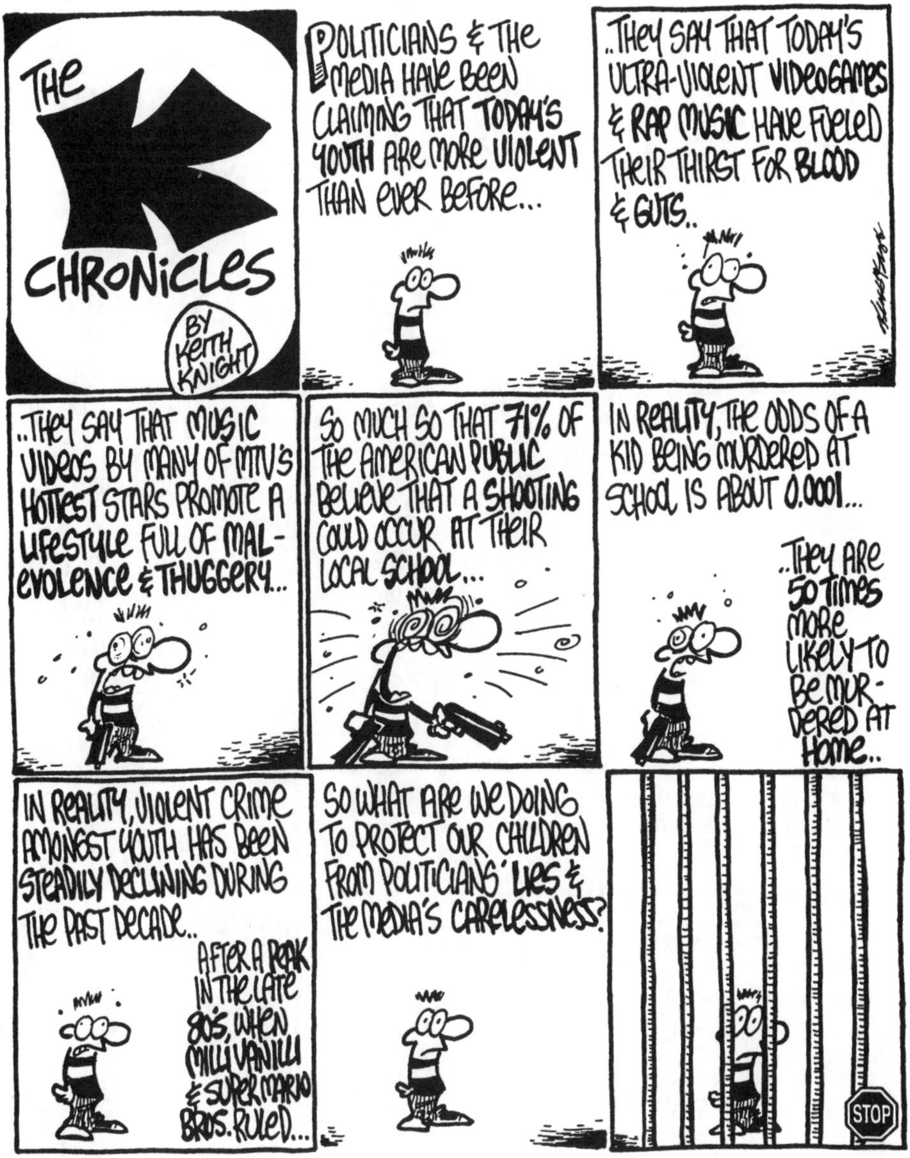
THE K CHRONICLES
BY KEITH KNIGHT
POLITICIANS & THE MEDIA HAVE BEEN CLAIMING THAT TODAY'S YOUTH ARE MORE VIOLENT THAN EVER BEFORE...
..THEY SAY THAT TODAY'S ULTRA-VIOLENT VIDEOGAMES & RAP MUSIC HAVE FUELED THEIR THIRST FOR BLOOD & GUTS..
..THEY SAY THAT MUSIC VIDEOS BY MANY OF MTV'S HOTTEST STARS PROMOTE A LIFESTYLE FULL OF MAL-EVOLENCE & THUGGERY...
SO MUCH SO THAT 71% OF THE AMERICAN PUBLIC BELIEVE THAT A SHOOTING COULD OCCUR AT THEIR LOCAL SCHOOL...
IN REALITY, THE ODDS OF A KID BEING MURDERED AT SCHOOL IS ABOUT 0.0001...
..THEY ARE 50 TIMES MORE LIKELY TO BE MUR-DERED AT HOME..
IN REALITY, VIOLENT CRIME AMONGST YOUTH HAS BEEN STEADILY DECLINING DURING THE PAST DECADE..
AFTER A PEAK IN THE LATE 80'S, WHEN MILLI VANILLI & SUPER MARIO BROS. RULED...
SO WHAT ARE WE DOING TO PROTECT OUR CHILDREN FROM POLITICIANS' LIES & THE MEDIA'S CARELESSNESS?
STOP

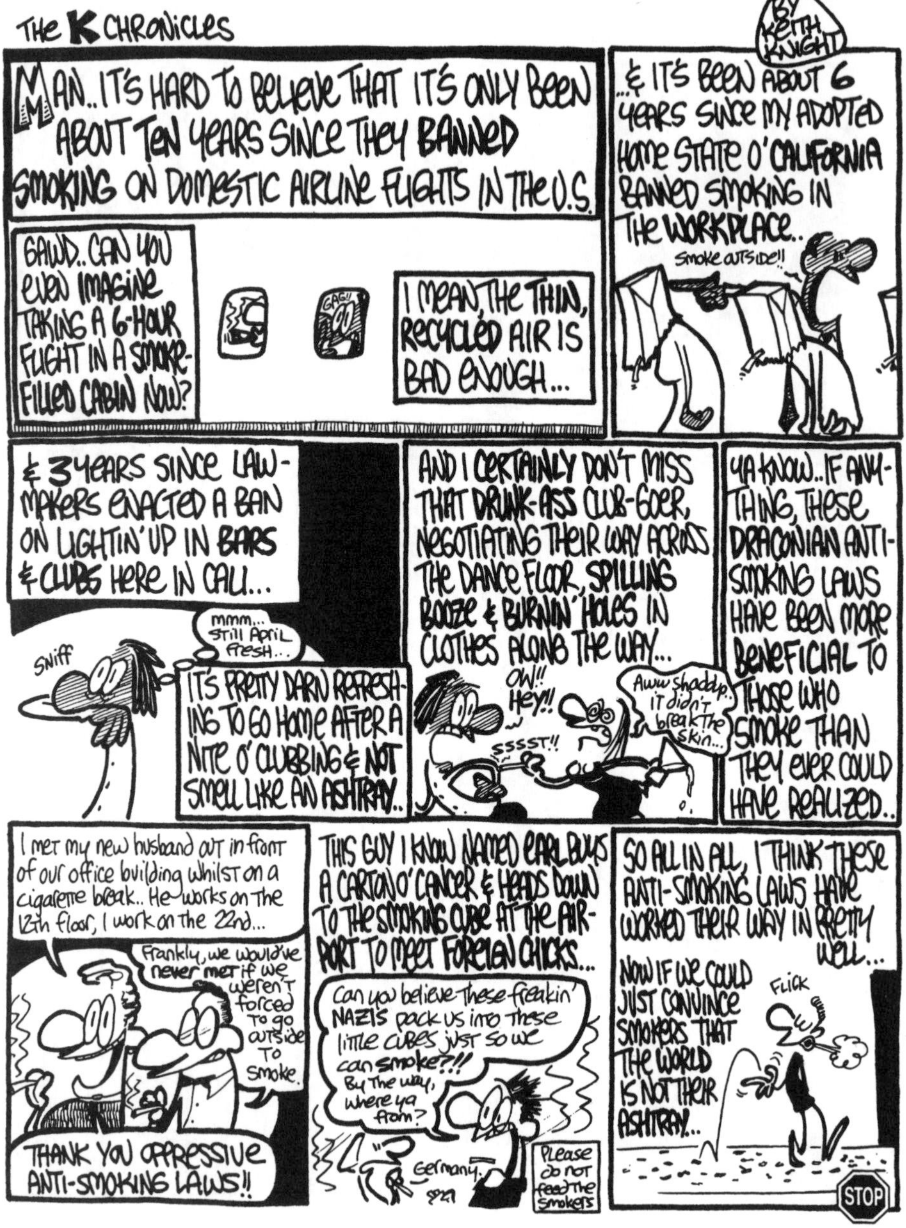

The K Chronicles
By Keith Knight
MAN.. IT'S HARD TO BELIEVE THAT IT'S ONLY BEEN ABOUT TEN YEARS SINCE THEY BANNED SMOKING ON DOMESTIC AIRLINE FLIGHTS IN THE U.S.
GAWD.. CAN YOU EVEN IMAGINE TAKING A 6-HOUR FLIGHT IN A SMOKE-FILLED CABIN NOW?
GAG!!
I MEAN, THE THIN, RECYCLED AIR IS BAD ENOUGH...
...& IT'S BEEN ABOUT 6 YEARS SINCE MY ADOPTED HOME STATE O' CALIFORNIA BANNED SMOKING IN THE WORKPLACE..
SMOKE OUTSIDE!!
& 3 YEARS SINCE LAW-MAKERS ENACTED A BAN ON LIGHTIN' UP IN BARS & CLUBS HERE IN CALI...
SNIFF
mmm... still April fresh...
IT'S PRETTY DARN REFRESHING TO GO HOME AFTER A NITE O' CLUBBING & NOT SMELL LIKE AN ASHTRAY..
AND I CERTAINLY DON'T MISS THAT DRUNK-ASS CLUB-GOER, NEGOTIATING THEIR WAY ACROSS THE DANCE FLOOR, SPILLING BOOZE & BURNIN' HOLES IN CLOTHES ALONG THE WAY...
OW!! Hey!!
SSSST!!
Aww shaddup.. It didn't break the skin...
YA KNOW.. IF ANYTHING, THESE DRACONIAN ANTI-SMOKING LAWS HAVE BEEN MORE BENEFICIAL TO THOSE WHO SMOKE THAN THEY EVER COULD HAVE REALIZED..
I met my new husband out in front of our office building whilst on a cigarette break.. He works on the 12th floor, I work on the 22nd...
Frankly, we would've never met if we weren't forced to go outside to smoke.
THANK YOU OPPRESSIVE ANTI-SMOKING LAWS!!
THIS GUY I KNOW NAMED EARL BUYS A CARTON O' CANCER & HEADS DOWN TO THE SMOKING CUBE AT THE AIRPORT TO MEET FOREIGN CHICKS...
Can you believe these freakin' NAZIS pack us into these little cubes just so we can smoke?!!
By the way, where ya from?
Germany.
Please do not feed the smokers
SO ALL IN ALL, I THINK THESE ANTI-SMOKING LAWS HAVE WORKED THEIR WAY IN PRETTY WELL...
NOW IF WE COULD JUST CONVINCE SMOKERS THAT THE WORLD IS NOT THEIR ASHTRAY..
FLICK
STOP

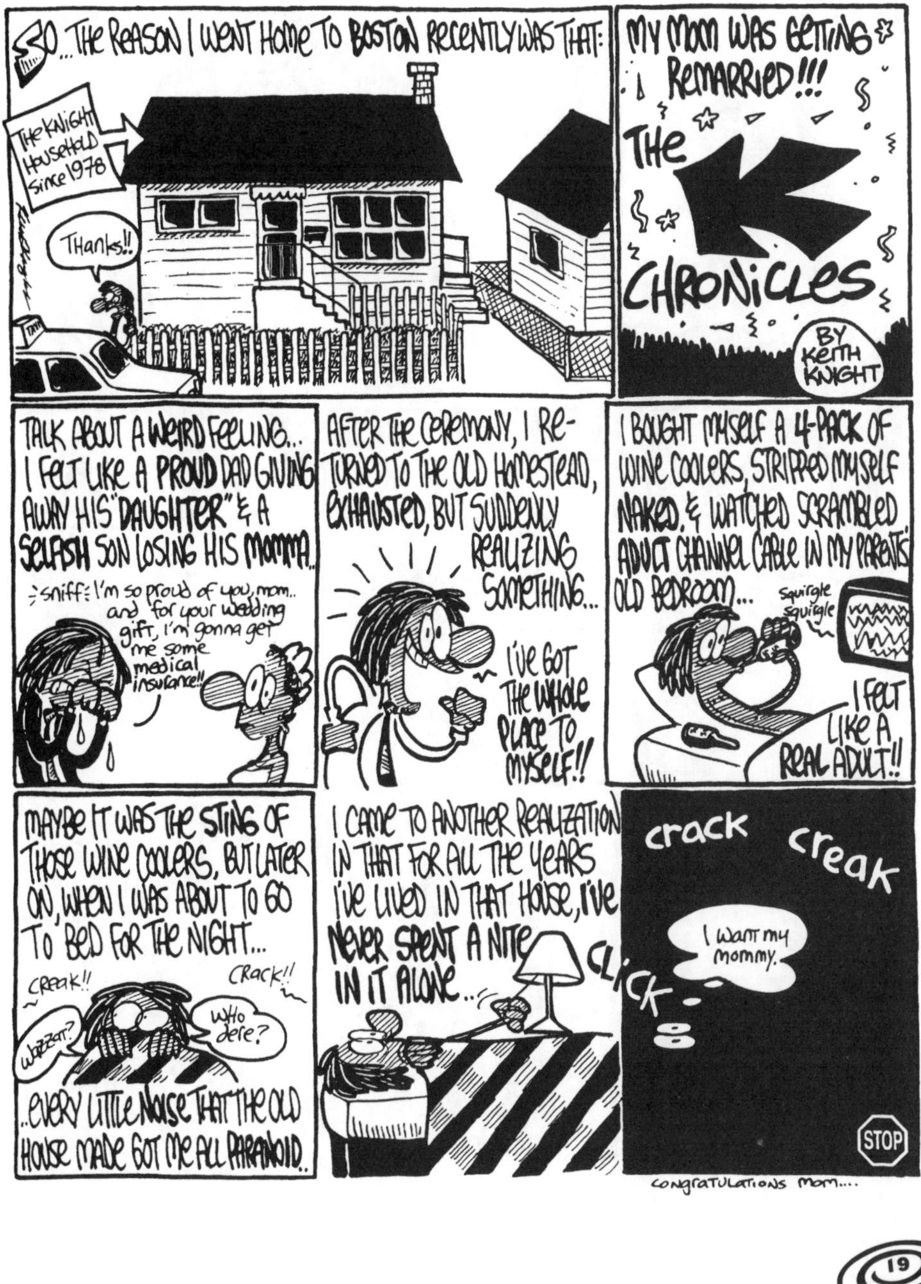
SO... THE REASON I WENT HOME TO BOSTON RECENTLY WAS THAT:
THE KNIGHT HOUSEHOLD SINCE 1978
THANKS!!
MY MOM WAS GETTING REMARRIED!!!
THE K CHRONICLES
BY KEITH KNIGHT
TALK ABOUT A WEIRD FEELING... I FELT LIKE A PROUD DAD GIVING AWAY HIS "DAUGHTER" & A SELFISH SON LOSING HIS MOMMA...
sniff I'm so proud of you, mom.. and for your wedding gift, I'm gonna get me some medical insurance!!
AFTER THE CEREMONY, I RETURNED TO THE OLD HOMESTEAD, EXHAUSTED, BUT SUDDENLY REALIZING SOMETHING...
I'VE GOT THE WHOLE PLACE TO MYSELF!!
I BOUGHT MYSELF A 4-PACK OF WINE COOLERS, STRIPPED MYSELF NAKED, & WATCHED SCRAMBLED ADULT CHANNEL CABLE IN MY PARENTS' OLD BEDROOM...
squiggle squiggle
I FELT LIKE A REAL ADULT!!
MAYBE IT WAS THE STING OF THOSE WINE COOLERS, BUT LATER ON, WHEN I WAS ABOUT TO GO TO BED FOR THE NIGHT...
CREAK!!
CRACK!!
WAZZAT?
WHO DERE?
..EVERY LITTLE NOISE THAT THE OLD HOUSE MADE GOT ME ALL PARANOID..
I CAME TO ANOTHER REALIZATION IN THAT FOR ALL THE YEARS I'VE LIVED IN THAT HOUSE, I'VE NEVER SPENT A NITE IN IT ALONE...
CLICK
crack
creak
I want my mommy.
STOP
congratulations mom....

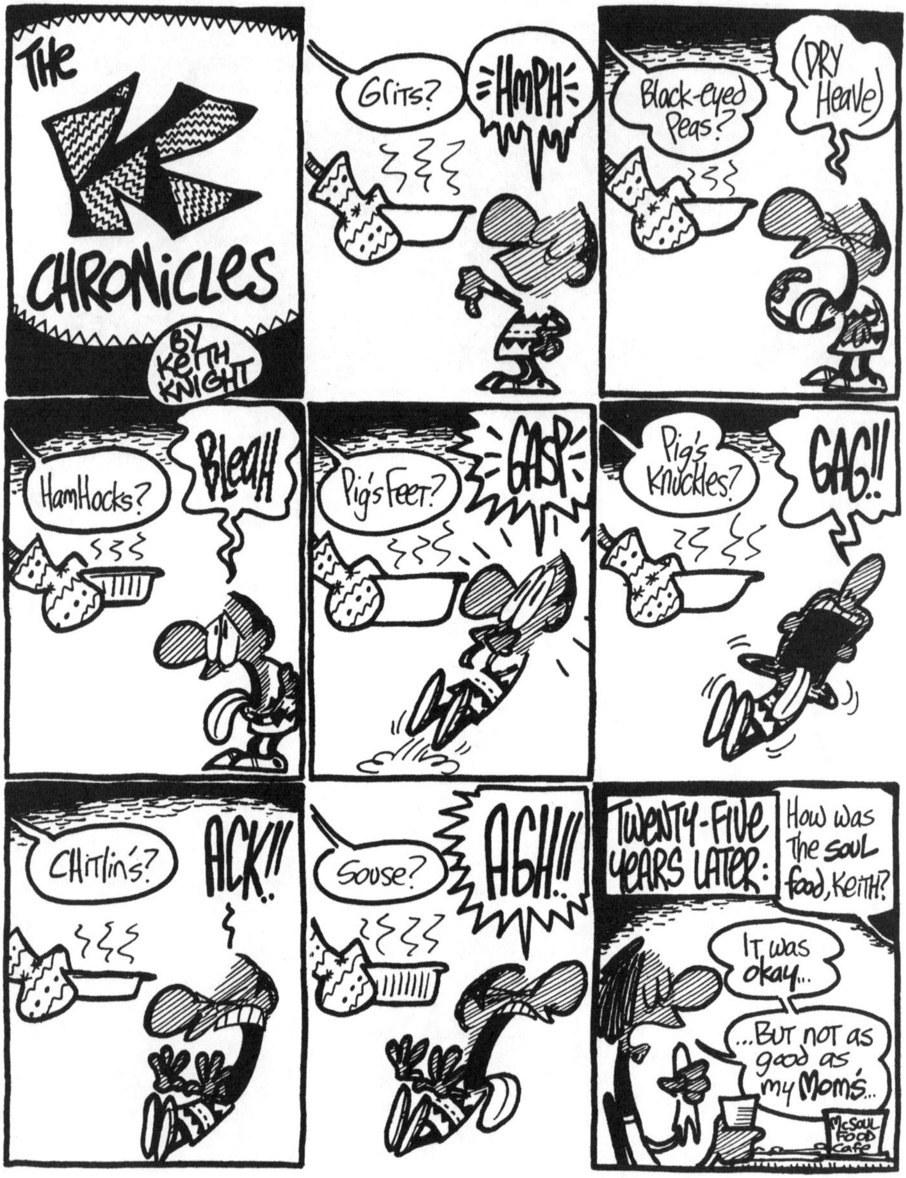
THE K CHRONICLES
BY KEITH KNIGHT
Grits?
HMPH
Black-eyed Peas?
(DRY Heave)
HamHocks?
BLeaH
Pig's Feet?
GASP
Pig's Knuckles?
GAG!!..
CHitlin's?
ACK!!..
Souse?
AGH!!..
TWENTY-FIVE YEARS LATER:
How was The SOUL food, KeiTH?
IT was okay...
...BUT NOT as good as my Mom's...
McSOUL FOOD Cafe

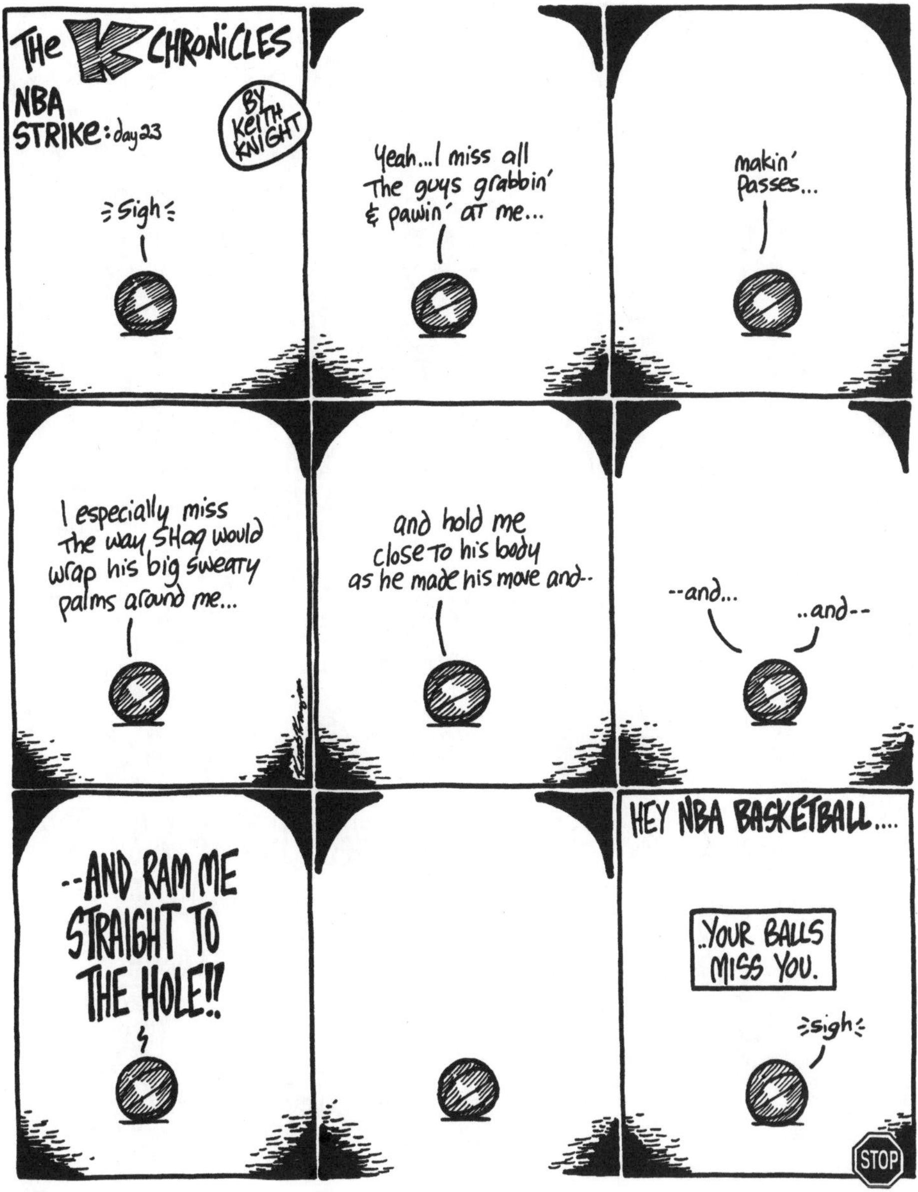
THE K CHRONICLES
NBA STRIKE: day 23
BY KEITH KNIGHT
Sigh
Yeah... I miss all the guys grabbin' & pawin' at me...
makin' passes...
I especially miss the way SHaq would wrap his big sweaty palms around me...
and hold me close to his body as he made his move and--
--and...
..and--
--AND RAM ME STRAIGHT TO THE HOLE!!
HEY NBA BASKETBALL....
..YOUR BALLS MISS YOU.
sigh
STOP

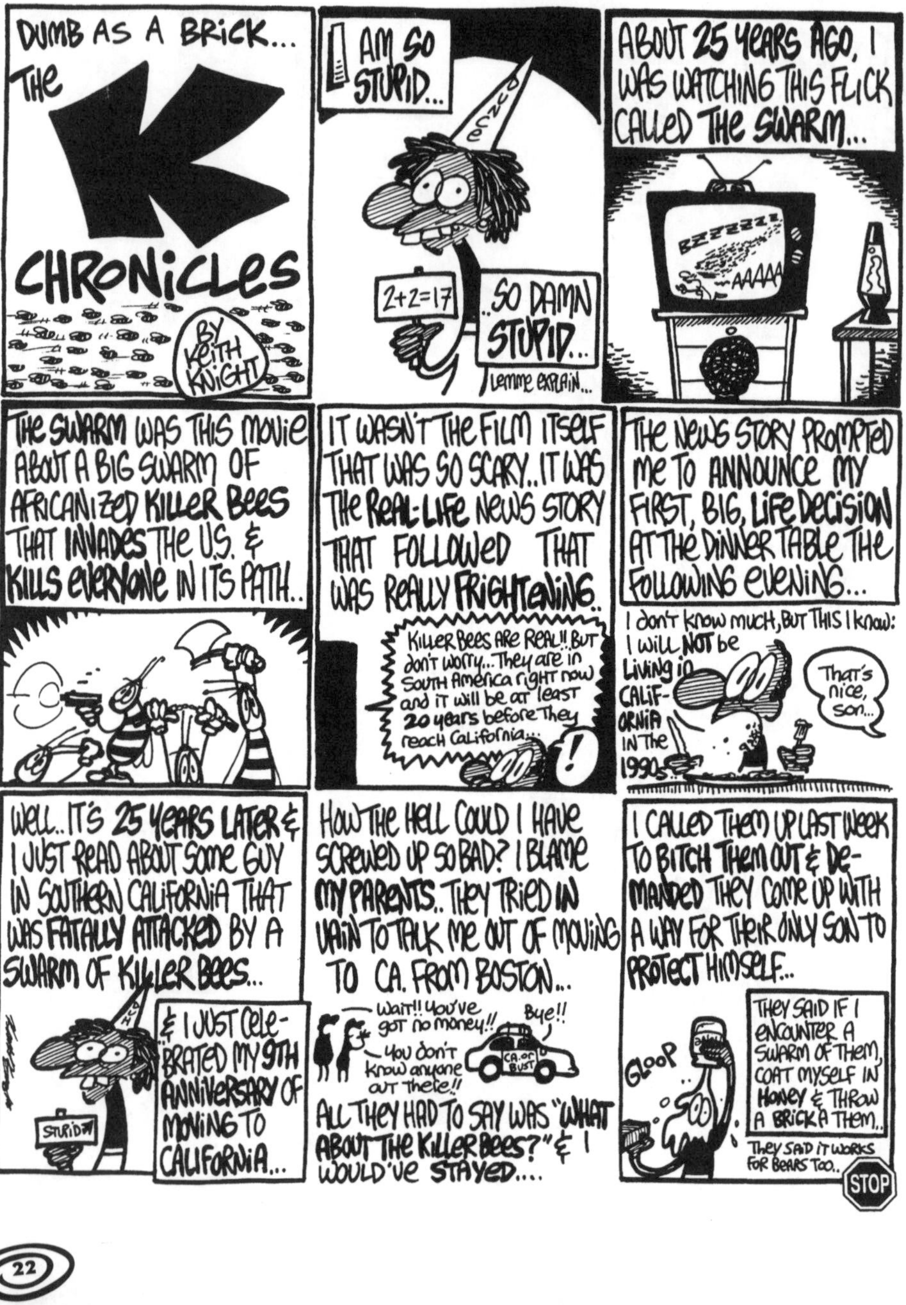

DUMB AS A BRICK...
THE K CHRONICLES
BY KEITH KNIGHT
I AM SO STUPID...
2+2=17
..SO DAMN STUPID...
LEMME EXPLAIN...
ABOUT 25 YEARS AGO, I WAS WATCHING THIS FLICK CALLED THE SWARM...
ZZZZZZZ
AAAAA
THE SWARM WAS THIS MOVIE ABOUT A BIG SWARM OF AFRICANIZED KILLER BEES THAT INVADES THE U.S. & KILLS EVERYONE IN ITS PATH..
IT WASN'T THE FILM ITSELF THAT WAS SO SCARY.. IT WAS THE REAL-LIFE NEWS STORY THAT FOLLOWED THAT WAS REALLY FRIGHTENING..
KILLER BEES ARE REAL!! BUT DON'T WORRY... THEY ARE IN SOUTH AMERICA RIGHT NOW AND IT WILL BE AT LEAST 20 YEARS BEFORE THEY REACH CALIFORNIA...
!
THE NEWS STORY PROMPTED ME TO ANNOUNCE MY FIRST, BIG, LIFE DECISION AT THE DINNER TABLE THE FOLLOWING EVENING...
I DON'T KNOW MUCH, BUT THIS I KNOW: I WILL NOT BE LIVING IN CALIFORNIA IN THE 1990S...
THAT'S NICE, SON...
WELL.. IT'S 25 YEARS LATER & I JUST READ ABOUT SOME GUY IN SOUTHERN CALIFORNIA THAT WAS FATALLY ATTACKED BY A SWARM OF KILLER BEES...
STUPID
& I JUST CELEBRATED MY 9TH ANNIVERSARY OF MOVING TO CALIFORNIA...
HOW THE HELL COULD I HAVE SCREWED UP SO BAD? I BLAME MY PARENTS.. THEY TRIED IN VAIN TO TALK ME OUT OF MOVING TO CA. FROM BOSTON...
WAIT!! YOU'VE GOT NO MONEY!!
YOU DON'T KNOW ANYONE OUT THERE!!
BYE!!
CA. OR BUST
ALL THEY HAD TO SAY WAS "WHAT ABOUT THE KILLER BEES?" & I WOULD'VE STAYED....
I CALLED THEM UP LAST WEEK TO BITCH THEM OUT & DEMANDED THEY COME UP WITH A WAY FOR THEIR ONLY SON TO PROTECT HIMSELF...
GLOOP
THEY SAID IF I ENCOUNTER A SWARM OF THEM, COAT MYSELF IN HONEY & THROW A BRICK A THEM..
THEY SAID IT WORKS FOR BEARS TOO..
STOP

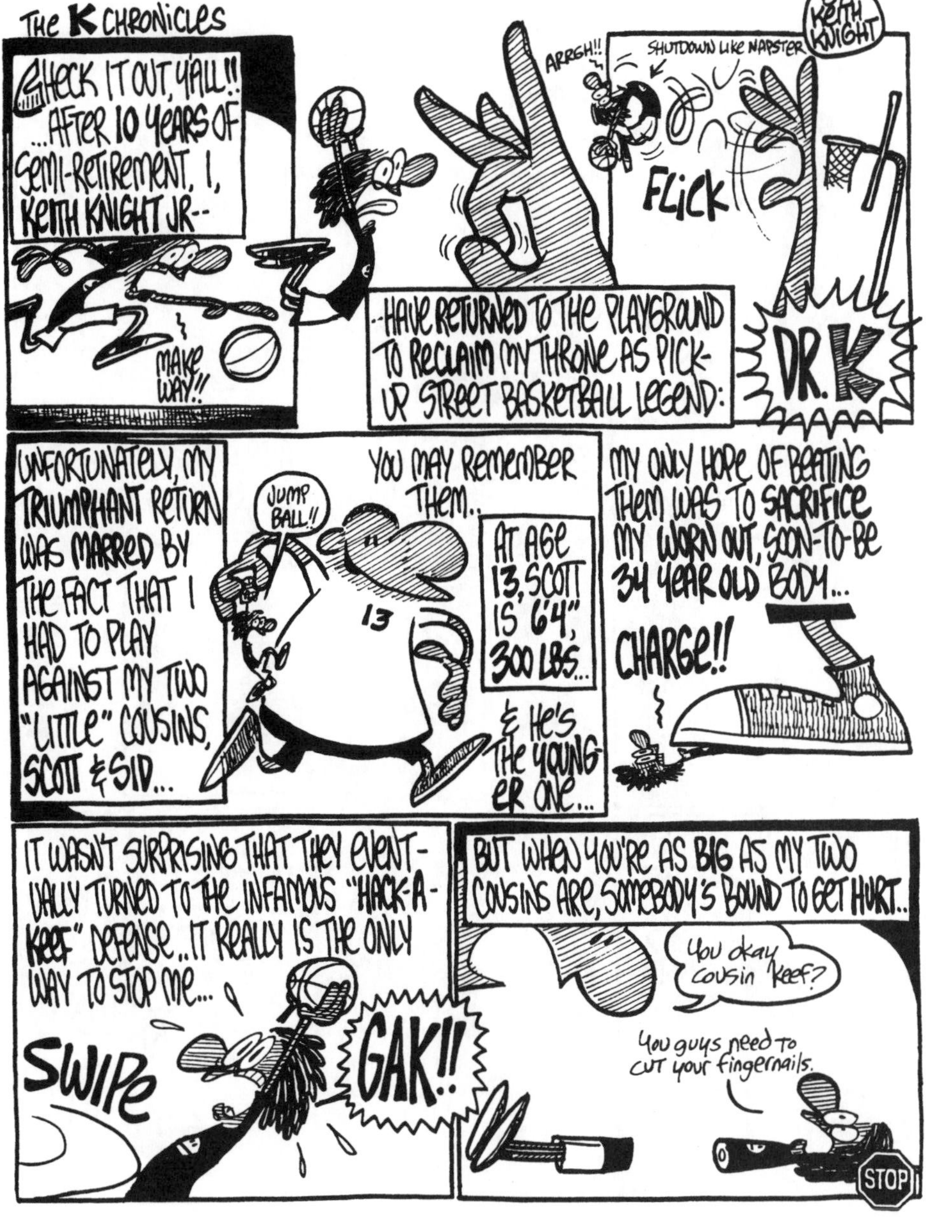
THE K CHRONICLES
BY KEITH KNIGHT
CHECK IT OUT, Y'ALL!! ...AFTER 10 YEARS OF SEMI-RETIREMENT, I, KEITH KNIGHT JR--
MAKE WAY!!
..HAVE RETURNED TO THE PLAYGROUND TO RECLAIM MY THRONE AS PICK-UP STREET BASKETBALL LEGEND:
ARRGH!!
SHUTDOWN LIKE NAPSTER
FLICK
DR. K
UNFORTUNATELY, MY TRIUMPHANT RETURN WAS MARRED BY THE FACT THAT I HAD TO PLAY AGAINST MY TWO "LITTLE" COUSINS, SCOTT & SID...
YOU MAY REMEMBER THEM..
JUMP BALL!!
13
AT AGE 13, SCOTT IS 6'4", 300 LBS...
& HE'S THE YOUNGER ONE...
MY ONLY HOPE OF BEATING THEM WAS TO SACRIFICE MY WORN OUT, SOON-TO-BE 34 YEAR OLD BODY...
CHARGE!!
IT WASN'T SURPRISING THAT THEY EVENTUALLY TURNED TO THE INFAMOUS "HACK-A-KEEF" DEFENSE..IT REALLY IS THE ONLY WAY TO STOP ME...
SWIPE
GAK!!
BUT WHEN YOU'RE AS BIG AS MY TWO COUSINS ARE, SOMEBODY'S BOUND TO GET HURT..
You okay cousin Keef?
You guys need to cut your fingernails.
STOP

THE K CHRONICLES

BY KEITH KNIGHT

Since most newspapers pay me **SQUAT** for all the hard work I do, I must resort to very innovative and frugal ways of amusing myself to remain sane in this very insane world... here is my short list of **CHEAP THRILLS**....

ART GALLERY OPENINGS

FREE FOOD!! FREE DRINKS!! THE ART IS EVEN GOOD SOMETIMES!!

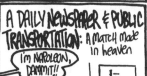

HOW TO RATE GALLERY OPENINGS:

1 star: Raw Veggies
2 stars: Beer & Wine
3 stars: Hot food
4 stars: Liquor
5 stars: Seafood!!

COLLEGE CAMPUSES

SIT IN ON LECTURES!! ATTEND THE CONCERTS!! SEE THE SPORTING EVENTS & PLAYS!! THE YOUTHFUL ENTHUSIASM FOR LEARNING IS CONTAGIOUS!! (LIKE HERPES)

GETTING A PINT OF BEN & JERRY'S & STANDING OUTSIDE THE WINDOW OF A FITNESS PLACE

Bastard!!

SINFULLY AMUSING!!

A DAILY NEWSPAPER & PUBLIC TRANSPORTATION: A MATCH MADE IN HEAVEN

I'M NAPOLEON, DAMMIT!!

IF YOU'RE LUCKY, YOU MAY ENCOUNTER A NUT.

KINKOS, REALLY LATE AT NITE

IT IS HERE WHERE YOU WILL FIND THE FUTURE UNABOMBERS OF THE WORLD...

THUNDERSTORMS...

BOOM

'NUFF SAID.

AND LAST BUT NOT LEAST, THAT OLD STANDBY:

A BEEPER DOWN THE UNDERPANTS...

...SET ON "VIBRATE."

BZZZ BZZZ

STOP

24

BY (K)EITH

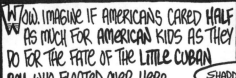

WOW. IMAGINE IF AMERICANS CARED **HALF** AS MUCH FOR AMERICAN KIDS AS THEY DO FOR THE FATE OF THE **LITTLE CUBAN BOY** WHO FLOATED OVER HERE IN AN INNER TUBE...

SHADDAP.. Why don't you go watch **Pokemon** or something?

Hey!! What about us?

WELL.. OUT HERE ON THE WEST COAST, CALIFORNIANS ARE ABOUT TO VOTE ON PROPOSITION 21: THE **GANG VIOLENCE & JUVENILE CRIME PREVENTION ACT**...

CORPORATE CONTRIBUTORS FOR THE CAMPAIGN INCLUDE UNOCAL, TRANSAMERICA, CHEVRON, PRICE WATERHOUSE...

IT SOUNDS GOOD, NO?.. BUT IF PASSED ON THE MARCH 2000 BALLOT, PROP. 21 WILL ALLOW POLICE & PROSECUTORS TO ARREST, TRY AS ADULTS, IMPRISON & EXECUTE JUVENILES AS YOUNG AS **14 YEARS OF AGE**!!

Bring da lil kids on in!!

Yeah!! We'll start a mentor program!!

PROP. 21 WOULD ALSO EXPAND THE LIST OF "3 STRIKES" OFFENSES FOR BOTH KIDS AND ADULTS...

CURRENTLY, "FELONY VANDALISM" IS DEFINED AS DAMAGE OVER $50,000... PROP. 21 WOULD BRING THE LIMIT DOWN TO $400.

NOW... I DON'T KNOW ABOUT YOU, BUT I MYSELF & EVERY SINGLE ONE OF MY FRIENDS BOTH BLACK & WHITE, BOY & GIRL, JEW & GENTILE HAVE DONE AT LEAST $400 DAMAGE TO PUBLIC PROPERTY WAY BACK WHEN!

IN FACT, MANY PROVISIONS OF THE INITIATIVE WOULD'VE QUALIFIED ME & MY PALS FOR SOME SERIOUS POLICE HARASSMENT & JAILTIME...

Similar clothing + permanent markers + 3 or more hanging TOGETHER = GANG!!

THE TRUTH IS THAT **ALL CRIME,** INCLUDING JUVENILE CRIME, HAS DROPPED SIGNIFICANTLY OVER THE PAST DECADE... LONG BEFORE THE "3 STRIKES" LAW WAS PASSED... DURING THIS SAME TIME PERIOD, CALIFORNIA HAS BUILT **21 PRISONS & ONE UNIVERSITY.** WITH A FALLING CRIME RATE, WHO ARE THEY GONNA GET TO FILL ALL THOSE PRISONS?

PROP. 21 IS BASICALLY A **WAR ON YOUTH**... IT'S EMPHASIS IS ON FILLING PRISONS.. NOT REHABILITATION.. WE'VE PRACTICALLY GIVEN UP ON ADULTS.. ARE WE READY TO GIVE UP ON OUR CHILDREN TOO?

BY THE WAY, HERE'S WHAT HAPPENED TO ME & MY "GANG MEMBER" FRIENDS:

works for IRS   CHEF   PRO WRESTLER   CARTOONIST   POET (you can't win 'em all)

VOTE **NO** ON PROP. 21!!

STOP

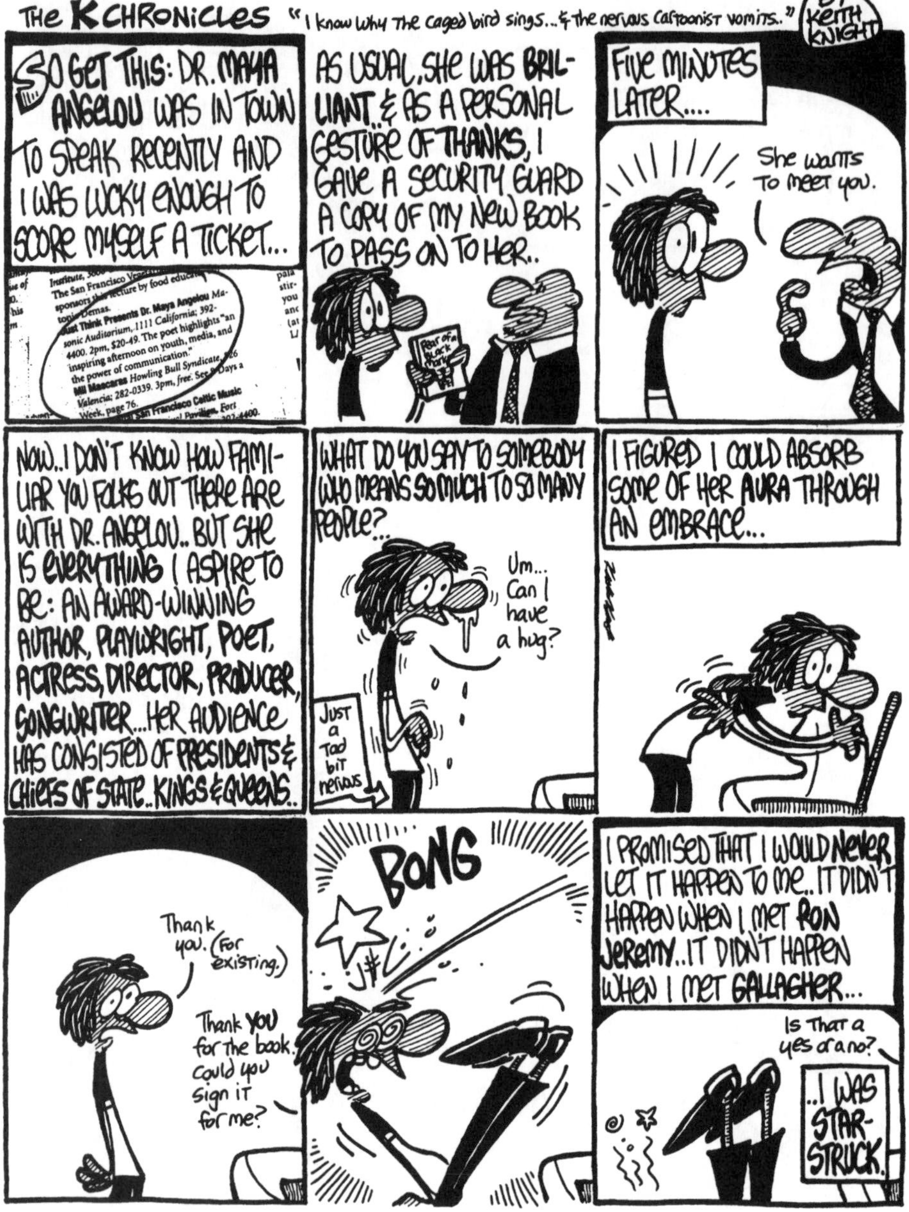
THE K CHRONICLES
"I know why the caged bird sings... & the nervous cartoonist vomits."
BY KEITH KNIGHT
SO GET THIS: DR. MAYA ANGELOU WAS IN TOWN TO SPEAK RECENTLY AND I WAS LUCKY ENOUGH TO SCORE MYSELF A TICKET...
The San Francisco Vegetarian Society sponsors this lecture by food educator Antonia Demas.
Just Think Presents Dr. Maya Angelou Masonic Auditorium, 1111 California; 392-4400. 2pm, $20-49. The poet highlights "an inspiring afternoon on youth, media, and the power of communication."
Mil Mascaras Howling Bull Syndicate, 826 Valencia; 282-0339. 3pm, free. See 8 Days a Week, page 76.
San Francisco Celtic Music
AS USUAL, SHE WAS BRILLIANT.. & AS A PERSONAL GESTURE OF THANKS, I GAVE A SECURITY GUARD A COPY OF MY NEW BOOK TO PASS ON TO HER..
Fear of a Black Marker
FIVE MINUTES LATER....
She wants to meet you.
NOW.. I DON'T KNOW HOW FAMILIAR YOU FOLKS OUT THERE ARE WITH DR. ANGELOU.. BUT SHE IS EVERYTHING I ASPIRE TO BE: AN AWARD-WINNING AUTHOR, PLAYWRIGHT, POET, ACTRESS, DIRECTOR, PRODUCER, SONGWRITER... HER AUDIENCE HAS CONSISTED OF PRESIDENTS & CHIEFS OF STATE.. KINGS & QUEENS..
WHAT DO YOU SAY TO SOMEBODY WHO MEANS SO MUCH TO SO MANY PEOPLE?...
Um... Can I have a hug?
JUST a Tad bit nervous
I FIGURED I COULD ABSORB SOME OF HER AURA THROUGH AN EMBRACE...
Thank you. (For existing.)
Thank YOU for the book. Could you sign it for me?
BONG
I PROMISED THAT I WOULD NEVER LET IT HAPPEN TO ME.. IT DIDN'T HAPPEN WHEN I MET RON JEREMY.. IT DIDN'T HAPPEN WHEN I MET GALLAGHER...
Is that a yes or a no?
..I WAS STAR-STRUCK.

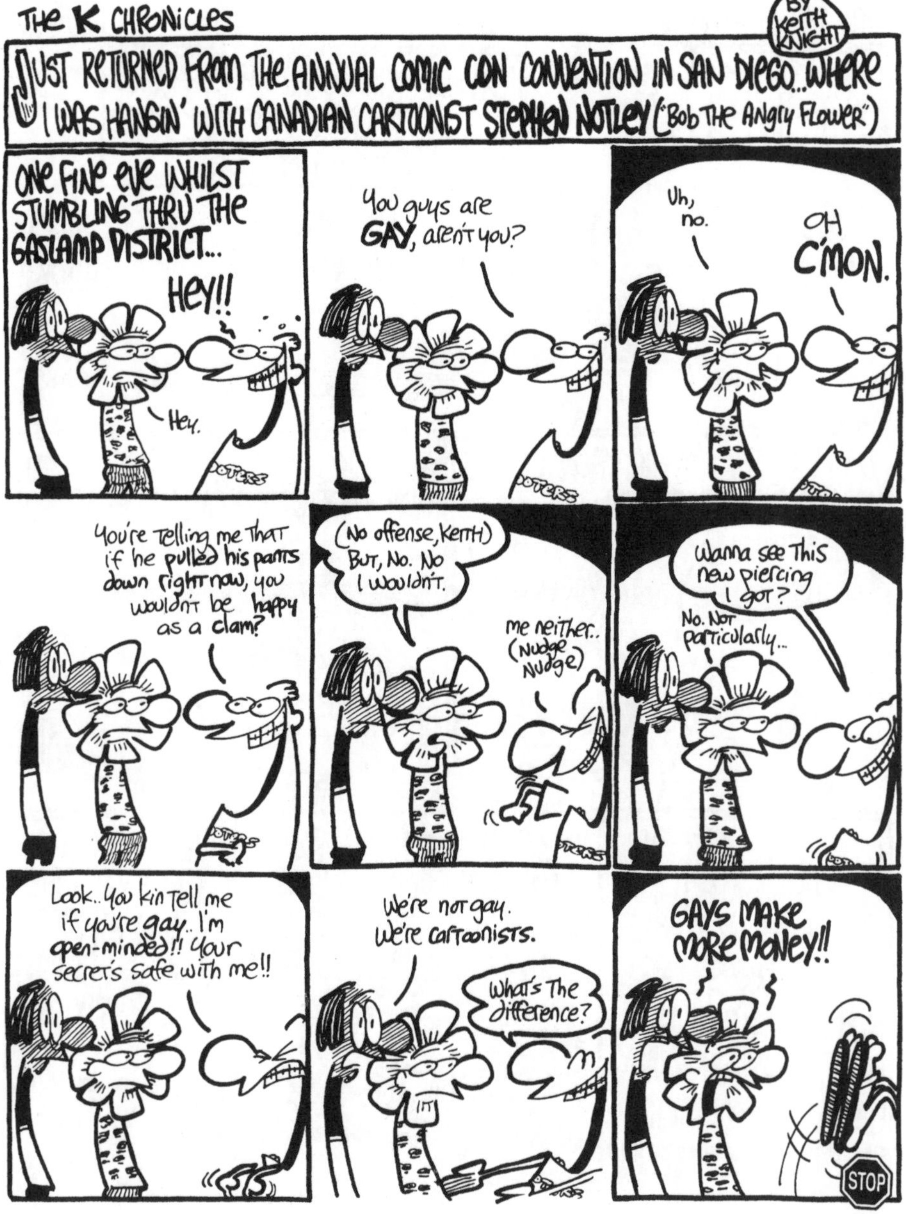
THE K CHRONICLES
BY KEITH KNIGHT
JUST RETURNED FROM THE ANNUAL COMIC CON CONVENTION IN SAN DIEGO...WHERE I WAS HANGIN' WITH CANADIAN CARTOONIST STEPHEN NOTLEY ("Bob The Angry Flower")
ONE FINE EVE WHILST STUMBLING THRU THE GASLAMP DISTRICT...
HEY!!
Hey.
You guys are GAY, aren't you?
Uh, no.
OH C'MON.
You're Telling me That if he pulled his pants down right now, you wouldn't be happy as a clam?
(No offense, Keith) But, No. No I wouldn't.
me neither.. (Nudge Nudge)
Wanna see This new piercing I got?
No. Not particularly...
Look.. You kin Tell me if you're gay.. I'm open-minded!! Your secret's safe with me!!
We're not gay. We're cartoonists.
What's The difference?
GAYS MAKE MORE MONEY!!
STOP

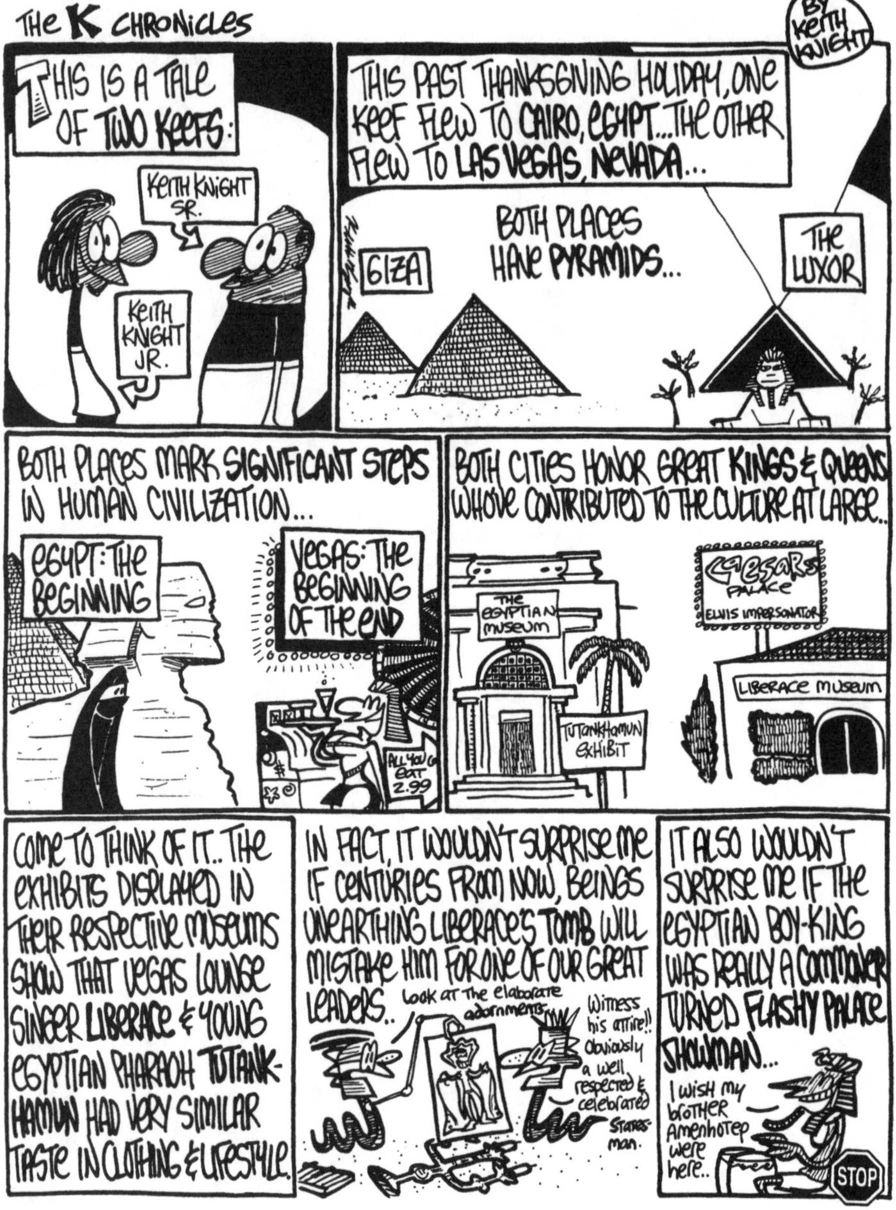
THE K CHRONICLES
BY KEITH KNIGHT
THIS IS A TALE OF TWO KEEFS:
KEITH KNIGHT SR.
KEITH KNIGHT JR.
THIS PAST THANKSGIVING HOLIDAY, ONE KEEF FLEW TO CAIRO, EGYPT... THE OTHER FLEW TO LAS VEGAS, NEVADA...
BOTH PLACES HAVE PYRAMIDS...
GIZA
THE LUXOR
BOTH PLACES MARK SIGNIFICANT STEPS IN HUMAN CIVILIZATION...
EGYPT: THE BEGINNING
VEGAS: THE BEGINNING OF THE END
ALL YOU CAN EAT 2.99
BOTH CITIES HONOR GREAT KINGS & QUEENS WHO'VE CONTRIBUTED TO THE CULTURE AT LARGE...
THE EGYPTIAN MUSEUM
TUTANKHAMUN EXHIBIT
CAESARS PALACE
ELVIS IMPERSONATOR
LIBERACE MUSEUM
COME TO THINK OF IT.. THE EXHIBITS DISPLAYED IN THEIR RESPECTIVE MUSEUMS SHOW THAT VEGAS LOUNGE SINGER LIBERACE & YOUNG EGYPTIAN PHARAOH TUTANKHAMUN HAD VERY SIMILAR TASTE IN CLOTHING & LIFESTYLE.
IN FACT, IT WOULDN'T SURPRISE ME IF CENTURIES FROM NOW, BEINGS UNEARTHING LIBERACE'S TOMB WILL MISTAKE HIM FOR ONE OF OUR GREAT LEADERS..
LOOK AT THE ELABORATE ADORNMENTS..
WITNESS HIS ATTIRE!! OBVIOUSLY A WELL RESPECTED & CELEBRATED STATESMAN.
IT ALSO WOULDN'T SURPRISE ME IF THE EGYPTIAN BOY-KING WAS REALLY A COMMONER TURNED FLASHY PALACE SHOWMAN...
I WISH MY BROTHER AMENHOTEP WERE HERE..
STOP

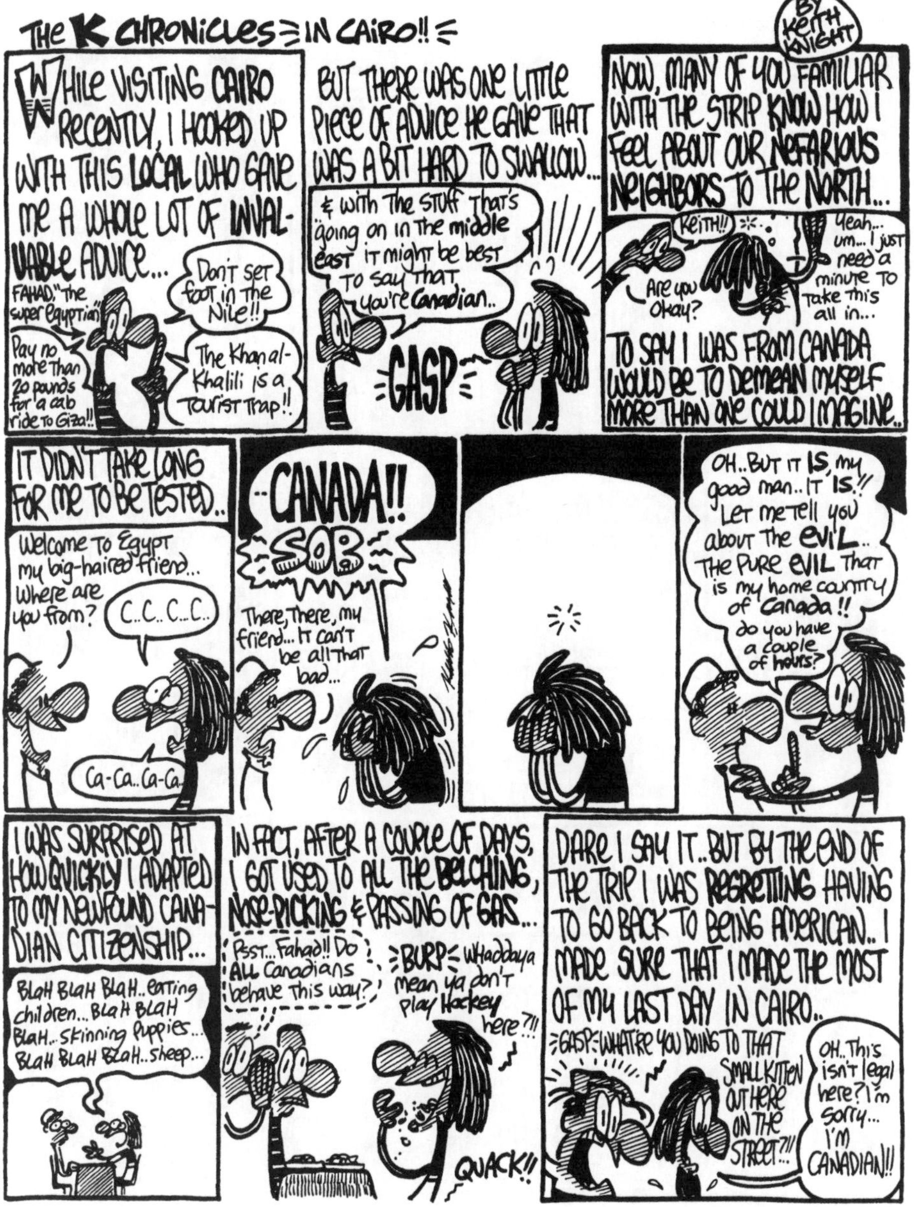

THE K CHRONICLES IN CAIRO!!
BY KEITH KNIGHT
WHILE VISITING CAIRO RECENTLY, I HOOKED UP WITH THIS LOCAL WHO GAVE ME A WHOLE LOT OF INVALUABLE ADVICE...
FAHAD, "The super Egyptian"
Don't set foot in the Nile!!
Pay no more than 20 pounds for a cab ride to Giza!!
The Khan al-Khalili is a Tourist Trap!!
BUT THERE WAS ONE LITTLE PIECE OF ADVICE HE GAVE THAT WAS A BIT HARD TO SWALLOW...
& with the stuff that's going on in the middle east it might be best to say that you're Canadian..
GASP
NOW, MANY OF YOU FAMILIAR WITH THE STRIP KNOW HOW I FEEL ABOUT OUR NEFARIOUS NEIGHBORS TO THE NORTH...
KEITH!!
Are you okay?
Yeah... um... I just need a minute to take this all in...
TO SAY I WAS FROM CANADA WOULD BE TO DEMEAN MYSELF MORE THAN ONE COULD IMAGINE..
IT DIDN'T TAKE LONG FOR ME TO BE TESTED..
Welcome to Egypt my big-haired friend... Where are you from?
C..C..C..C..
Ca-Ca..Ca-Ca..
..CANADA!!
SOB
There, there, my friend... It can't be all that bad...
OH..BUT IT IS, my good man.. IT IS!! Let me tell you about the evil.. The pure evil that is my home country of Canada!! do you have a couple of hours?
I WAS SURPRISED AT HOW QUICKLY I ADAPTED TO MY NEWFOUND CANADIAN CITIZENSHIP...
Blah Blah Blah..eating children...Blah Blah Blah..skinning puppies... Blah Blah Blah..sheep...
IN FACT, AFTER A COUPLE OF DAYS, I GOT USED TO ALL THE BELCHING, NOSE-PICKING & PASSING OF GAS...
Psst...Fahad!! Do ALL Canadians behave this way?
BURP
Whaddaya mean ya don't play Hockey here?!!
QUACK!!
DARE I SAY IT..BUT BY THE END OF THE TRIP I WAS REGRETTING HAVING TO GO BACK TO BEING AMERICAN.. I MADE SURE THAT I MADE THE MOST OF MY LAST DAY IN CAIRO..
GASP WHAT'RE YOU DOING TO THAT SMALL KITTEN OUT HERE ON THE STREET?!!
OH..This isn't legal here? I'm sorry... I'm CANADIAN!!

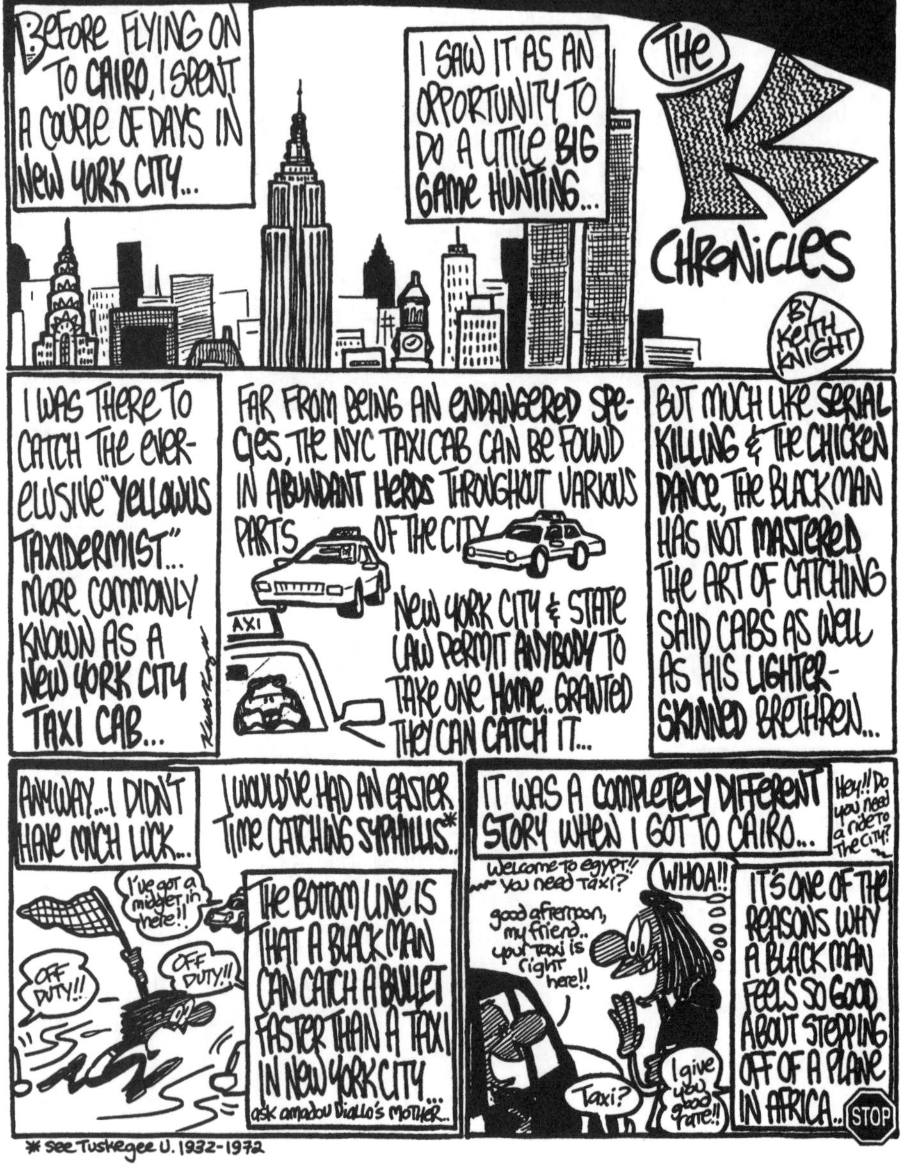
Before flying on to Cairo, I spent a couple of days in New York City...
I saw it as an opportunity to do a little big game hunting...
The K Chronicles
by Keith Knight
I was there to catch the ever-elusive "Yellowus Taxidermist"... more commonly known as a New York City taxi cab...
Far from being an endangered species, the NYC taxicab can be found in abundant herds throughout various parts of the city
AXI
New York City & State law permit anybody to take one home.. granted they can catch it...
But much like serial killing & the chicken dance, the black man has not mastered the art of catching said cabs as well as his lighter-skinned brethren...
Anyway...I didn't have much luck...
I would've had an easier time catching syphilis*..
I've got a midget in here!!
Off duty!!
Off duty!!
The bottom line is that a black man can catch a bullet faster than a taxi in New York City...
ask Amadou Diallo's mother..
It was a completely different story when I got to Cairo...
Hey!! Do you need a ride to the city?
Welcome to Egypt!! You need taxi?
WHOA!!
good afternoon, my friend.. your taxi is right here!!
Taxi?
I give you good rate!!
It's one of the reasons why a black man feels so good about stepping off of a plane in Africa..
STOP

* see Tuskegee U. 1932-1972

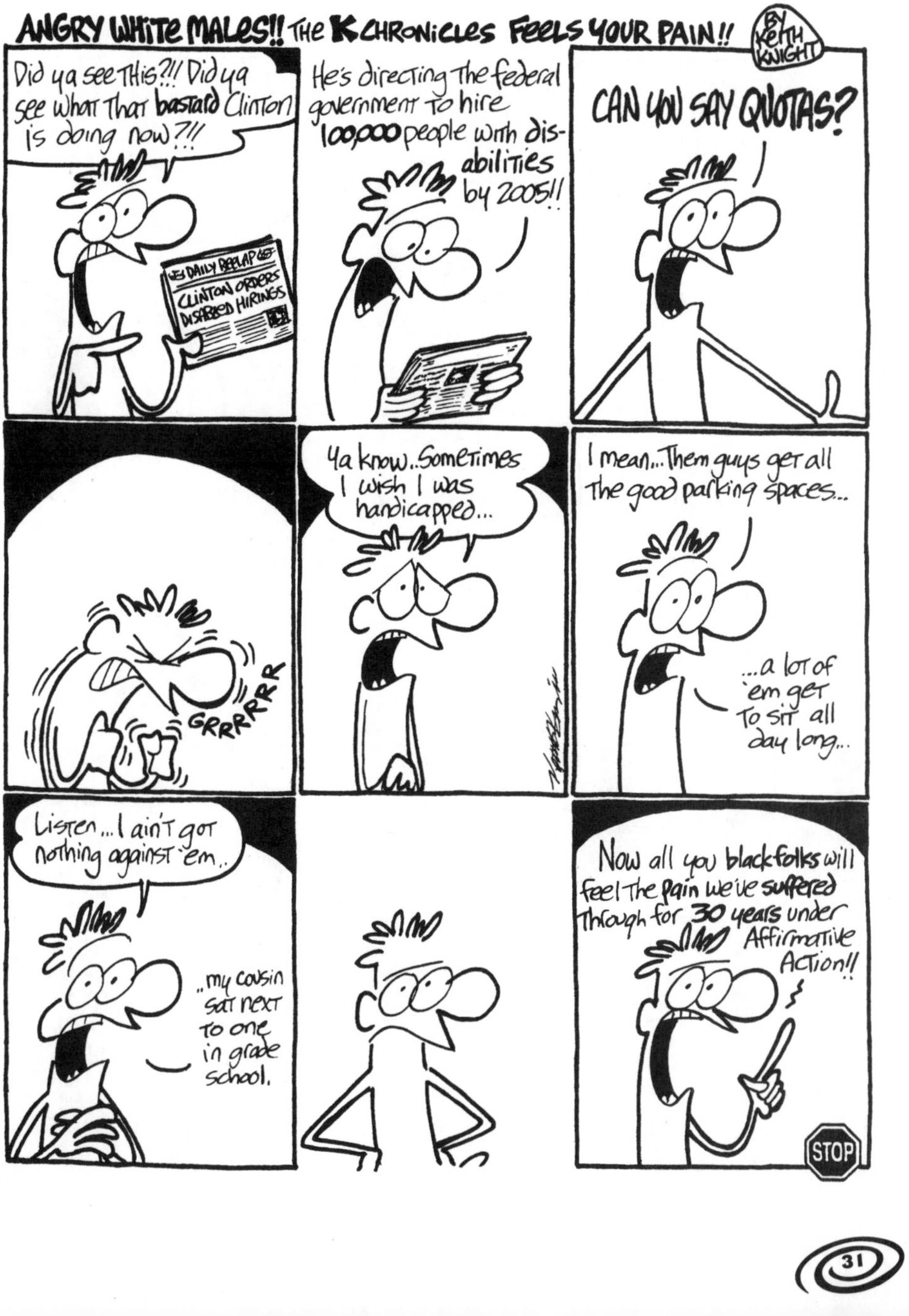
ANGRY WHITE MALES!! THE K CHRONICLES FEELS YOUR PAIN!!
BY KEITH KNIGHT
Did ya see THIS?!! Did ya see what That bastard Clinton is doing now?!!
DAILY BEELAP
CLINTON ORDERS DISABLED HIRINGS
He's directing The federal government To hire 100,000 people with dis-abilities by 2005!!
CAN YOU SAY QUOTAS?
GRRRRRR
Ya know..Sometimes I wish I was handicapped...
I mean...Them guys get all The good parking spaces...
...a lot of 'em get To sit all day long...
Listen...I ain't got nothing against 'em..
..my cousin sat next to one in grade school.
Now all you blackfolks will feel The pain we've suffered Through for 30 years under Affirmative Action!!
STOP

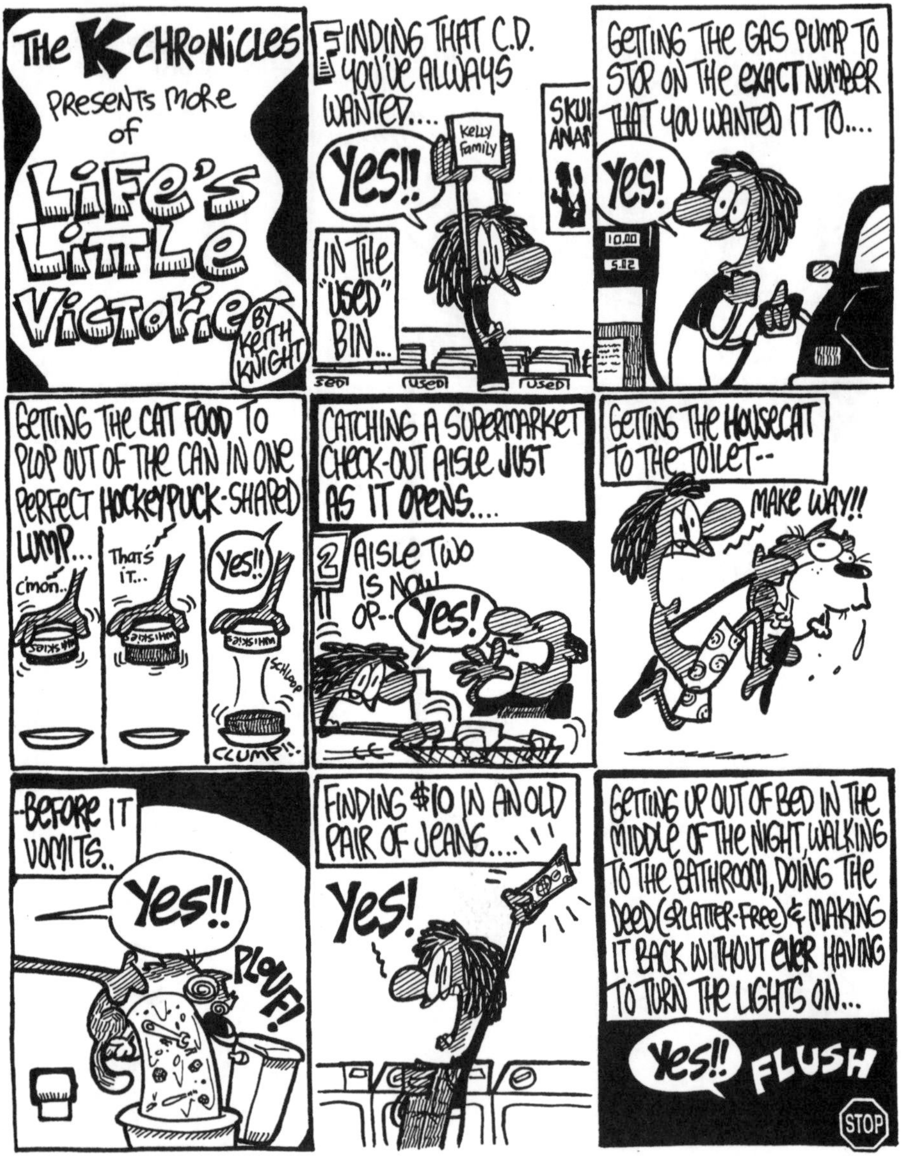

THE K CHRONICLES
PRESENTS MORE OF
LIFE'S LITTLE VICTORIES
BY KEITH KNIGHT
FINDING THAT C.D. YOU'VE ALWAYS WANTED....
IN THE "USED" BIN...
Yes!!
KELLY FAMILY
USED
USED
USED
GETTING THE GAS PUMP TO STOP ON THE EXACT NUMBER THAT YOU WANTED IT TO....
Yes!
10.00
GETTING THE CAT FOOD TO PLOP OUT OF THE CAN IN ONE PERFECT HOCKEYPUCK-SHAPED LUMP...
C'MON..
THAT'S IT...
Yes!!
SCHLOOP
CLUMP!!
CATCHING A SUPERMARKET CHECK-OUT AISLE JUST AS IT OPENS....
2
AISLE TWO IS NOW OP--
Yes!
GETTING THE HOUSECAT TO THE TOILET--
MAKE WAY!!
--BEFORE IT VOMITS..
Yes!!
PLOUF!
FINDING $10 IN AN OLD PAIR OF JEANS....
Yes!
GETTING UP OUT OF BED IN THE MIDDLE OF THE NIGHT, WALKING TO THE BATHROOM, DOING THE DEED (SPLATTER-FREE) & MAKING IT BACK WITHOUT EVER HAVING TO TURN THE LIGHTS ON...
Yes!!
FLUSH
STOP

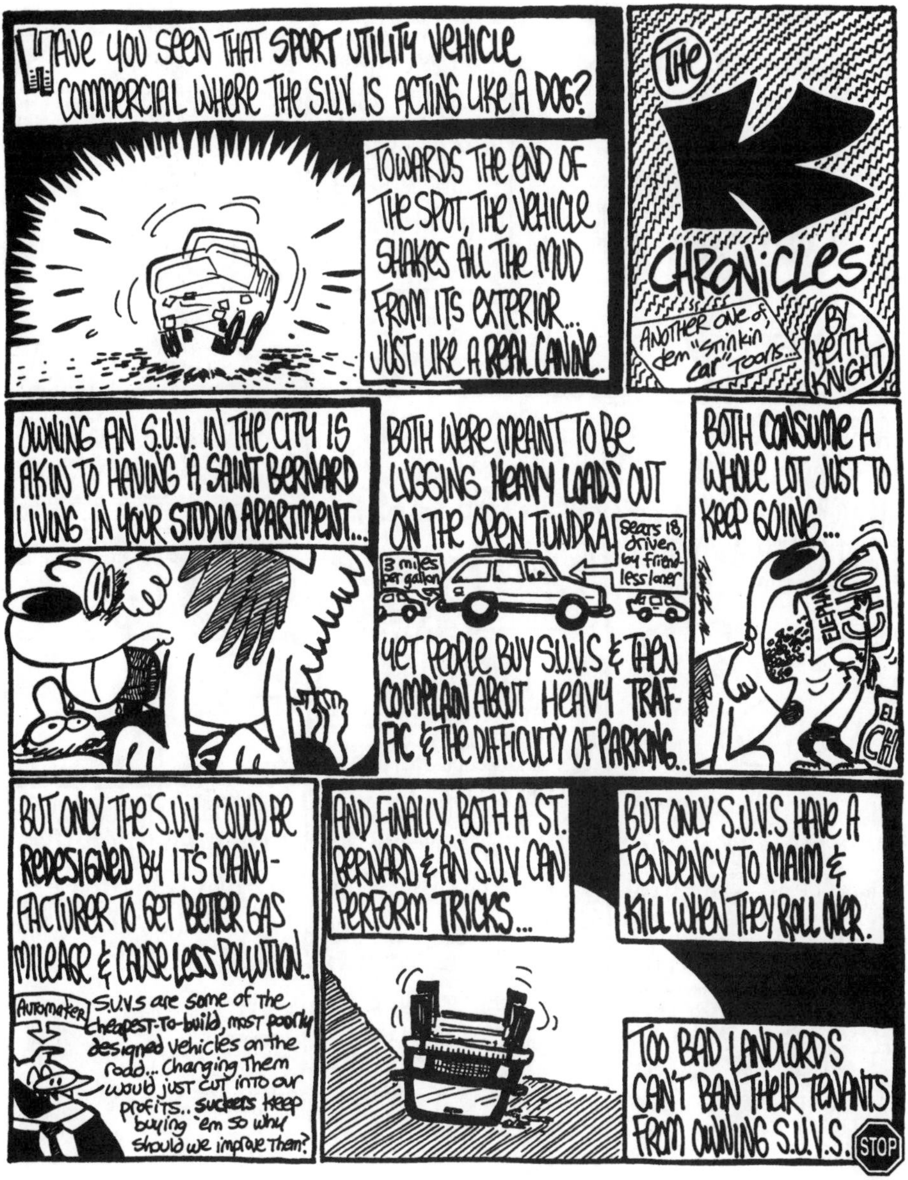
HAVE YOU SEEN THAT SPORT UTILITY VEHICLE COMMERCIAL WHERE THE S.U.V. IS ACTING LIKE A DOG?
TOWARDS THE END OF THE SPOT, THE VEHICLE SHAKES ALL THE MUD FROM ITS EXTERIOR... JUST LIKE A REAL CANINE.
THE K CHRONICLES
ANOTHER ONE OF dem "Stinkin Car" Toons...
BY KEITH KNIGHT
OWNING AN S.U.V. IN THE CITY IS AKIN TO HAVING A SAINT BERNARD LIVING IN YOUR STUDIO APARTMENT...
BOTH WERE MEANT TO BE LUGGING HEAVY LOADS OUT ON THE OPEN TUNDRA.
3 miles per gallon
Seats 18, driven by friendless loner
YET PEOPLE BUY S.U.V.S & THEN COMPLAIN ABOUT HEAVY TRAFFIC & THE DIFFICULTY OF PARKING..
BOTH CONSUME A WHOLE LOT JUST TO KEEP GOING...
ELEPHANT CHOW
BUT ONLY THE S.U.V. COULD BE REDESIGNED BY IT'S MANUFACTURER TO GET BETTER GAS MILEAGE & CAUSE LESS POLLUTION..
AUTOMAKER
S.U.V.S are some of the cheapest-to-build, most poorly designed vehicles on the road... Changing them would just cut into our profits.. suckers keep buying 'em so why should we improve them?
AND FINALLY, BOTH A ST. BERNARD & AN S.U.V. CAN PERFORM TRICKS...
BUT ONLY S.U.V.S HAVE A TENDENCY TO MAIM & KILL WHEN THEY ROLL OVER.
TOO BAD LANDLORDS CAN'T BAN THEIR TENANTS FROM OWNING S.U.V.S.
STOP

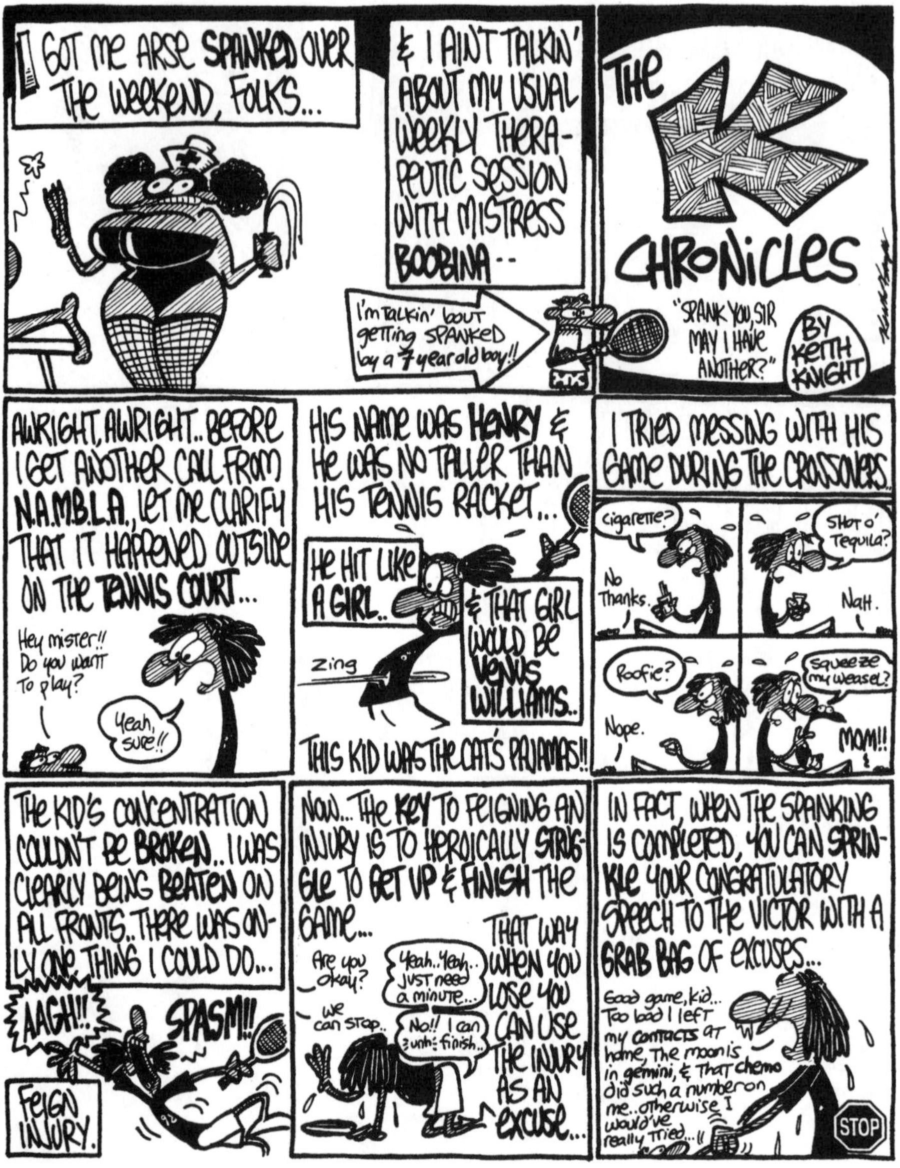
I GOT ME ARSE SPANKED OVER THE WEEKEND, FOLKS...
& I AIN'T TALKIN' ABOUT MY USUAL WEEKLY THERA-PEUTIC SESSION WITH MISTRESS BOOBINA--
I'm TALKin' 'bout getting SPANKED by a 7 year old boy!!
THE K CHRONICLES
"SPANK YOU, SIR MAY I HAVE ANOTHER?"
BY KEITH KNIGHT
AWRIGHT, AWRIGHT... BEFORE I GET ANOTHER CALL FROM N.A.M.B.L.A., LET ME CLARIFY THAT IT HAPPENED OUTSIDE ON THE TENNIS COURT...
Hey mister!! Do you want to play?
Yeah, sure!!
HIS NAME WAS HENRY & HE WAS NO TALLER THAN HIS TENNIS RACKET...
HE HIT LIKE A GIRL..
& THAT GIRL WOULD BE VENUS WILLIAMS..
Zing
THIS KID WAS THE CAT'S PAJAMAS!!
I TRIED MESSING WITH HIS GAME DURING THE CROSSOVERS..
Cigarette?
No Thanks.
Shot o' Tequila?
Nah.
Roofie?
Nope.
Squeeze my weasel?
MOM!!
THE KID'S CONCENTRATION COULDN'T BE BROKEN.. I WAS CLEARLY BEING BEATEN ON ALL FRONTS.. THERE WAS ONLY ONE THING I COULD DO...
AAGH!!
SPASM!!
FEIGN INJURY.
NOW... THE KEY TO FEIGNING AN INJURY IS TO HEROICALLY STRUG-GLE TO GET UP & FINISH THE GAME...
Are you okay?
Yeah.. Yeah.. JUST need a minute...
We can stop..
No!! I can ...unh.. finish..
THAT WAY WHEN YOU LOSE YOU CAN USE THE INJURY AS AN EXCUSE...
IN FACT, WHEN THE SPANKING IS COMPLETED, YOU CAN SPRIN-KLE YOUR CONGRATULATORY SPEECH TO THE VICTOR WITH A GRAB BAG OF EXCUSES...
Good game, kid... Too bad I left my contacts at home, the moon is in gemini, & that chemo did such a number on me.. otherwise I would've really tried...!!
STOP

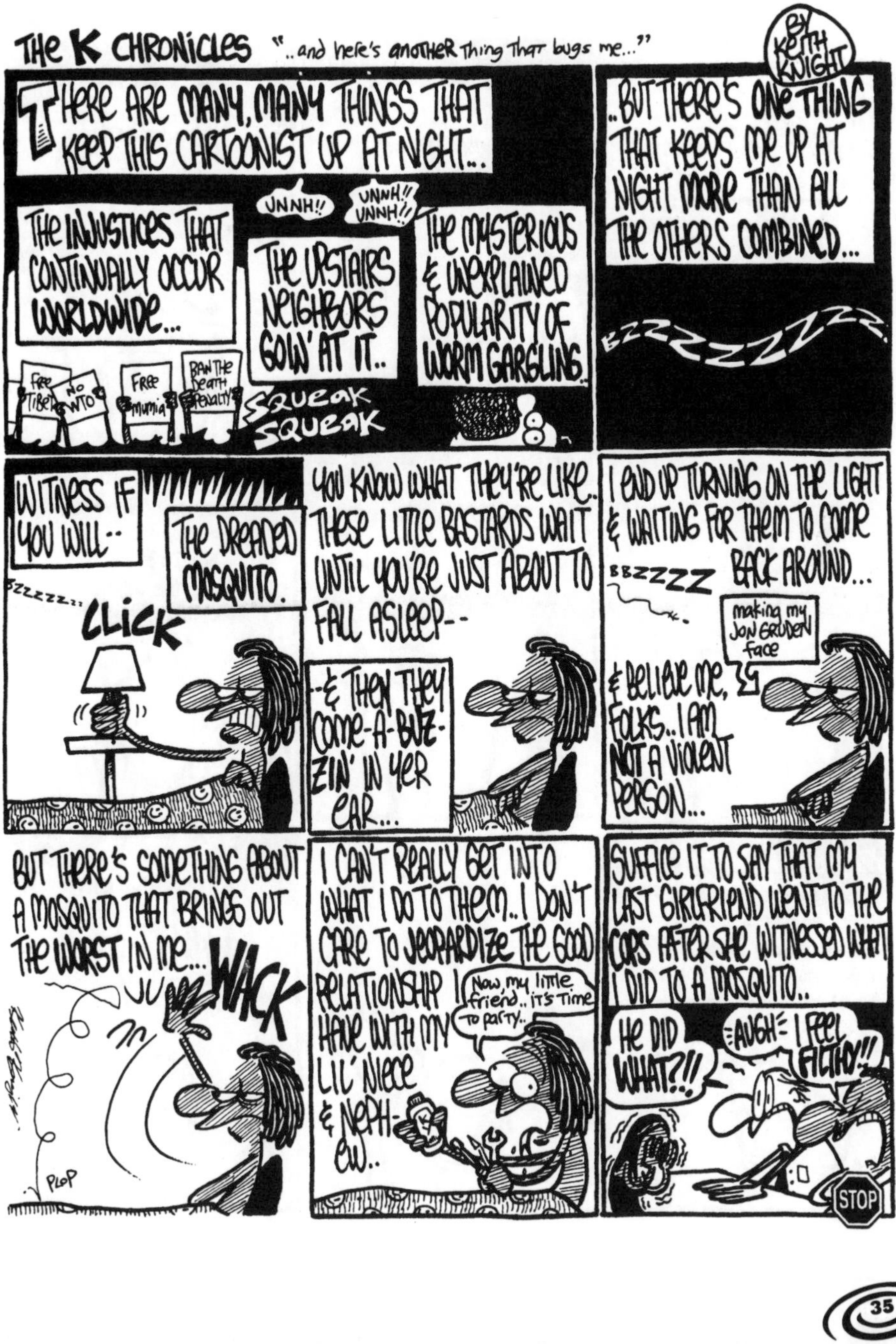
THE K CHRONICLES "..and here's ANOTHER thing that bugs me..."
BY KEITH KNIGHT
THERE ARE MANY, MANY THINGS THAT KEEP THIS CARTOONIST UP AT NIGHT...
THE INJUSTICES THAT CONTINUALLY OCCUR WORLDWIDE...
FREE TIBET
NO WTO
FREE MUMIA
BAN THE DEATH PENALTY
UNNH!!
UNNH!! UNNH!!
THE UPSTAIRS NEIGHBORS GOIN' AT IT..
SQUEAK SQUEAK
THE MYSTERIOUS & UNEXPLAINED POPULARITY OF WORM GARGLING..
..BUT THERE'S ONE THING THAT KEEPS ME UP AT NIGHT MORE THAN ALL THE OTHERS COMBINED...
BZZZZZZZZ
WITNESS IF YOU WILL--
THE DREADED MOSQUITO.
CLICK
YOU KNOW WHAT THEY'RE LIKE.. THESE LITTLE BASTARDS WAIT UNTIL YOU'RE JUST ABOUT TO FALL ASLEEP--
--& THEN THEY COME-A-BUZZIN' IN YER EAR...
I END UP TURNING ON THE LIGHT & WAITING FOR THEM TO COME BACK AROUND...
BBZZZZ
making my JON GRUDEN face
& BELIEVE ME, FOLKS.. I AM NOT A VIOLENT PERSON...
BUT THERE'S SOMETHING ABOUT A MOSQUITO THAT BRINGS OUT THE WORST IN ME...
WACK
PLOP
I CAN'T REALLY GET INTO WHAT I DO TO THEM.. I DON'T CARE TO JEOPARDIZE THE GOOD RELATIONSHIP I HAVE WITH MY LIL' NIECE & NEPHEW..
Now my little friend.. it's time to party..
SUFFICE IT TO SAY THAT MY LAST GIRLFRIEND WENT TO THE COPS AFTER SHE WITNESSED WHAT I DID TO A MOSQUITO..
HE DID WHAT?!!
AUGH! I FEEL FILTHY!!
STOP

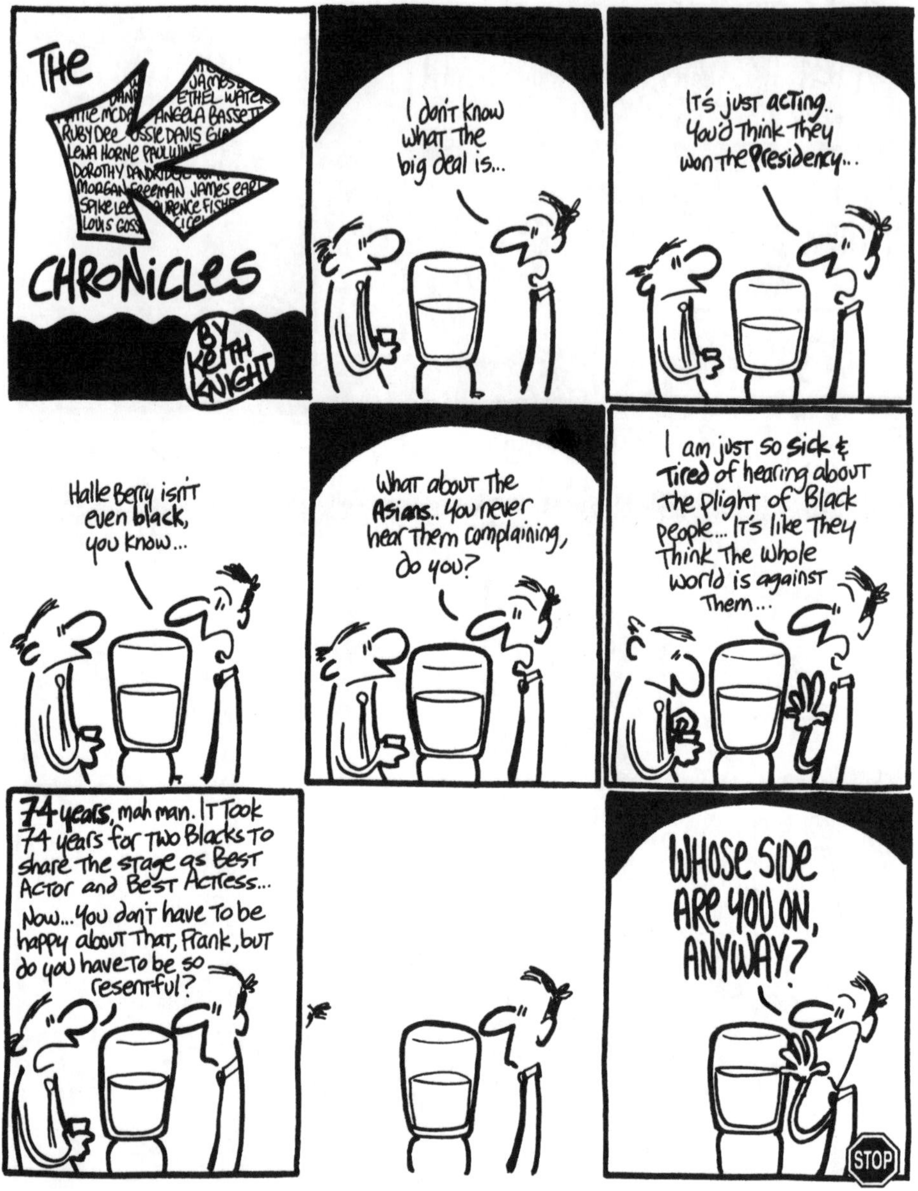
THE K CHRONICLES
BY KEITH KNIGHT
I don't know what the big deal is...
It's just acting.. You'd think they won the Presidency...
Halle Berry isn't even black, you know...
What about the Asians.. You never hear them complaining, do you?
I am just so sick & tired of hearing about the plight of Black people... It's like they think the whole world is against them...
74 years, mah man. It took 74 years for two Blacks to share the stage as Best Actor and Best Actress...
Now... You don't have to be happy about that, Frank, but do you have to be so resentful?
WHOSE SIDE ARE YOU ON, ANYWAY?
STOP

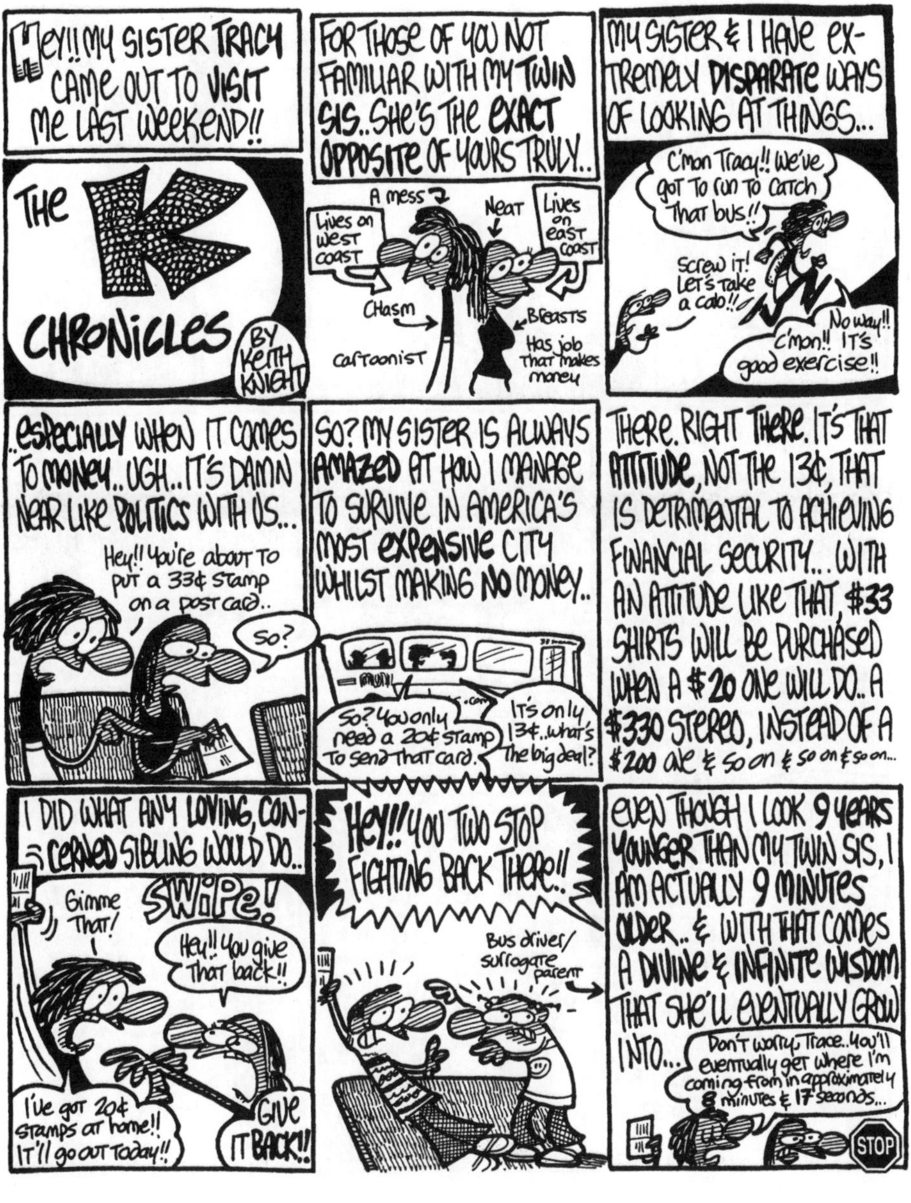
Hey!! My sister Tracy came out to visit me last weekend!!
The K Chronicles
By Keith Knight
For those of you not familiar with my twin sis.. she's the exact opposite of yours truly..
A mess
Neat
Lives on west coast
Lives on east coast
Chasm
Breasts
Cartoonist
Has job that makes money
My sister & I have extremely disparate ways of looking at things...
C'mon Tracy!! We've got to run to catch that bus!!
Screw it! Let's take a cab!!
No way!! C'mon!! It's good exercise!!
..especially when it comes to money.. ugh.. it's damn near like politics with us...
Hey!! You're about to put a 33¢ stamp on a post card..
So?
So? My sister is always amazed at how I manage to survive in America's most expensive city whilst making no money..
So? You only need a 20¢ stamp to send that card.
It's only 13¢.. what's the big deal?
There. Right there. It's that attitude, not the 13¢, that is detrimental to achieving financial security... with an attitude like that, $33 shirts will be purchased when a $20 one will do.. a $330 stereo, instead of a $200 one & so on & so on & so on...
I did what any loving, concerned sibling would do..
Gimme that!
Swipe!
Hey!! You give that back!!
I've got 20¢ stamps at home!! It'll go out today!!
Give it back!!
Hey!! You two stop fighting back there!!
Bus driver/ surrogate parent
Even though I look 9 years younger than my twin sis, I am actually 9 minutes older.. & with that comes a divine & infinite wisdom that she'll eventually grow into...
Don't worry, Trace.. You'll eventually get where I'm coming from in approximately 8 minutes & 17 seconds...
STOP

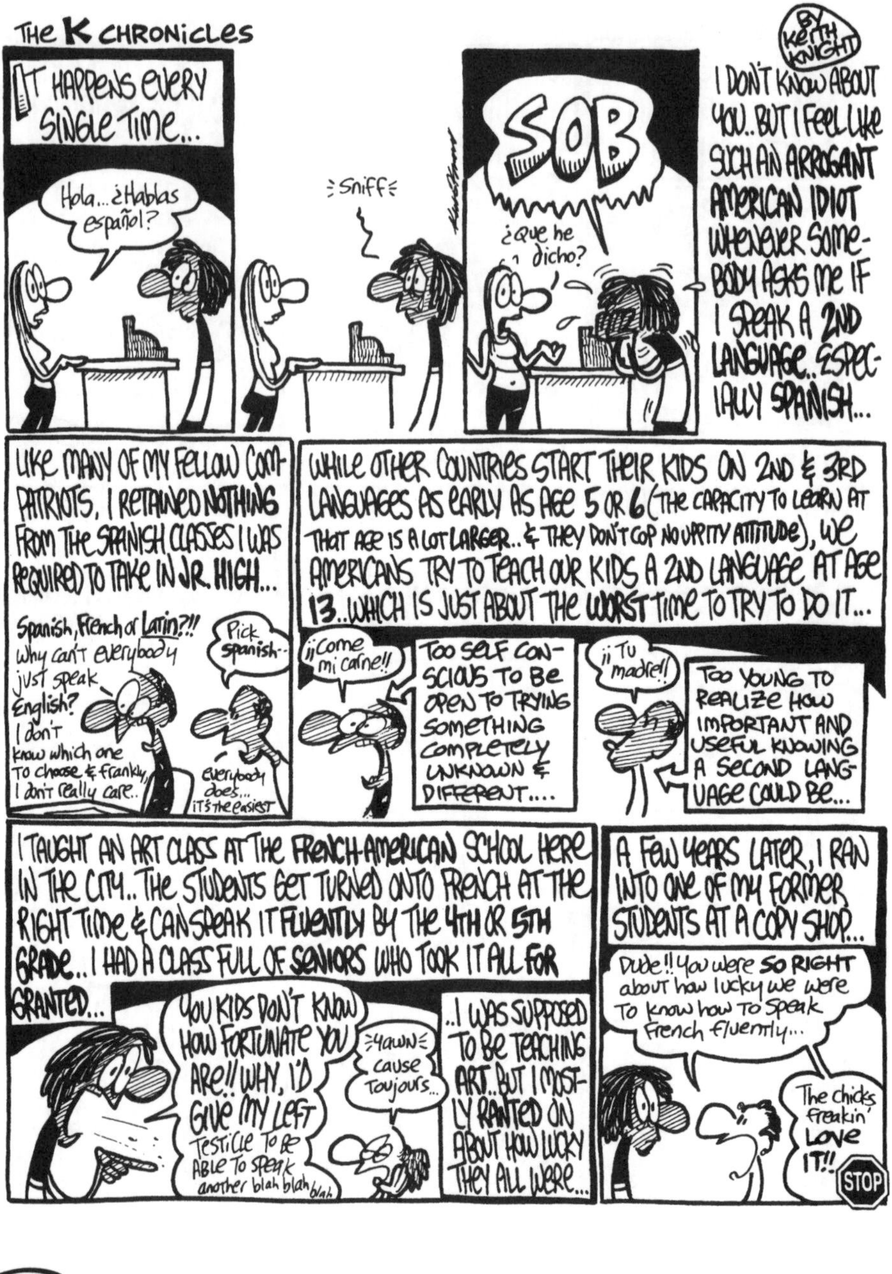
THE K CHRONICLES
BY KEITH KNIGHT
IT HAPPENS EVERY SINGLE TIME...
Hola... ¿Hablas español?
Sniff
SOB
¿Que he dicho?
I DON'T KNOW ABOUT YOU.. BUT I FEEL LIKE SUCH AN ARROGANT AMERICAN IDIOT WHENEVER SOMEBODY ASKS ME IF I SPEAK A 2ND LANGUAGE.. ESPECIALLY SPANISH...
LIKE MANY OF MY FELLOW COMPATRIOTS, I RETAINED NOTHING FROM THE SPANISH CLASSES I WAS REQUIRED TO TAKE IN JR. HIGH...
Spanish, French or Latin?!! Why can't everybody just speak English? I don't know which one to choose & frankly, I don't really care..
Pick Spanish..
everybody does... it's the easiest
WHILE OTHER COUNTRIES START THEIR KIDS ON 2ND & 3RD LANGUAGES AS EARLY AS AGE 5 OR 6 (THE CAPACITY TO LEARN AT THAT AGE IS A LOT LARGER.. & THEY DON'T COP NO UPPITY ATTITUDE), WE AMERICANS TRY TO TEACH OUR KIDS A 2ND LANGUAGE AT AGE 13.. WHICH IS JUST ABOUT THE WORST TIME TO TRY TO DO IT...
¡¡Come mi carne!!
TOO SELF CONSCIOUS TO BE OPEN TO TRYING SOMETHING COMPLETELY UNKNOWN & DIFFERENT....
¡¡Tu madre!!
TOO YOUNG TO REALIZE HOW IMPORTANT AND USEFUL KNOWING A SECOND LANGUAGE COULD BE...
I TAUGHT AN ART CLASS AT THE FRENCH-AMERICAN SCHOOL HERE IN THE CITY.. THE STUDENTS GET TURNED ONTO FRENCH AT THE RIGHT TIME & CAN SPEAK IT FLUENTLY BY THE 4TH OR 5TH GRADE... I HAD A CLASS FULL OF SENIORS WHO TOOK IT ALL FOR GRANTED...
YOU KIDS DON'T KNOW HOW FORTUNATE YOU ARE!! WHY, I'D GIVE MY LEFT TESTICLE TO BE ABLE TO SPEAK another blah blah blah
yawn
cause toujours...
..I WAS SUPPOSED TO BE TEACHING ART.. BUT I MOSTLY RANTED ON ABOUT HOW LUCKY THEY ALL WERE...
A FEW YEARS LATER, I RAN INTO ONE OF MY FORMER STUDENTS AT A COPY SHOP...
Dude!! You were SO RIGHT about how lucky we were to know how to speak French fluently...
The chicks freakin' LOVE IT!!
STOP

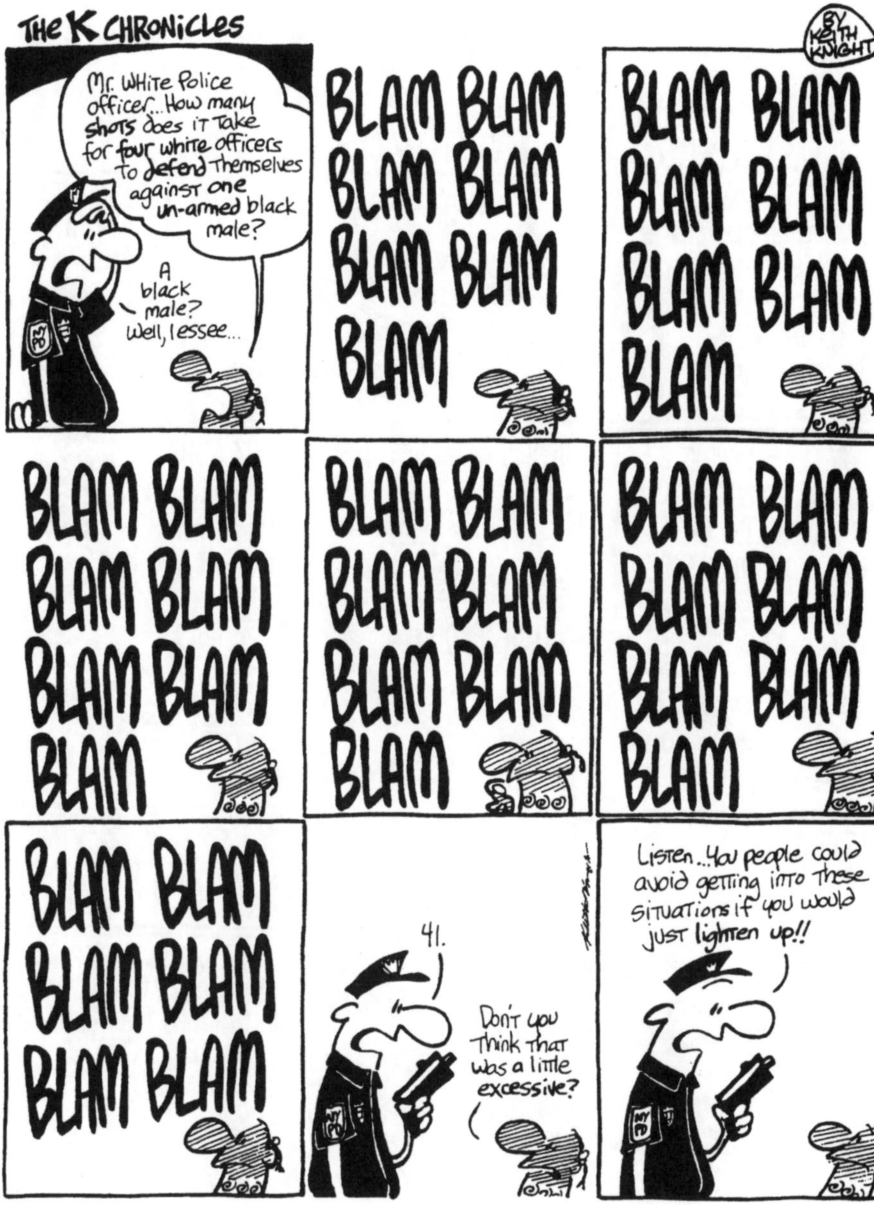

THE K CHRONICLES
BY KEITH KNIGHT
Mr. WHITE Police officer... How many shots does it take for four white officers to defend themselves against one un-armed black male?
A black male? Well, lessee...
BLAM BLAM BLAM BLAM BLAM BLAM BLAM
BLAM BLAM BLAM BLAM BLAM BLAM BLAM
BLAM BLAM BLAM BLAM BLAM BLAM BLAM
BLAM BLAM BLAM BLAM BLAM BLAM BLAM
BLAM BLAM BLAM BLAM BLAM BLAM BLAM
BLAM BLAM BLAM BLAM BLAM BLAM
41.
Don't you think that was a little excessive?
Listen... You people could avoid getting into these situations if you would just lighten up!!

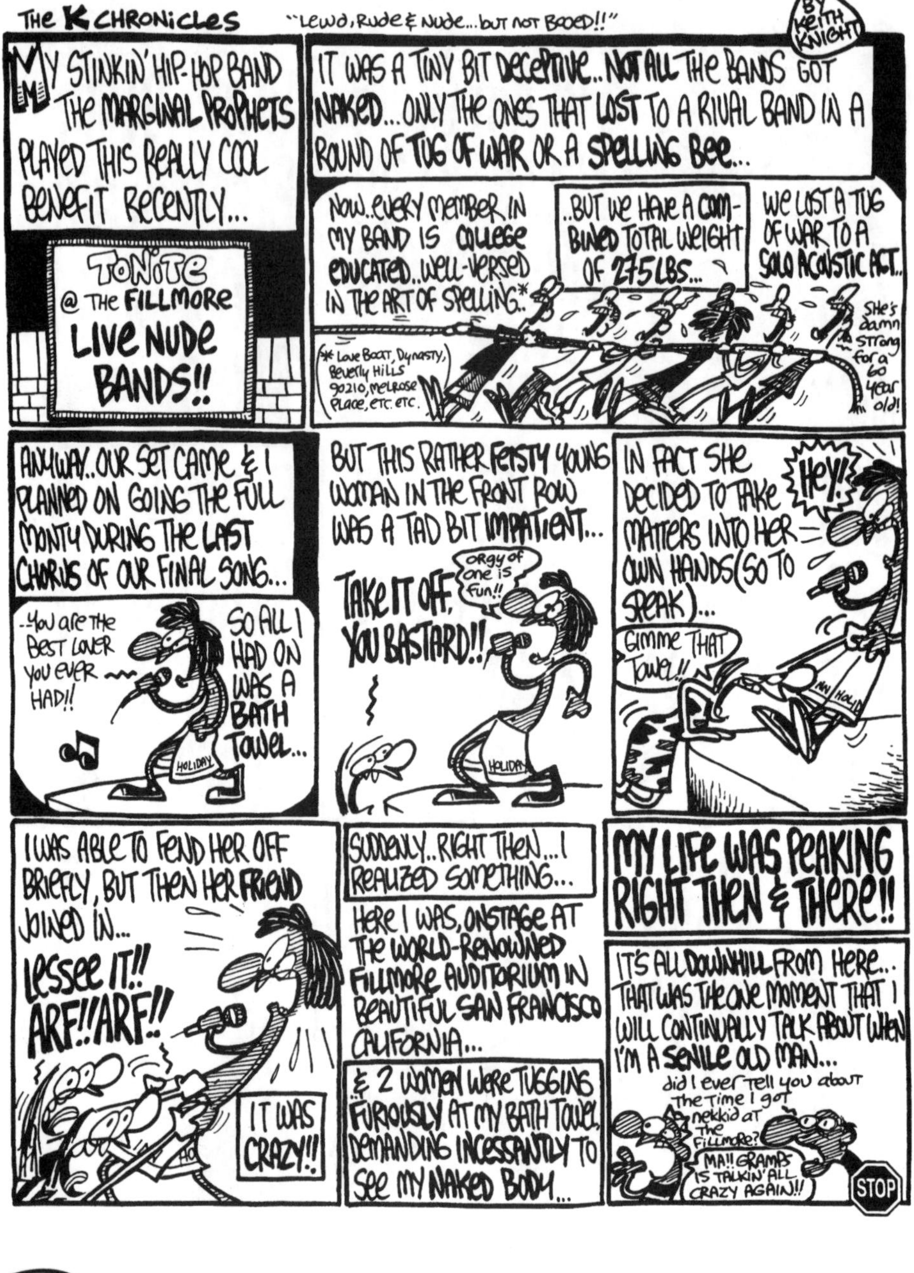
THE K CHRONICLES
"LEWD, RUDE & NUDE... BUT NOT BOOED!!"
BY KEITH KNIGHT
MY STINKIN' HIP-HOP BAND THE MARGINAL PROPHETS PLAYED THIS REALLY COOL BENEFIT RECENTLY...
TONITE @ THE FILLMORE LIVE NUDE BANDS!!
IT WAS A TINY BIT DECEPTIVE.. NOT ALL THE BANDS GOT NAKED... ONLY THE ONES THAT LOST TO A RIVAL BAND IN A ROUND OF TUG OF WAR OR A SPELLING BEE...
NOW.. EVERY MEMBER IN MY BAND IS COLLEGE EDUCATED.. WELL-VERSED IN THE ART OF SPELLING.*
..BUT WE HAVE A COMBINED TOTAL WEIGHT OF 275 LBS...
WE LOST A TUG OF WAR TO A SOLO ACOUSTIC ACT..
SHE'S DAMN STRONG FOR A 60 YEAR OLD!
* LOVE BOAT, DYNASTY, BEVERLY HILLS 90210, MELROSE PLACE, ETC. ETC.
ANYWAY.. OUR SET CAME & I PLANNED ON GOING THE FULL MONTY DURING THE LAST CHORUS OF OUR FINAL SONG...
-YOU ARE THE BEST LOVER YOU EVER HAD!!
SO ALL I HAD ON WAS A BATH TOWEL...
HOLIDAY
BUT THIS RATHER FEISTY YOUNG WOMAN IN THE FRONT ROW WAS A TAD BIT IMPATIENT...
TAKE IT OFF, YOU BASTARD!!
ORGY OF ONE IS FUN!!
HOLIDAY
IN FACT SHE DECIDED TO TAKE MATTERS INTO HER OWN HANDS (SO TO SPEAK)...
HEY!!
GIMME THAT TOWEL!!
I WAS ABLE TO FEND HER OFF BRIEFLY, BUT THEN HER FRIEND JOINED IN...
LESSEE IT!!
ARF!! ARF!!
IT WAS CRAZY!!
SUDDENLY.. RIGHT THEN... I REALIZED SOMETHING...
HERE I WAS, ONSTAGE AT THE WORLD-RENOWNED FILLMORE AUDITORIUM IN BEAUTIFUL SAN FRANCISCO CALIFORNIA...
& 2 WOMEN WERE TUGGING FURIOUSLY AT MY BATH TOWEL, DEMANDING INCESSANTLY TO SEE MY NAKED BODY...
MY LIFE WAS PEAKING RIGHT THEN & THERE!!
IT'S ALL DOWNHILL FROM HERE... THAT WAS THE ONE MOMENT THAT I WILL CONTINUALLY TALK ABOUT WHEN I'M A SENILE OLD MAN...
DID I EVER TELL YOU ABOUT THE TIME I GOT NEKKID AT THE FILLMORE?
MA!! GRAMPS IS TALKIN' ALL CRAZY AGAIN!!
STOP

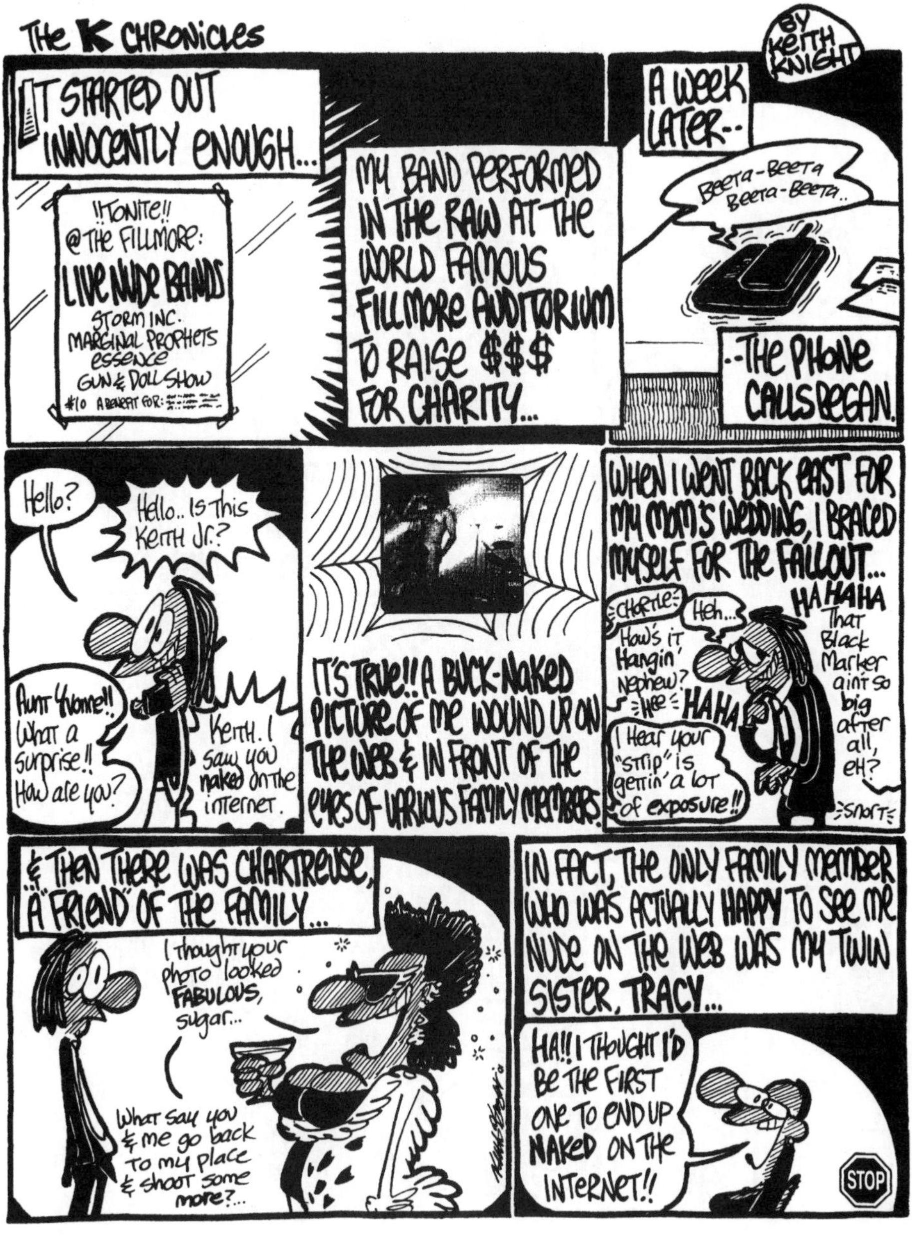

The K Chronicles
By Keith Knight
IT STARTED OUT INNOCENTLY ENOUGH...
!!TONITE!! @THE FILLMORE: LIVE NUDE BANDS
STORM INC.
MARGINAL PROPHETS
ESSENCE
GUN & DOLL SHOW
#10 A BENEFIT FOR:
MY BAND PERFORMED IN THE RAW AT THE WORLD FAMOUS FILLMORE AUDITORIUM TO RAISE $$$ FOR CHARITY...
A WEEK LATER...
Beeta-Beeta Beeta-Beeta..
..THE PHONE CALLS BEGAN.
Hello?
Hello.. Is this Keith Jr.?
Aunt Yvonne!! What a surprise!! How are you?
Keith. I saw you naked on the internet.
IT'S TRUE!! A BUCK-NAKED PICTURE OF ME WOUND UP ON THE WEB & IN FRONT OF THE EYES OF VARIOUS FAMILY MEMBERS.
WHEN I WENT BACK EAST FOR MY MOM'S WEDDING, I BRACED MYSELF FOR THE FALLOUT...
Chortle
How's it Hangin' Nephew?
Hee
Heh...
HA HAHA
HAHA
That Black Marker ain't so big after all, eH?
I Hear your "strip" is gettin' a lot of exposure!!
Snort
& THEN THERE WAS CHARTREUSE, "A FRIEND" OF THE FAMILY...
I thought your photo looked FABULOUS, sugar...
What say you & me go back to my place & shoot some more?...
IN FACT, THE ONLY FAMILY MEMBER WHO WAS ACTUALLY HAPPY TO SEE ME NUDE ON THE WEB WAS MY TWIN SISTER, TRACY...
HA!! I THOUGHT I'D BE THE FIRST ONE TO END UP NAKED ON THE INTERNET!!
STOP

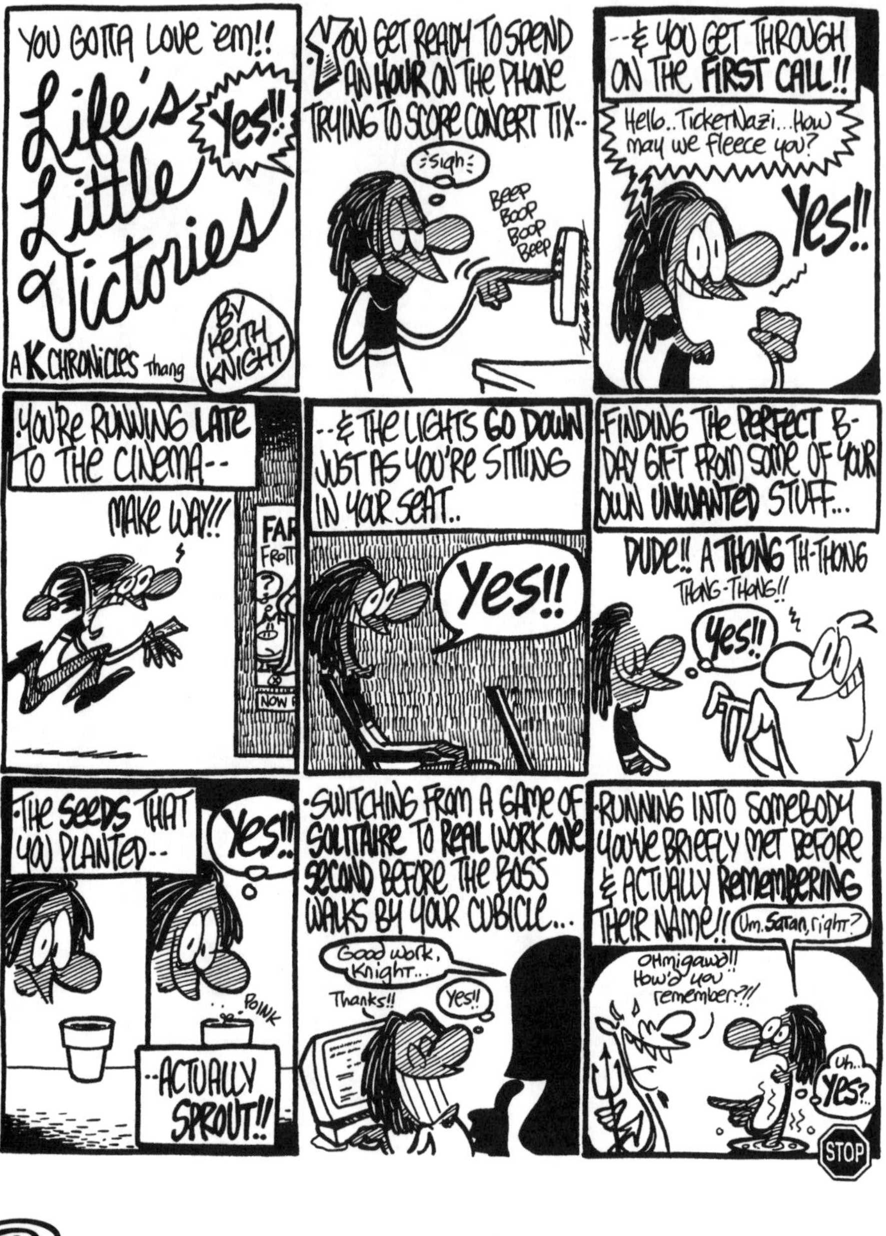
YOU GOTTA LOVE 'EM!!
Life's Little Victories
Yes!!
A K CHRONICLES thang
BY KEITH KNIGHT
YOU GET READY TO SPEND AN HOUR ON THE PHONE TRYING TO SCORE CONCERT TIX..
Sigh
BEEP BOOP BOOP BOOP BEEP
--& YOU GET THROUGH ON THE FIRST CALL!!
Hello..TicketNazi...How may we fleece you?
Yes!!..
YOU'RE RUNNING LATE TO THE CINEMA--
MAKE WAY!!
--& THE LIGHTS GO DOWN JUST AS YOU'RE SITTING IN YOUR SEAT..
Yes!!
FINDING THE PERFECT B-DAY GIFT FROM SOME OF YOUR OWN UNWANTED STUFF...
DUDE!! A THONG TH-THONG THONG-THONG!!
Yes!!
THE SEEDS THAT YOU PLANTED--
Yes!!..
POINK
--ACTUALLY SPROUT!!
SWITCHING FROM A GAME OF SOLITAIRE TO REAL WORK ONE SECOND BEFORE THE BOSS WALKS BY YOUR CUBICLE...
Good work, Knight...
Thanks!!
Yes!!
RUNNING INTO SOMEBODY YOU'VE BRIEFLY MET BEFORE & ACTUALLY REMEMBERING THEIR NAME!!
Um..Satan, right?
OHmigawd!! How'd you remember?!!
Uh... Yes?..
STOP

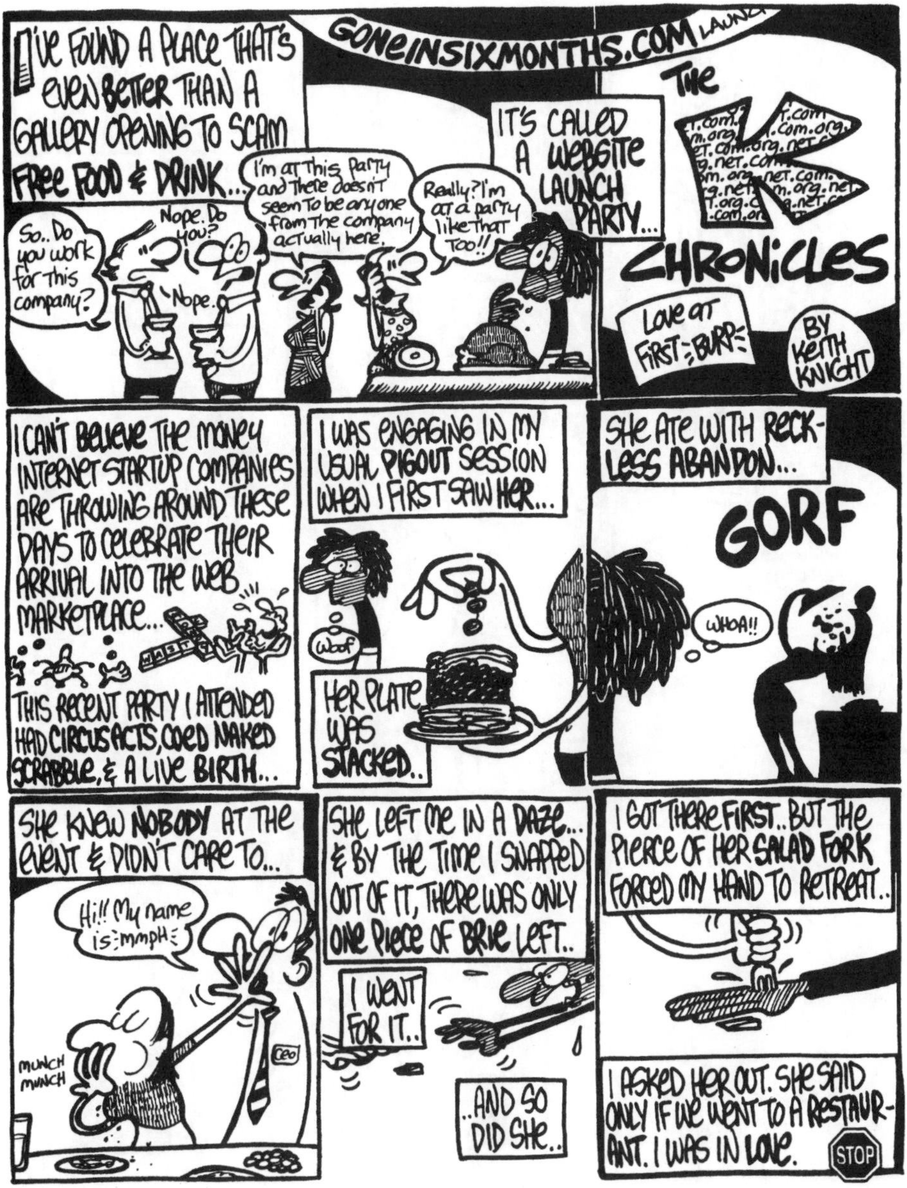
GONEINSIXMONTHS.COM
THE K CHRONICLES
Love at FIRST BURP
BY KEITH KNIGHT
I've found a place that's even better than a gallery opening to scam free food & drink...
It's called a website launch party...
So.. Do you work for this company?
Nope. Do you?
Nope.
I'm at this party and there doesn't seem to be anyone from the company actually here.
Really? I'm at a party like that too!!
I can't believe the money internet startup companies are throwing around these days to celebrate their arrival into the web marketplace...
This recent party I attended had circus acts, coed naked scrabble, & a live birth...
I was engaging in my usual pigout session when I first saw her...
Woof
Her plate was stacked..
She ate with reckless abandon...
GORF
WHOA!!
She knew nobody at the event & didn't care to...
Hi!! My name is mmpH
MUNCH MUNCH
CEO
She left me in a daze... & by the time I snapped out of it, there was only one piece of brie left..
I went for it..
..and so did she..
I got there first.. but the pierce of her salad fork forced my hand to retreat..
I asked her out. She said only if we went to a restaurant. I was in love.
STOP

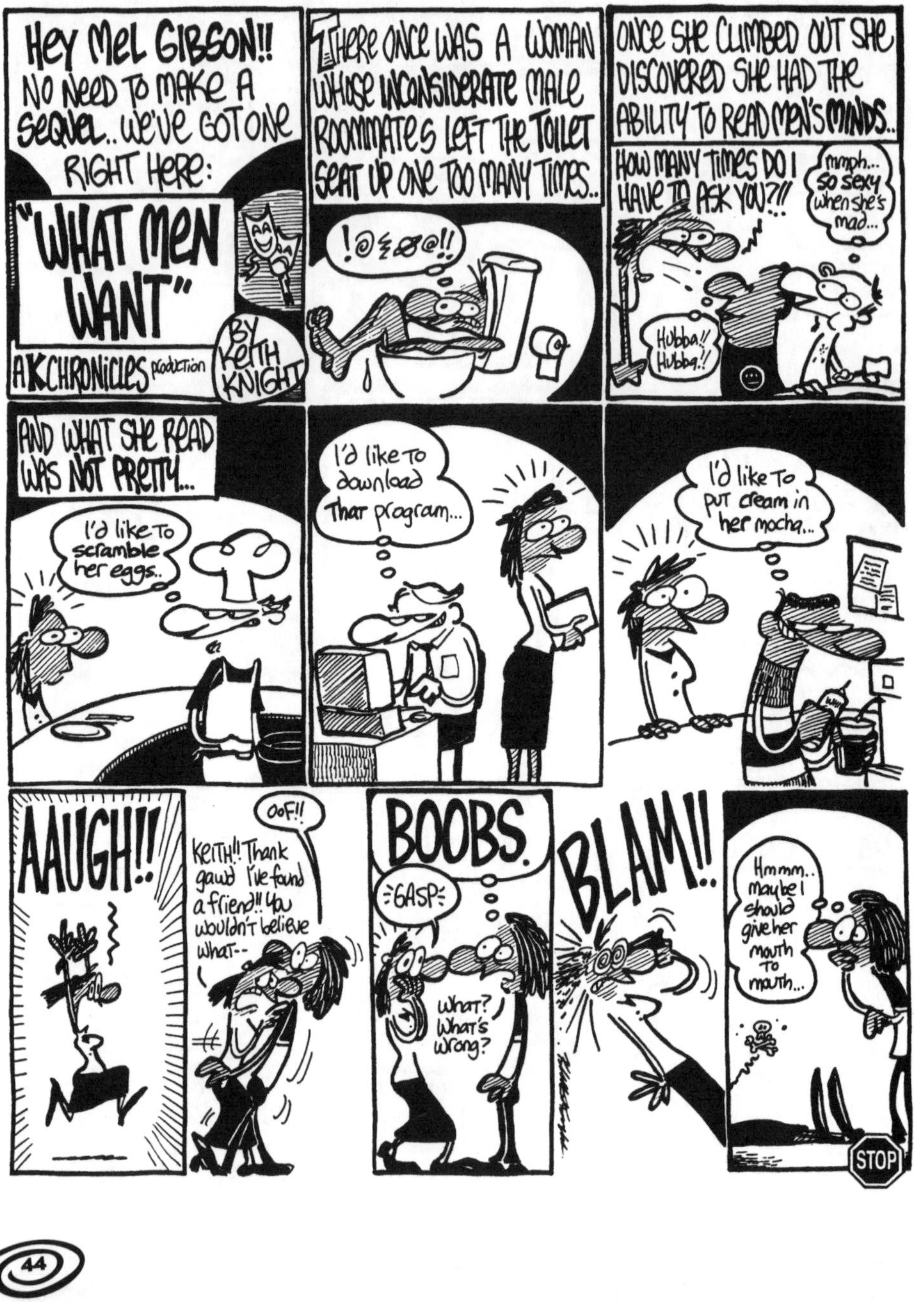
HEY MEL GIBSON!! NO NEED TO MAKE A SEQUEL.. WE'VE GOT ONE RIGHT HERE:
"WHAT MEN WANT"
A K CHRONICLES production
BY KEITH KNIGHT
THERE ONCE WAS A WOMAN WHOSE INCONSIDERATE MALE ROOMMATES LEFT THE TOILET SEAT UP ONE TOO MANY TIMES..
ONCE SHE CLIMBED OUT SHE DISCOVERED SHE HAD THE ABILITY TO READ MEN'S MINDS..
HOW MANY TIMES DO I HAVE TO ASK YOU?!!
mmph... so sexy when she's mad...
Hubba!! Hubba!!
AND WHAT SHE READ WAS NOT PRETTY...
I'd like to scramble her eggs..
I'd like to download that program...
I'd like to put cream in her mocha...
AAUGH!!
OOF!!
KEITH!! Thank gawd I've found a friend!! You wouldn't believe what--
BOOBS.
GASP
What? What's wrong?
BLAM!!
Hmmm.. maybe I should give her mouth to mouth...
STOP

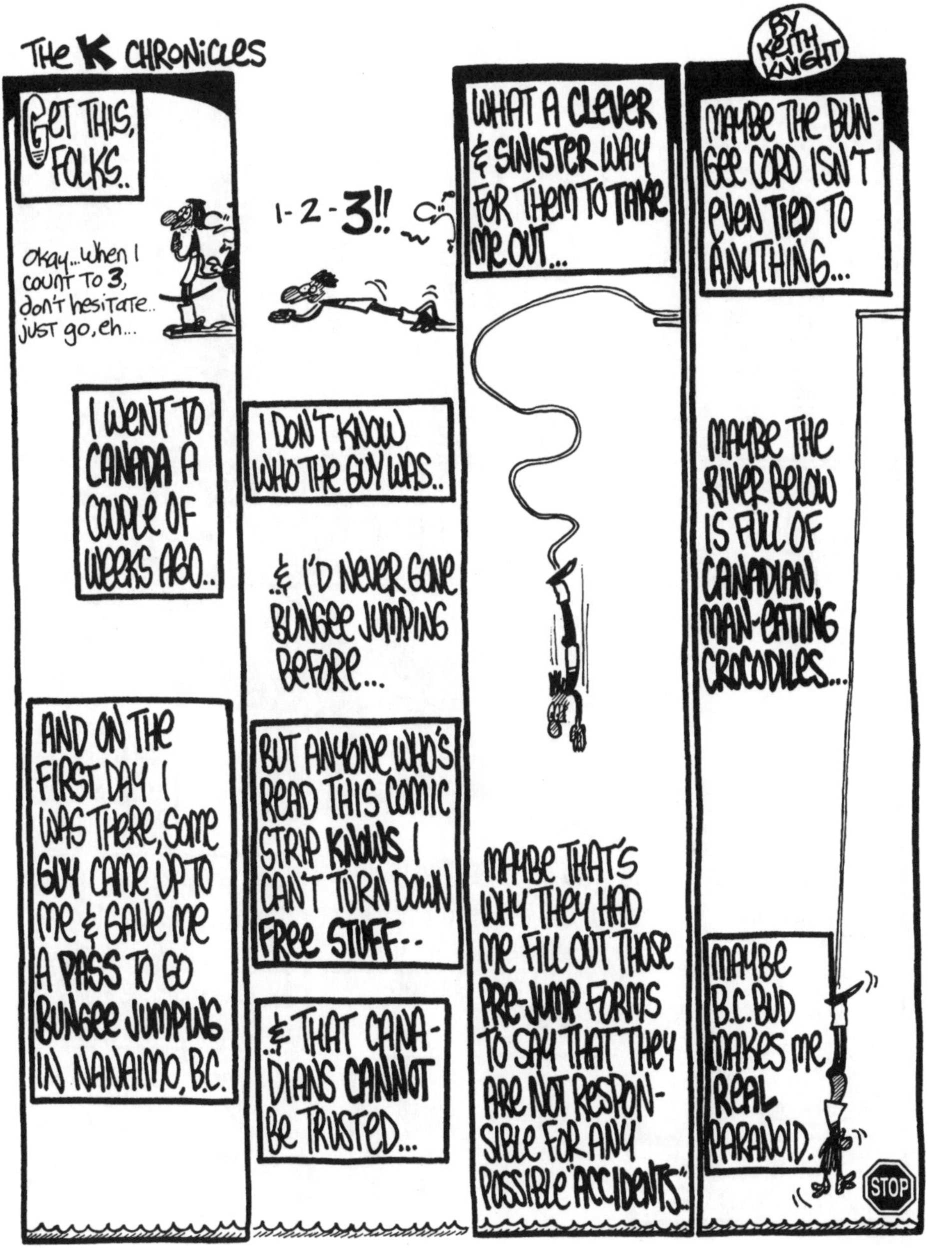
THE K CHRONICLES
BY KEITH KNIGHT
GET THIS, FOLKS..
Okay...When I count to 3, don't hesitate.. just go, eh...
I WENT TO CANADA A COUPLE OF WEEKS AGO..
AND ON THE FIRST DAY I WAS THERE, SOME GUY CAME UP TO ME & GAVE ME A PASS TO GO BUNGEE JUMPING IN NANAIMO, B.C.
1-2-3!!
I DON'T KNOW WHO THE GUY WAS..
..& I'D NEVER GONE BUNGEE JUMPING BEFORE...
BUT ANYONE WHO'S READ THIS COMIC STRIP KNOWS I CAN'T TURN DOWN FREE STUFF..
..& THAT CANADIANS CANNOT BE TRUSTED...
WHAT A CLEVER & SINISTER WAY FOR THEM TO TAKE ME OUT...
MAYBE THAT'S WHY THEY HAD ME FILL OUT THOSE PRE-JUMP FORMS TO SAY THAT THEY ARE NOT RESPONSIBLE FOR ANY POSSIBLE "ACCIDENTS."
MAYBE THE BUNGEE CORD ISN'T EVEN TIED TO ANYTHING...
MAYBE THE RIVER BELOW IS FULL OF CANADIAN, MAN-EATING CROCODILES...
MAYBE B.C. BUD MAKES ME REAL PARANOID.
STOP

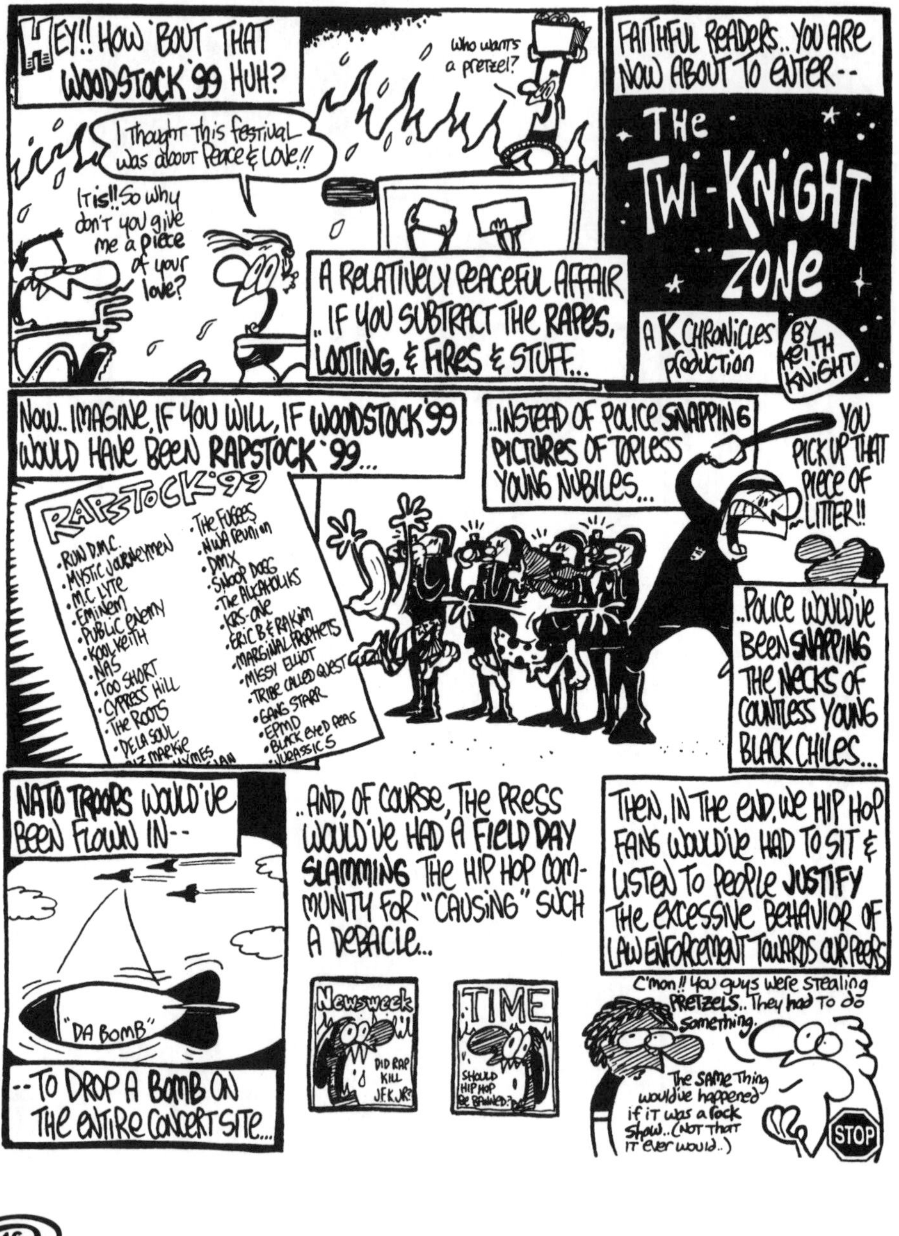
HEY!! HOW 'BOUT THAT WOODSTOCK '99 HUH?
I thought this festival was about Peace & Love!!
It is!! So why don't you give me a piece of your love?
Who wants a pretzel?
A RELATIVELY PEACEFUL AFFAIR .. IF YOU SUBTRACT THE RAPES, LOOTING, & FIRES & STUFF...
FAITHFUL READERS.. YOU ARE NOW ABOUT TO ENTER--
THE TWI-KNIGHT ZONE
A K CHRONICLES PRODUCTION
BY KEITH KNIGHT
NOW.. IMAGINE, IF YOU WILL, IF WOODSTOCK '99 WOULD HAVE BEEN RAPSTOCK '99...
RAPSTOCK '99
•RUN D.M.C.
•MYSTIC JOURNEYMEN
•M.C LYTE
•EMINEM
•PUBLIC ENEMY
•KOOL KEITH
•NAS
•TOO SHORT
•CYPRESS HILL
•THE ROOTS
•DE LA SOUL
•THE FUGEES
•NWA REUNION
•DMX
•SNOOP DOGG
•THE ALKAHOLIKS
•KRS-ONE
•ERIC B & RAKIM
•MARGINAL PROPHETS
•MISSY ELLIOT
•TRIBE CALLED QUEST
•GANG STARR
•EPMD
•BLACK EYED PEAS
•JURASSIC 5
...INSTEAD OF POLICE SNAPPING PICTURES OF TOPLESS YOUNG NUBILES...
YOU PICK UP THAT PIECE OF LITTER!!
..POLICE WOULD'VE BEEN SNAPPING THE NECKS OF COUNTLESS YOUNG BLACK CHILES...
NATO TROOPS WOULD'VE BEEN FLOWN IN--
"DA BOMB"
--TO DROP A BOMB ON THE ENTIRE CONCERT SITE...
..AND, OF COURSE, THE PRESS WOULD'VE HAD A FIELD DAY SLAMMING THE HIP HOP COMMUNITY FOR "CAUSING" SUCH A DEBACLE...
Newsweek
DID RAP KILL J.F.K. JR?
TIME
SHOULD HIP HOP BE BANNED?
THEN, IN THE END, WE HIP HOP FANS WOULD'VE HAD TO SIT & LISTEN TO PEOPLE JUSTIFY THE EXCESSIVE BEHAVIOR OF LAW ENFORCEMENT TOWARDS OUR PEERS
C'mon!! You guys were stealing PRETZELS.. They had to do something.
The same thing would've happened if it was a rock show.. (NOT THAT IT ever would..)
STOP

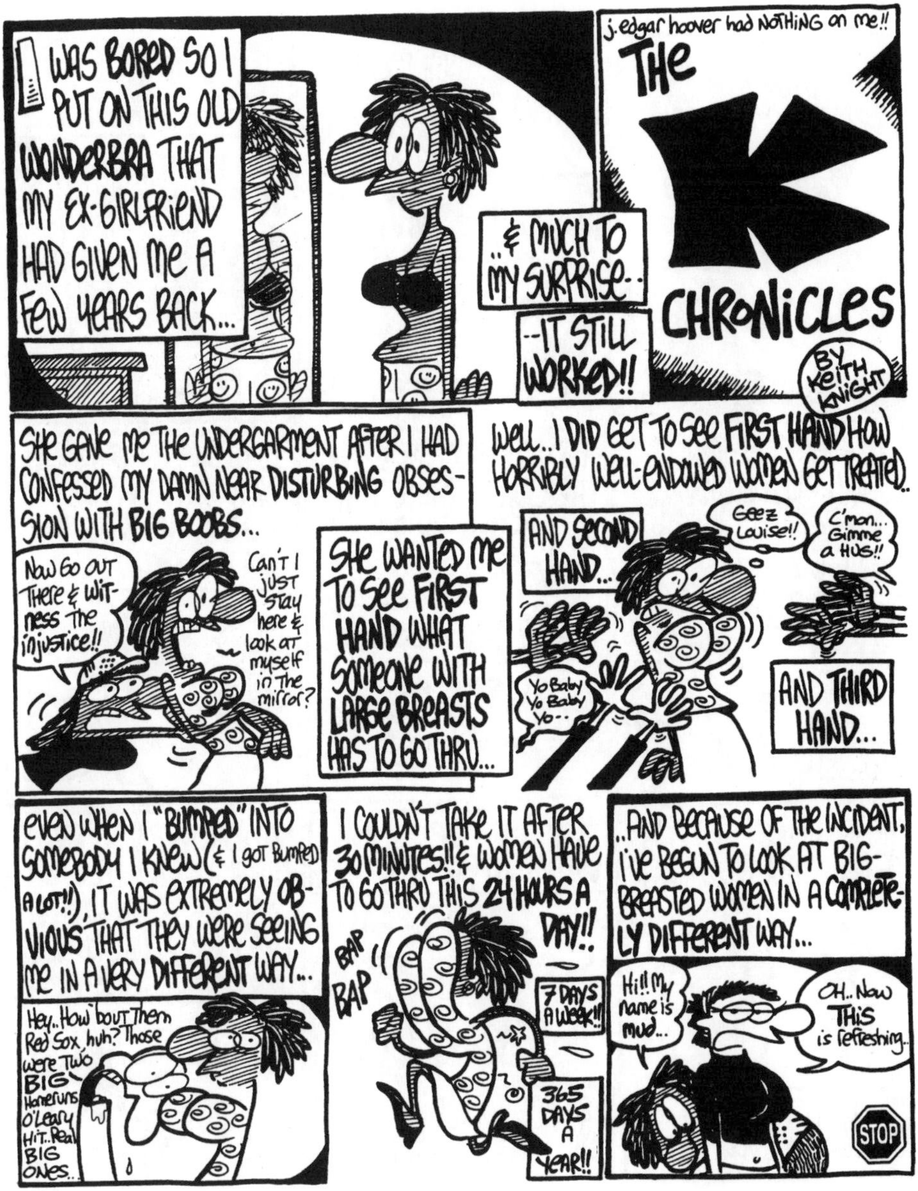
I WAS BORED SO I PUT ON THIS OLD WONDERBRA THAT MY EX-GIRLFRIEND HAD GIVEN ME A FEW YEARS BACK...
..& MUCH TO MY SURPRISE--
--IT STILL WORKED!!
j. edgar hoover had NOTHING on me!!
THE K CHRONICLES
BY KEITH KNIGHT
SHE GAVE ME THE UNDERGARMENT AFTER I HAD CONFESSED MY DAMN NEAR DISTURBING OBSES-SION WITH BIG BOOBS...
Now GO OUT There & WIT-ness The injustice!!
Can't I just stay here & look at myself in the mirror?
SHE WANTED ME TO SEE FIRST HAND WHAT SOMEONE WITH LARGE BREASTS HAS TO GO THRU...
WELL...I DID GET TO SEE FIRST HAND HOW HORRIBLY WELL-ENDOWED WOMEN GET TREATED..
AND SECOND HAND...
Geez Louise!!
C'mon... Gimme a HUG!!
Yo Baby Yo Baby Yo--
AND THIRD HAND...
EVEN WHEN I "BUMPED" INTO SOMEBODY I KNEW (& I GOT BUMPED A LOT!!), IT WAS EXTREMELY OB-VIOUS THAT THEY WERE SEEING ME IN A VERY DIFFERENT WAY...
Hey..How 'bout Them Red Sox, huh? Those were TWO BIG Homeruns O'Leary HIT..Real BIG ONES..
I COULDN'T TAKE IT AFTER 30 MINUTES!! & WOMEN HAVE TO GO THRU THIS 24 HOURS A DAY!!
7 DAYS A WEEK!!
365 DAYS A YEAR!!
BAP BAP
..AND BECAUSE OF THE INCIDENT, I'VE BEGUN TO LOOK AT BIG-BREASTED WOMEN IN A COMPLETE-LY DIFFERENT WAY...
Hi!! My name is mud...
OH.. Now THIS is refreshing..
STOP

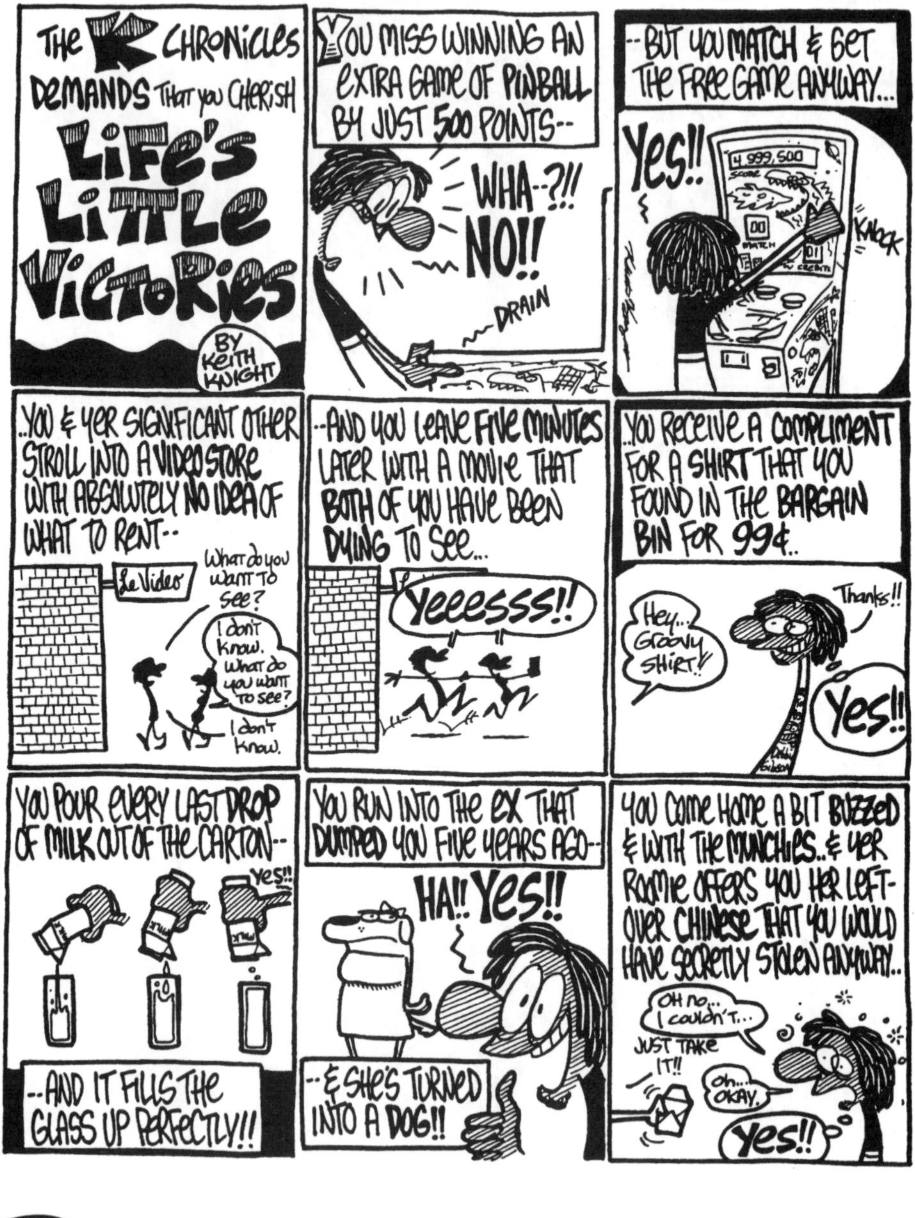
THE K CHRONICLES DEMANDS THAT YOU CHERISH
LIFE'S LITTLE VICTORIES
BY KEITH KNIGHT
YOU MISS WINNING AN EXTRA GAME OF PINBALL BY JUST 500 POINTS--
WHA--?!!
NO!!
DRAIN
--BUT YOU MATCH & GET THE FREE GAME ANYWAY...
YES!!
4,999,500
SCORE
MATCH
CREDITS
KNOCK
..YOU & YER SIGNIFICANT OTHER STROLL INTO A VIDEO STORE WITH ABSOLUTELY NO IDEA OF WHAT TO RENT--
Le Video
What do you want to see?
I don't know. What do you want to see?
I don't know.
--AND YOU LEAVE FIVE MINUTES LATER WITH A MOVIE THAT BOTH OF YOU HAVE BEEN DYING TO SEE...
YEEESSS!!
..YOU RECEIVE A COMPLIMENT FOR A SHIRT THAT YOU FOUND IN THE BARGAIN BIN FOR 99¢..
Hey... Groovy SHIRT!!
Thanks!!
YES!!
YOU POUR EVERY LAST DROP OF MILK OUT OF THE CARTON--
MILK
YES!!
--AND IT FILLS THE GLASS UP PERFECTLY!!
YOU RUN INTO THE EX THAT DUMPED YOU FIVE YEARS AGO--
HA!! YES!!
--& SHE'S TURNED INTO A DOG!!
YOU COME HOME A BIT BUZZED & WITH THE MUNCHIES..& YER ROOMIE OFFERS YOU HER LEFT-OVER CHINESE THAT YOU WOULD HAVE SECRETLY STOLEN ANYWAY..
OH NO... I COULDN'T...
JUST TAKE IT!!
Oh... OKAY.
YES!!

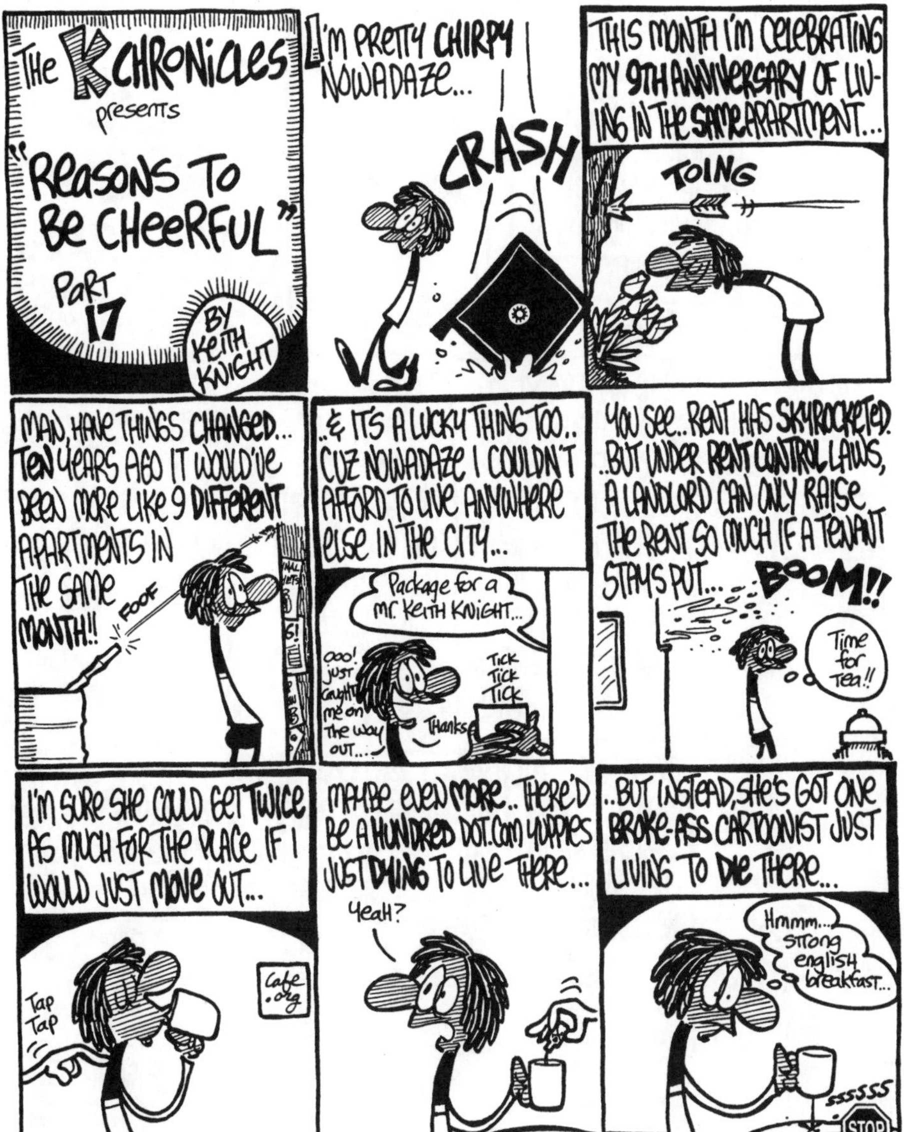

The K Chronicles presents
"Reasons to Be Cheerful"
Part 17
By Keith Knight
I'm pretty chirpy nowadaze...
CRASH
This month I'm celebrating my 9th anniversary of living in the same apartment...
TOING
Man, have things changed... Ten years ago it would've been more like 9 different apartments in the same month!!
FOOF
...& it's a lucky thing too... cuz nowadaze I couldn't afford to live anywhere else in the city...
Package for a mr. Keith Knight...
Ooo! Just caught me on the way out...
Tick Tick Tick
Thanks
You see... rent has skyrocketed. ...But under rent control laws, a landlord can only raise the rent so much if a tenant stays put...
BOOM!!
Time for Tea!!
I'm sure she could get twice as much for the place if I would just move out...
Tap Tap
Cafe .org
Maybe even more... There'd be a hundred dot.com yuppies just dying to live there...
Yeah?
...But instead, she's got one broke-ass cartoonist just living to die there...
Hmmm... strong english breakfast...
SSSSSS
STOP

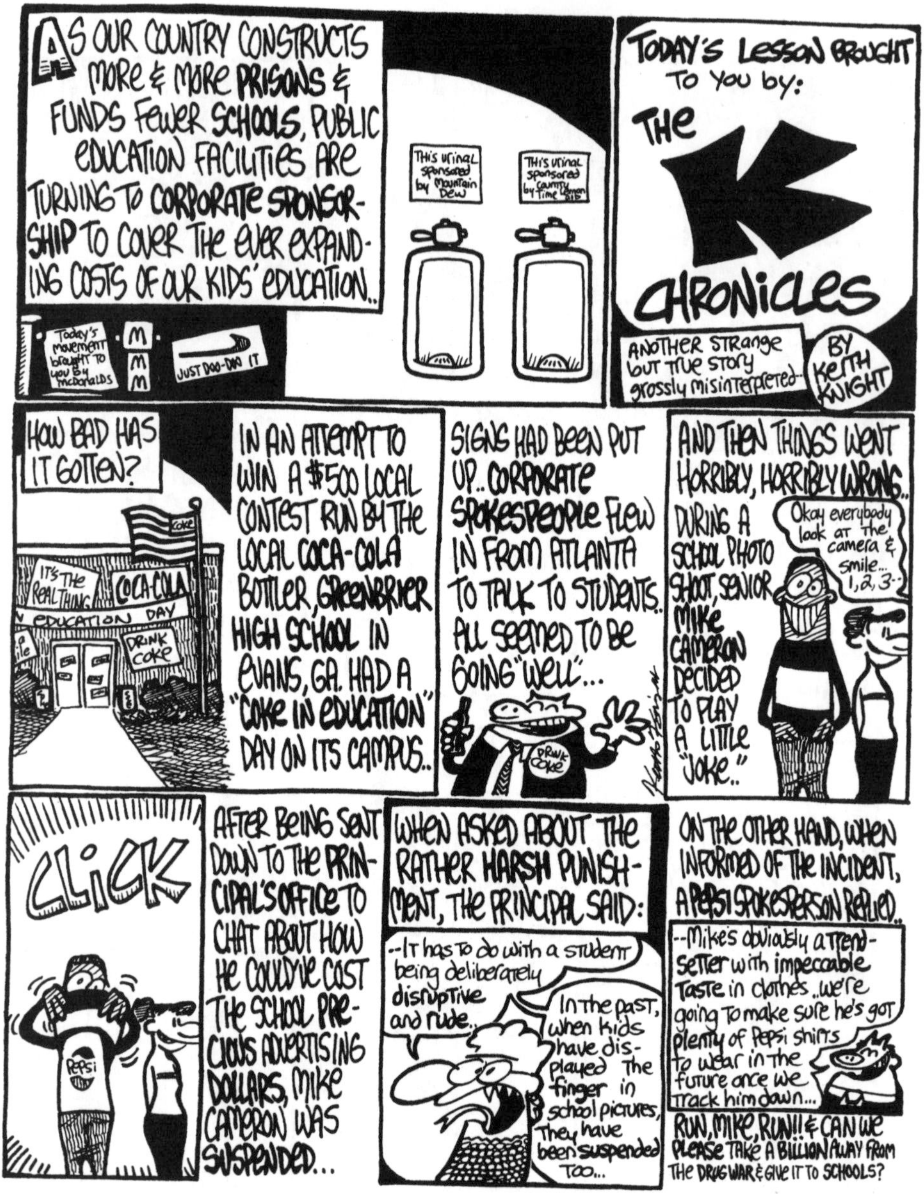
AS OUR COUNTRY CONSTRUCTS MORE & MORE PRISONS & FUNDS FEWER SCHOOLS, PUBLIC EDUCATION FACILITIES ARE TURNING TO CORPORATE SPONSORSHIP TO COVER THE EVER EXPANDING COSTS OF OUR KIDS' EDUCATION..
This urinal sponsored by Mountain Dew
This urinal sponsored by Country Time Lemonade
Today's movement brought to you by McDonalds
M
M
M
JUST DOO-DOO IT
TODAY'S LESSON BROUGHT TO YOU BY:
THE K CHRONICLES
ANOTHER STRANGE BUT TRUE STORY GROSSLY MISINTERPRETED...
BY KEITH KNIGHT
HOW BAD HAS IT GOTTEN?
COKE
IT'S THE REAL THING
COCA-COLA
EDUCATION DAY
DRINK COKE
IN AN ATTEMPT TO WIN A $500 LOCAL CONTEST RUN BY THE LOCAL COCA-COLA BOTTLER, GREENBRIER HIGH SCHOOL IN EVANS, GA. HAD A "COKE IN EDUCATION" DAY ON ITS CAMPUS..
SIGNS HAD BEEN PUT UP.. CORPORATE SPOKESPEOPLE FLEW IN FROM ATLANTA TO TALK TO STUDENTS.. ALL SEEMED TO BE GOING "WELL"...
DRINK COKE
AND THEN THINGS WENT HORRIBLY, HORRIBLY WRONG..
DURING A SCHOOL PHOTO SHOOT, SENIOR MIKE CAMERON DECIDED TO PLAY A LITTLE "JOKE"..
Okay everybody look at the camera & smile... 1, 2, 3--
CLICK
Pepsi
AFTER BEING SENT DOWN TO THE PRINCIPAL'S OFFICE TO CHAT ABOUT HOW HE COULD'VE COST THE SCHOOL PRECIOUS ADVERTISING DOLLARS, MIKE CAMERON WAS SUSPENDED...
WHEN ASKED ABOUT THE RATHER HARSH PUNISHMENT, THE PRINCIPAL SAID:
--It has to do with a student being deliberately disruptive and rude..
In the past, when kids have displayed the finger in school pictures, they have been suspended too...
ON THE OTHER HAND, WHEN INFORMED OF THE INCIDENT, A PEPSI SPOKESPERSON REPLIED..
--Mike's obviously a trend-setter with impeccable taste in clothes..we're going to make sure he's got plenty of Pepsi shirts to wear in the future once we track him down...
RUN, MIKE, RUN!! & CAN WE PLEASE TAKE A BILLION AWAY FROM THE DRUG WAR & GIVE IT TO SCHOOLS?

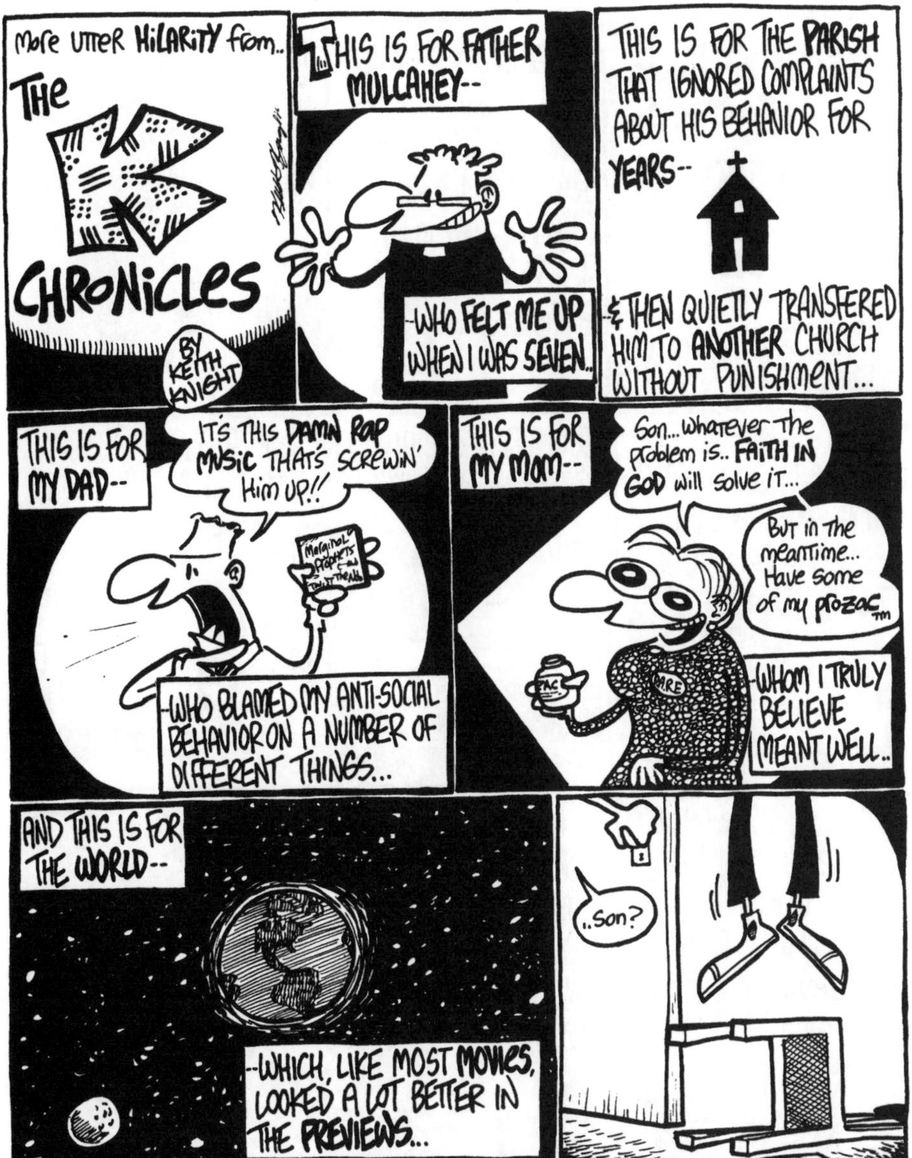
More UTTER HILARITY from..
THE K CHRONICLES
BY KEITH KNIGHT
THIS IS FOR FATHER MULCAHEY--
--WHO FELT ME UP WHEN I WAS SEVEN..
THIS IS FOR THE PARISH THAT IGNORED COMPLAINTS ABOUT HIS BEHAVIOR FOR YEARS--
--& THEN QUIETLY TRANSFERED HIM TO ANOTHER CHURCH WITHOUT PUNISHMENT...
THIS IS FOR MY DAD--
IT'S THIS DAMN RAP MUSIC THAT'S SCREWIN' HIM UP!!
--WHO BLAMED MY ANTI-SOCIAL BEHAVIOR ON A NUMBER OF DIFFERENT THINGS...
THIS IS FOR MY MOM--
Son... whatever the problem is.. FAITH IN GOD will solve it...
But in the meantime... Have some of my prozac™
--WHOM I TRULY BELIEVE MEANT WELL..
AND THIS IS FOR THE WORLD--
--WHICH, LIKE MOST MOVIES, LOOKED A LOT BETTER IN THE PREVIEWS...
..Son?
VICTIMS OF SEXUAL ABUSE: TELL ALL THAT YOU CAN TELL...

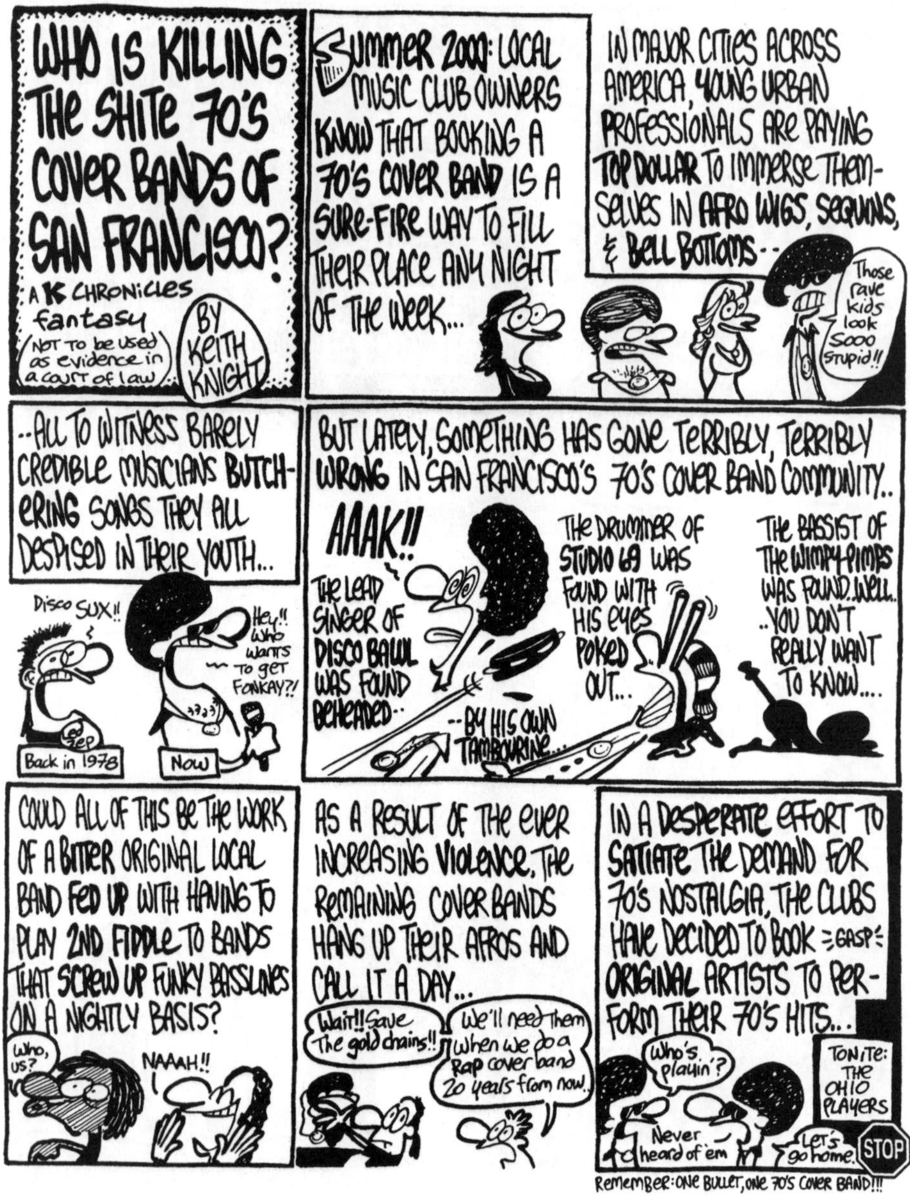
WHO IS KILLING THE SHITE 70'S COVER BANDS OF SAN FRANCISCO?
A K CHRONICLES fantasy
(NOT TO be used as evidence in a court of law)
BY KEITH KNIGHT
SUMMER 2000: LOCAL MUSIC CLUB OWNERS KNOW THAT BOOKING A 70'S COVER BAND IS A SURE-FIRE WAY TO FILL THEIR PLACE ANY NIGHT OF THE WEEK...
IN MAJOR CITIES ACROSS AMERICA, YOUNG URBAN PROFESSIONALS ARE PAYING TOP DOLLAR TO IMMERSE THEM-SELVES IN AFRO WIGS, SEQUINS, & BELL BOTTOMS--
Those rave kids look sooo stupid!!
--ALL TO WITNESS BARELY CREDIBLE MUSICIANS BUTCH-ERING SONGS THEY ALL DESPISED IN THEIR YOUTH...
Disco SUX!!
Led Zep
Back in 1978
Hey!! Who wants to get FONKAY?!
Now
BUT LATELY, SOMETHING HAS GONE TERRIBLY, TERRIBLY WRONG IN SAN FRANCISCO'S 70'S COVER BAND COMMUNITY..
AAAK!!
THE LEAD SINGER OF DISCO BAWL WAS FOUND BEHEADED--
--BY HIS OWN TAMBOURINE...
THE DRUMMER OF STUDIO 69 WAS FOUND WITH HIS EYES POKED OUT...
THE BASSIST OF THE WIMPY-PIMPS WAS FOUND..WELL.. ..YOU DON'T REALLY WANT TO KNOW....
COULD ALL OF THIS BE THE WORK OF A BITTER ORIGINAL LOCAL BAND FED UP WITH HAVING TO PLAY 2ND FIDDLE TO BANDS THAT SCREW UP FUNKY BASSLINES ON A NIGHTLY BASIS?
Who, us?
NAAAH!!
AS A RESULT OF THE EVER INCREASING VIOLENCE, THE REMAINING COVER BANDS HANG UP THEIR AFROS AND CALL IT A DAY...
Wait!! Save the gold chains!!
We'll need them when we do a Rap cover band 20 years from now..
IN A DESPERATE EFFORT TO SATIATE THE DEMAND FOR 70'S NOSTALGIA, THE CLUBS HAVE DECIDED TO BOOK =GASP= ORIGINAL ARTISTS TO PER-FORM THEIR 70'S HITS...
Who's playin'?
TONITE: THE OHIO PLAYERS
Never heard of 'em
Let's go home.
STOP
REMEMBER: ONE BULLET, ONE 70'S COVER BAND!!!

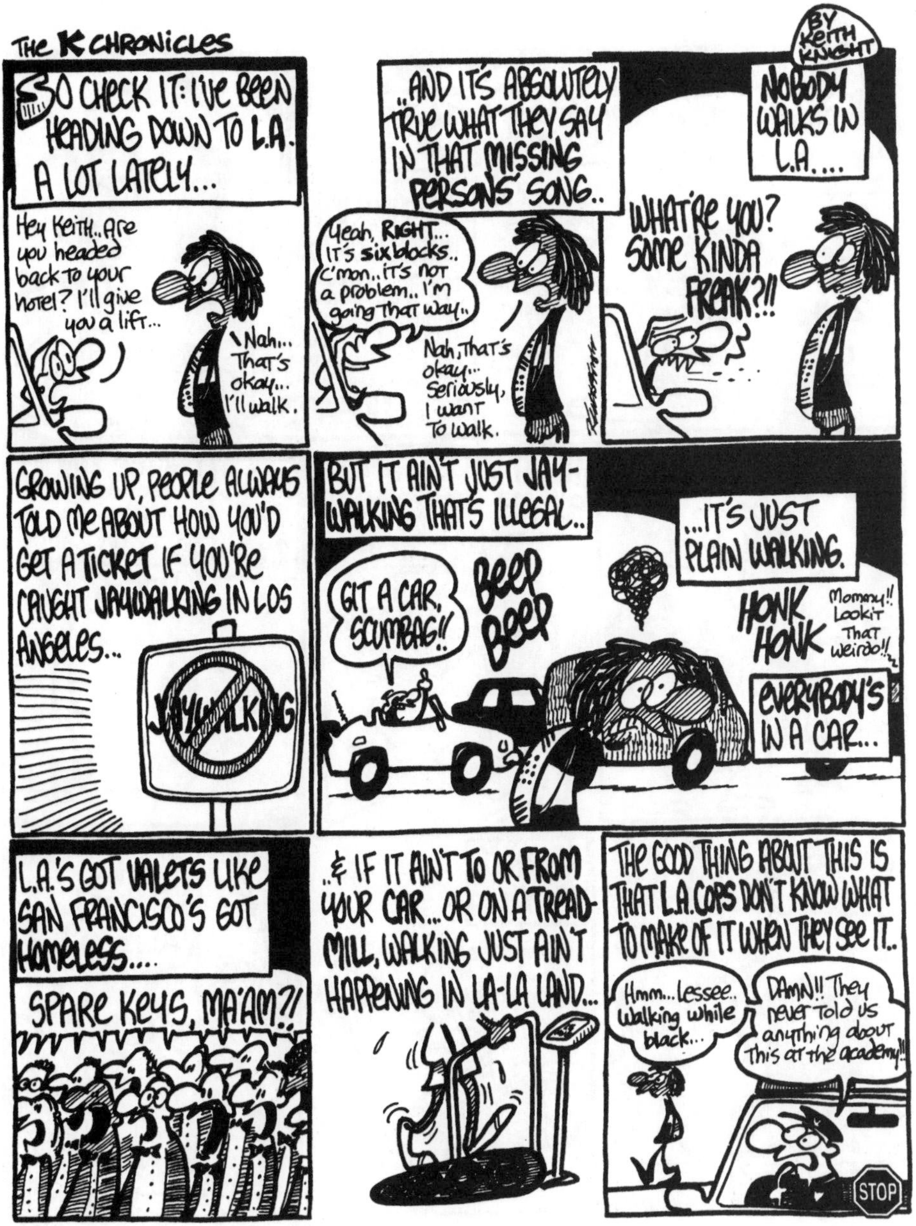
The K Chronicles
By Keith Knight
So check it: I've been heading down to L.A. a lot lately...
Hey Keith.. are you headed back to your hotel? I'll give you a lift...
Nah... That's okay... I'll walk.
..and it's absolutely true what they say in that Missing Persons' song..
Yeah, RIGHT... it's six blocks.. c'mon.. it's not a problem.. I'm going that way..
Nah, that's okay... Seriously, I want to walk.
Nobody walks in L.A....
What're you? Same kinda freak?!!
Growing up, people always told me about how you'd get a ticket if you're caught jaywalking in Los Angeles...
Jaywalking
But it ain't just jay-walking that's illegal..
...it's just plain walking.
Git a car, scumbag!!
Beep Beep
Honk Honk
Mommy!! Lookit that weirdo!!
Everybody's in a car...
L.A.'s got valets like San Francisco's got homeless....
Spare keys, ma'am?!
..& if it ain't to or from your car...or on a tread-mill, walking just ain't happening in La-La Land...
The good thing about this is that L.A. cops don't know what to make of it when they see it..
Hmm... lessee.. walking while black...
Damn!! They never told us anything about this at the academy!!
STOP

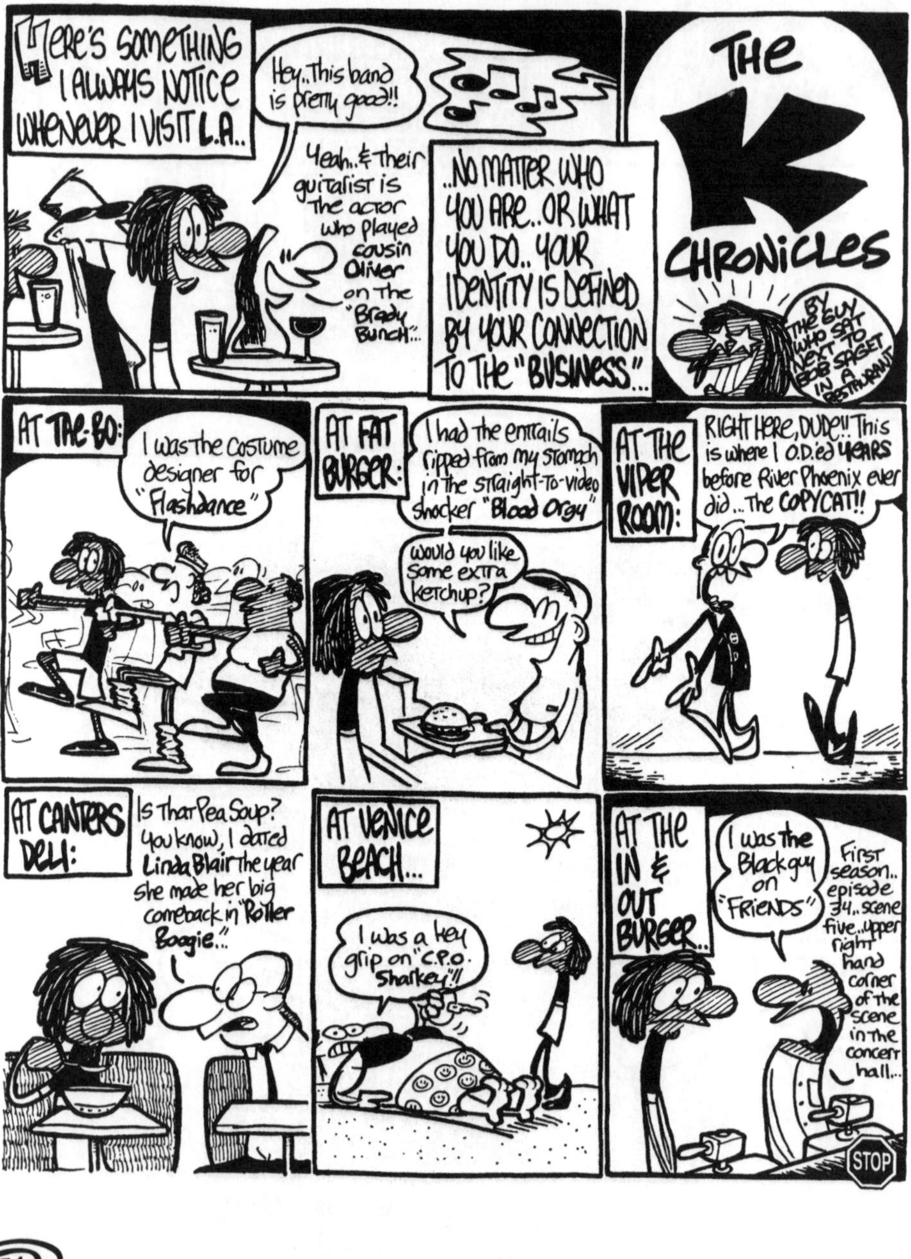
Here's something I always notice whenever I visit L.A..
Hey.. This band is pretty good!!
Yeah.. & their guitarist is the actor who played cousin Oliver on the "Brady Bunch"..
..No matter who you are.. or what you do.. your identity is defined by your connection to the "Business"...
THE K CHRONICLES
By the guy who sat next to Bob Saget in a restaurant
At Tae-Bo:
I was the costume designer for "Flashdance"
At Fat Burger:
I had the entrails ripped from my stomach in the straight-to-video shocker "Blood Orgy"
Would you like some extra ketchup?
At the Viper Room:
Right here, dude!! This is where I O.D.'ed years before River Phoenix ever did... The copycat!!
At Canters Deli:
Is that Pea Soup? You know, I dated Linda Blair the year she made her big comeback in "Roller Boogie."
At Venice Beach...
I was a key grip on "C.P.O. Sharkey"!!
At the In & Out Burger..
I was the Black guy on "Friends"
First season.. episode 34.. scene five.. upper right hand corner of the scene in the concert hall...
STOP

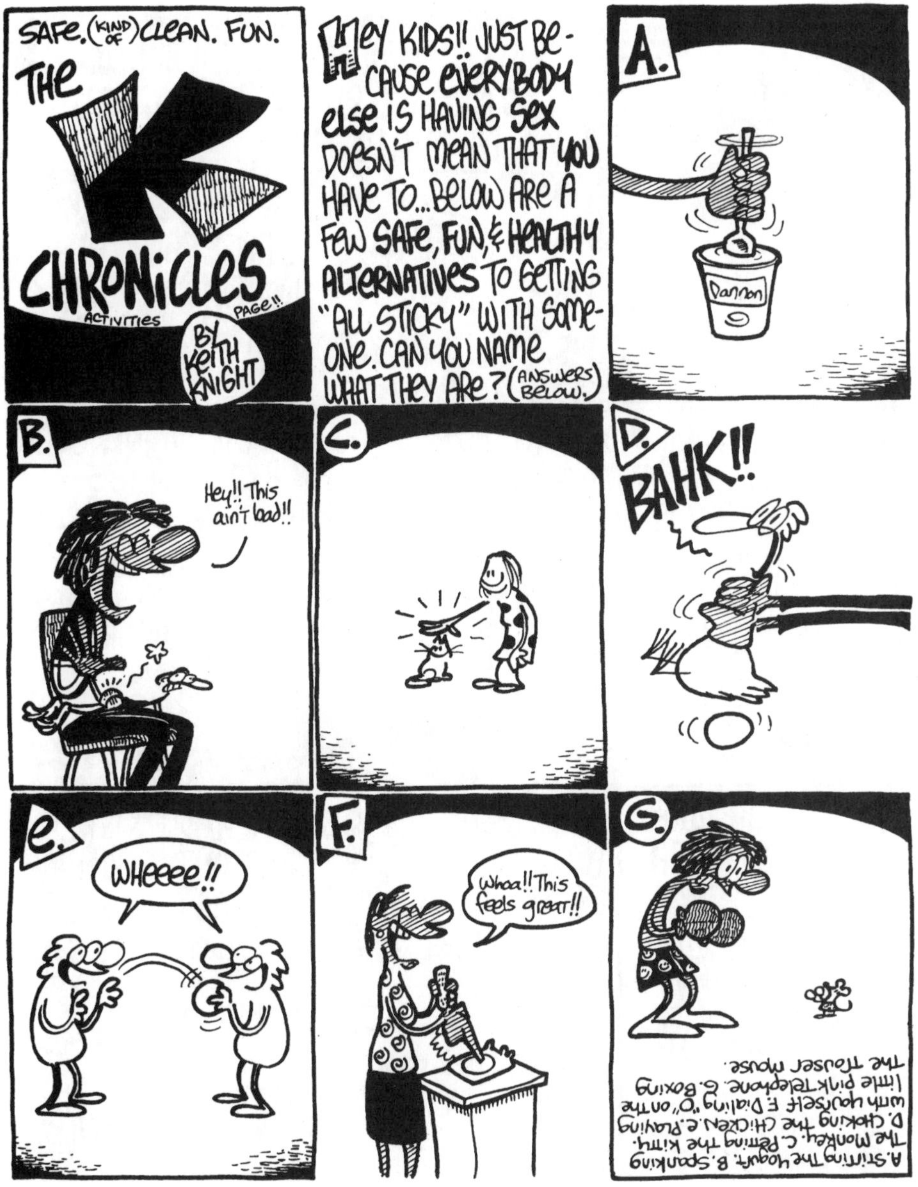
SAFE. (KIND OF) CLEAN. FUN.
THE K CHRONICLES ACTIVITIES PAGE!!
BY KEITH KNIGHT
HEY KIDS!! JUST BECAUSE EVERYBODY ELSE IS HAVING SEX DOESN'T MEAN THAT YOU HAVE TO... BELOW ARE A FEW SAFE, FUN, & HEALTHY ALTERNATIVES TO GETTING "ALL STICKY" WITH SOMEONE. CAN YOU NAME WHAT THEY ARE? (ANSWERS BELOW.)
A.
Dannon
B.
Hey!! This ain't bad!!
C.
D.
BAHK!!
e.
WHEEEE!!
F.
Whoa!! This feels great!!
G.
A. Stirring the Yogurt. B. Spanking the Monkey. C. Petting the kitty. D. Choking the Chicken. E. Playing with yourself. F. Dialing "O" on the little pink telephone. G. Boxing the trouser mouse.

RALPH NADER RALPH NADER RALPH NADER RALPH NADER RALPH NADER RALPH NADER... (background text)

THE **K** CHRONICLES

BREAKS DOWN THE PRESIDENTIAL ELECTION!!

BY KEITH KNIGHT

I DON'T CARE WHAT PEOPLE SAY.. IF BILL CLINTON WAS ALLOWED TO RUN FOR PRESIDENT AGAIN, HE'D WIN IN A LANDSLIDE...

munch munch munch

FLINT

THE GUY IS SMART, CRAFTY, & CHARISMATIC.. CAN HANG WITH ANY WORLD LEADER & AIN'T ABOVE HITTIN' THE LOCAL BBQ JOINT FOR A TUB O' RIBS..

BUT SADLY, THIS IS **REALITY**, & THE CURRENT DEMOCRATIC & REPUBLICAN CANDIDATES ARE BASICALLY CLINTON SPLIT IN HALF..

=SIGH=

Stiff as a board

AL GORE'S GOT THE SMARTS & **NONE** OF THE CHARISMA

BUT WHILE CLINTON WAS BORN WITH A PORK RIB IN HIS MOUTH, BUSH & GORE WERE BORN WITH SILVER SPOONS..

GEORGE W. BUSH HAS GOT THE CHARISMA AND **NONE** OF THE SMARTS

Dumb as a brick

SURE, BUSH IS THE TYPE OF GUY AMERICA CAN SIT DOWN & HAVE A BEER WITH.. HE'S PERSONABLE, IN A GOOFY, DOPEY TYPE OF WAY...

BUT TAKE A GOOD LOOK AT WHAT'S GOIN' ON IN THE MIDDLE EAST, FOLKS...

um... anybody want some coke?

CAN YOU IMAGINE BUSH TRYING TO WORK A DEAL WITH THESE GUYS?

AND I AIN'T JUST TALKING ABOUT PRONOUNCING THEIR NAMES CORRECTLY...

AND LESSEE.. THE COUNTRY HAS **PROSPERED** OVER THE PAST 8 YEARS UNDER THE CLINTON ADMINISTRATION.. THE DOLLAR IS STRONG... UNEMPLOYMENT & VIOLENT CRIME ARE AT THEIR LOWEST RATES IN YEARS...

SO HOW BIG OF A LAME-ASS DOES AL GORE HAVE TO BE FOR THIS ELECTION TO BE AS CLOSE AS IT IS? IT'S HIS ELECTION TO LOSE!!

TRIPLE X-TRA LARGE   SUPER-SIZED **MEGA** LAME-ASS

HEY AL GORE!! THIS IS ALL YOU WOULD HAVE TO SAY TO THE AMERICAN PEOPLE TO WIN THIS ELECTION:

IF YOU ELECT ME PRESIDENT, YOU WILL GET EXACTLY WHAT YOU'VE GOTTEN OVER THE PAST 8 YEARS--

--BUT INSTEAD OF MONICA ON HER KNEES IN THE OVAL OFFICE--IT'LL **BE MY WIFE!!**

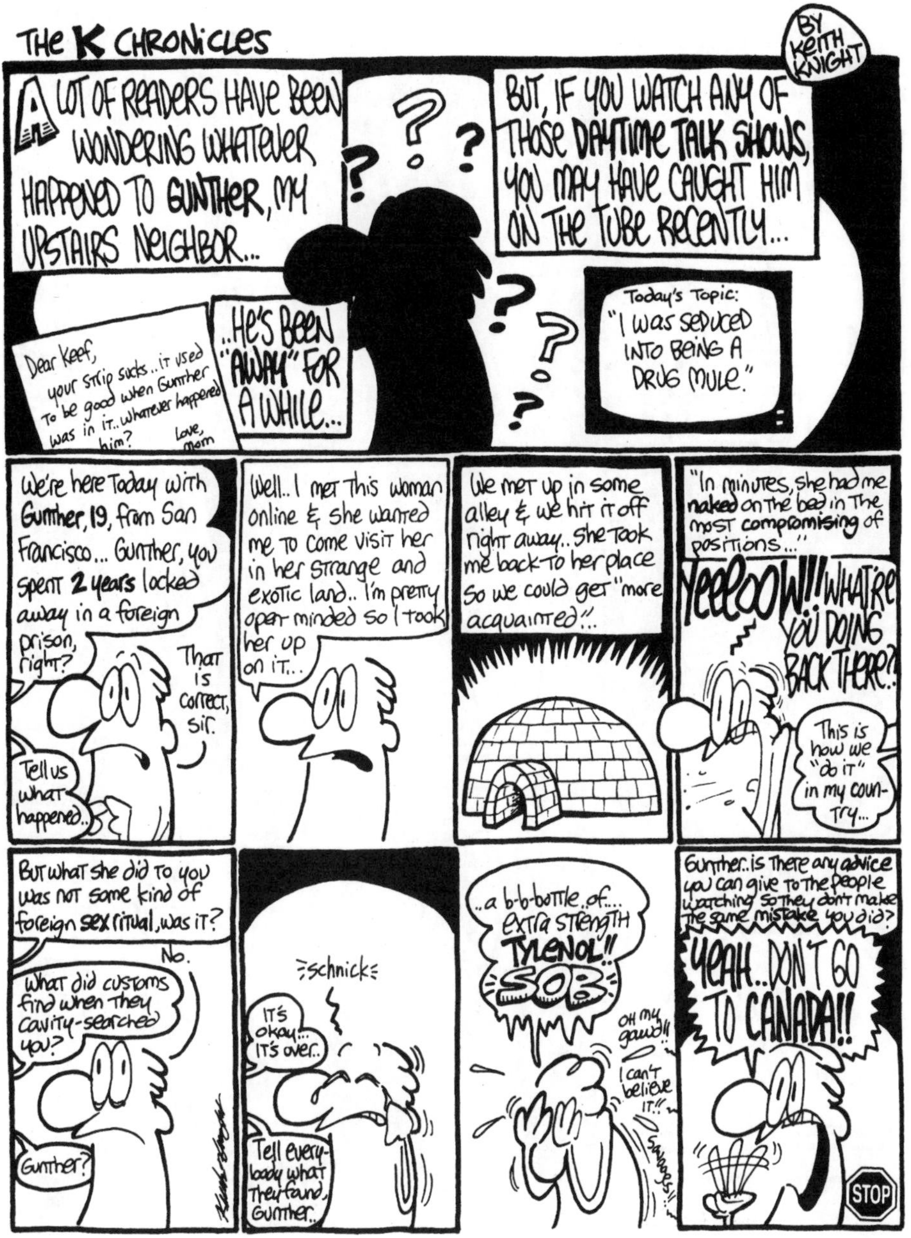

THE K CHRONICLES
BY KEITH KNIGHT
A LOT OF READERS HAVE BEEN WONDERING WHATEVER HAPPENED TO GUNTHER, MY UPSTAIRS NEIGHBOR...
Dear Keef, your strip sucks... it used to be good when Gunther was in it.. whatever happened to him? Love, mom
..HE'S BEEN "AWAY" FOR A WHILE...
BUT, IF YOU WATCH ANY OF THOSE DAYTIME TALK SHOWS, YOU MAY HAVE CAUGHT HIM ON THE TUBE RECENTLY...
Today's Topic: "I was seduced into being a drug mule."
We're here today with Gunther, 19, from San Francisco... Gunther, you spent 2 years locked away in a foreign prison, right?
That is correct, sir.
Tell us what happened..
Well.. I met this woman online & she wanted me to come visit her in her strange and exotic land.. I'm pretty open minded so I took her up on it...
We met up in some alley & we hit it off right away.. she took me back to her place so we could get "more acquainted"...
"In minutes, she had me naked on the bed in the most compromising of positions..."
YEELOOW!! WHAT'RE YOU DOING BACK THERE?!
This is how we "do it" in my country...
But what she did to you was not some kind of foreign sex ritual, was it?
No.
What did customs find when they cavity-searched you?
Gunther?
schnick
It's okay... It's over..
Tell everybody what they found, Gunther..
..a b-b-bottle..of.... extra strength TYLENOL!! SOB
OH MY GAWD!!
I can't believe it!!
Gunther..is there any advice you can give to the people watching so they don't make the same mistake you did?
YEAH..DON'T GO TO CANADA!!
STOP

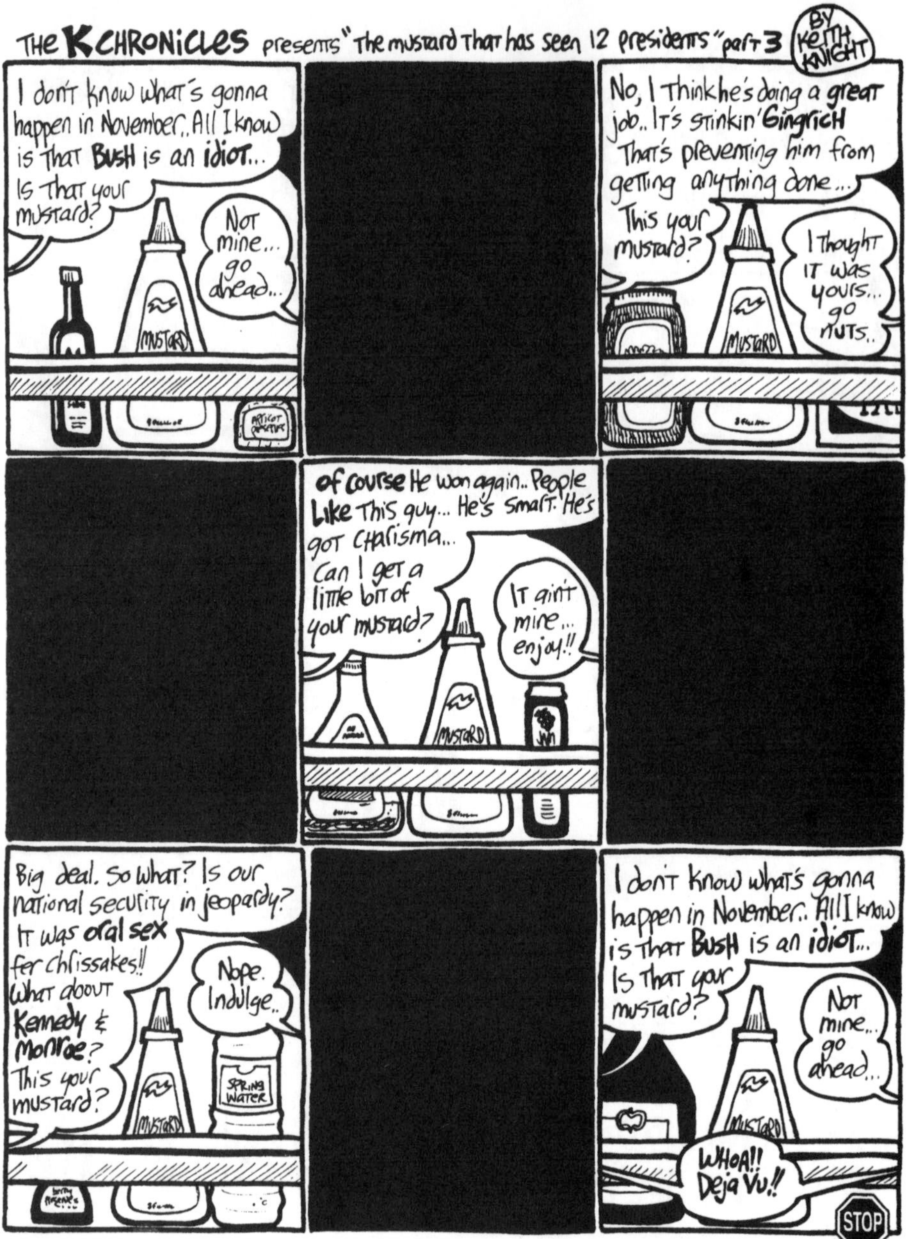
THE K CHRONICLES presents "The mustard that has seen 12 presidents" part 3
BY KEITH KNIGHT
I don't know what's gonna happen in November.. All I know is that BUSH is an idiot... Is that your mustard?
Not mine... go ahead...
MUSTARD
No, I think he's doing a great job.. It's stinkin' Gingrich that's preventing him from getting anything done... This your mustard?
I thought it was yours... go nuts..
MUSTARD
of course he won again.. People like this guy... He's smart. He's got charisma... Can I get a little bit of your mustard?
It ain't mine... enjoy!!
MUSTARD
Big deal. So what? Is our national security in jeopardy? It was oral sex fer chrissakes!! What about Kennedy & Monroe? This your mustard?
Nope. Indulge..
MUSTARD
SPRING WATER
I don't know what's gonna happen in November.. All I know is that BUSH is an idiot... Is that your mustard?
Not mine... go ahead...
MUSTARD
WHOA!! Deja Vu!!
STOP

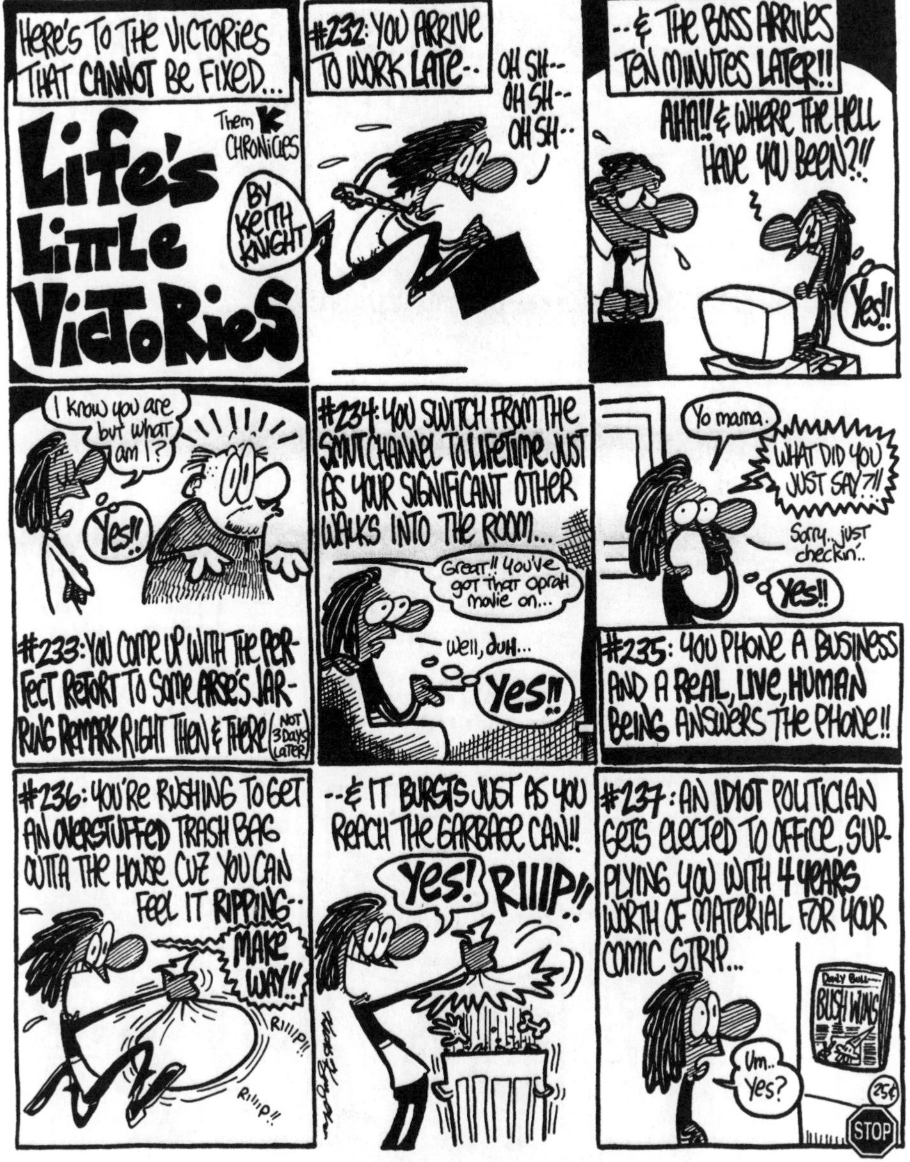
HERE'S TO THE VICTORIES THAT CANNOT BE FIXED...
Life's Little Victories
Them K CHRONICLES
BY KEITH KNIGHT
#232: YOU ARRIVE TO WORK LATE--
OH SH-- OH SH-- OH SH--
--& THE BOSS ARRIVES TEN MINUTES LATER!!
AHA!! & WHERE THE HELL HAVE YOU BEEN?!!
Yes!!
I know you are but what am I?
Yes!!
#233: YOU COME UP WITH THE PERFECT RETORT TO SOME ARSE'S JARRING REMARK RIGHT THEN & THERE (NOT 3 DAYS LATER)
#234: YOU SWITCH FROM THE SMUT CHANNEL TO LIFETIME JUST AS YOUR SIGNIFICANT OTHER WALKS INTO THE ROOM...
Great!! You've got that Oprah movie on...
Well, duh...
Yes!!
Yo mama.
WHAT DID YOU JUST SAY?!!
Sorry.. just checkin'..
Yes!!
#235: YOU PHONE A BUSINESS AND A REAL, LIVE, HUMAN BEING ANSWERS THE PHONE!!
#236: YOU'RE RUSHING TO GET AN OVERSTUFFED TRASH BAG OUTTA THE HOUSE CUZ YOU CAN FEEL IT RIPPING--
MAKE WAY!!
RIIIP!!
RIIIP!!
--& IT BURSTS JUST AS YOU REACH THE GARBAGE CAN!!
YES!
RIIIP!!
#237: AN IDIOT POLITICIAN GETS ELECTED TO OFFICE, SUPPLYING YOU WITH 4 YEARS WORTH OF MATERIAL FOR YOUR COMIC STRIP...
Daily Bull
BUSH WINS
25¢
STOP
Um.. Yes?

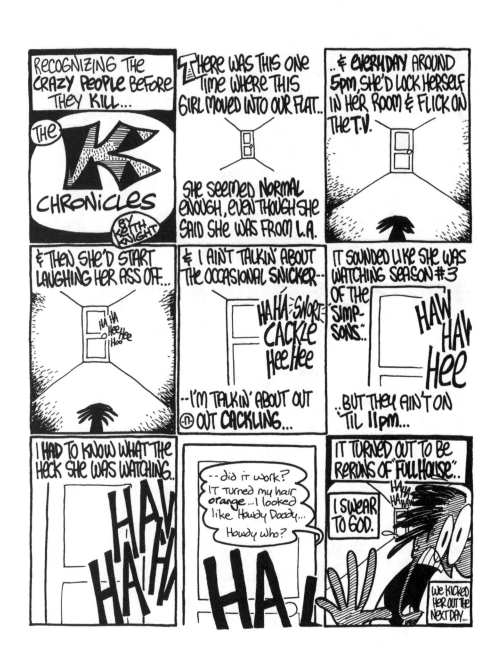

RECOGNIZING THE CRAZY PEOPLE BEFORE THEY KILL...

THE **K** CHRONICLES BY KEITH KNIGHT

THERE WAS THIS ONE TIME WHERE THIS GIRL MOVED INTO OUR FLAT..

SHE SEEMED NORMAL ENOUGH, EVEN THOUGH SHE SAID SHE WAS FROM L.A.

..& EVERYDAY AROUND 5PM, SHE'D LOCK HERSELF IN HER ROOM & FLICK ON THE T.V.

& THEN SHE'D START LAUGHING HER ASS OFF...

HA HA HEE HEE HOO

& I AIN'T TALKIN' ABOUT THE OCCASIONAL SNICKER--

HAHA SNORT CACKLE HEE HEE

--I'M TALKIN' ABOUT OUT OUT CACKLING...

IT SOUNDED LIKE SHE WAS WATCHING SEASON #3 OF THE "SIMPSONS"..

HAW HAW HEE

..BUT THEY AIN'T ON 'TIL 11PM...

I HAD TO KNOW WHAT THE HECK SHE WAS WATCHING..

HA HA HA

--did it work? IT turned my hair orange...I looked like Howdy Doody... Howdy who?

HA

IT TURNED OUT TO BE RERUNS OF "FULL HOUSE"..

HA HA HA HAW

I SWEAR TO GOD.

WE KICKED HER OUT THE NEXT DAY...

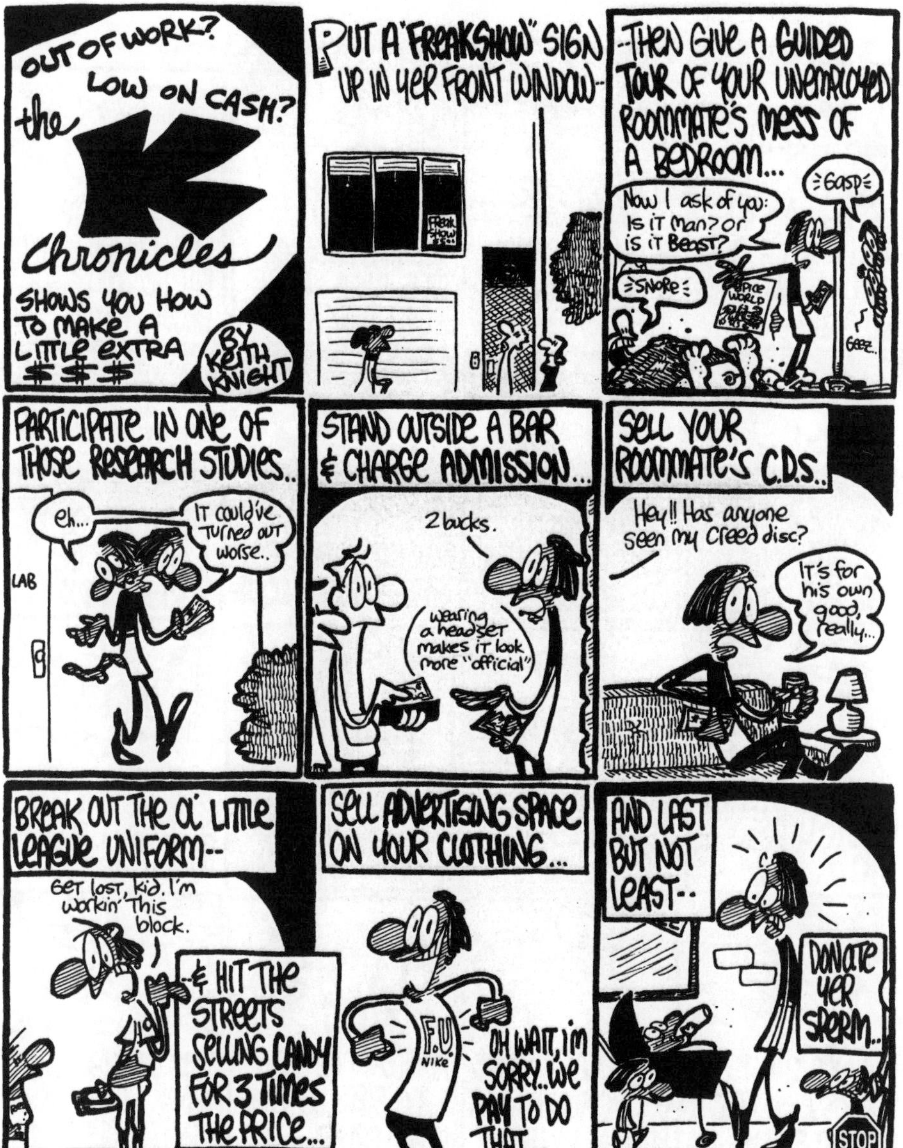

OUT OF WORK?
LOW ON CASH?
the K Chronicles
SHOWS YOU HOW TO MAKE A LITTLE EXTRA $ $ $
BY KEITH KNIGHT
PUT A "FREAKSHOW" SIGN UP IN YER FRONT WINDOW--
FREAK SHOW
--THEN GIVE A GUIDED TOUR OF YOUR UNEMPLOYED ROOMMATE'S MESS OF A BEDROOM...
Gasp
Now I ask of you: Is it Man? or is it Beast?
SNORE
SPICE WORLD
Geez..
PARTICIPATE IN ONE OF THOSE RESEARCH STUDIES..
eh...
It could've turned out worse..
LAB
STAND OUTSIDE A BAR & CHARGE ADMISSION...
2 bucks.
(wearing a headset makes it look more "official")
SELL YOUR ROOMMATE'S C.D.S..
Hey!! Has anyone seen my Creed disc?
It's for his own good, really...
BREAK OUT THE OL' LITTLE LEAGUE UNIFORM--
Get lost, kid. I'm workin' this block.
--& HIT THE STREETS SELLING CANDY FOR 3 TIMES THE PRICE...
SELL ADVERTISING SPACE ON YOUR CLOTHING...
F.U. NIKE
OH WAIT, I'M SORRY.. WE PAY TO DO THAT...
AND LAST BUT NOT LEAST--
DONATE YER SPERM...
STOP

32 LINES ABOUT 32 ROOMMATES

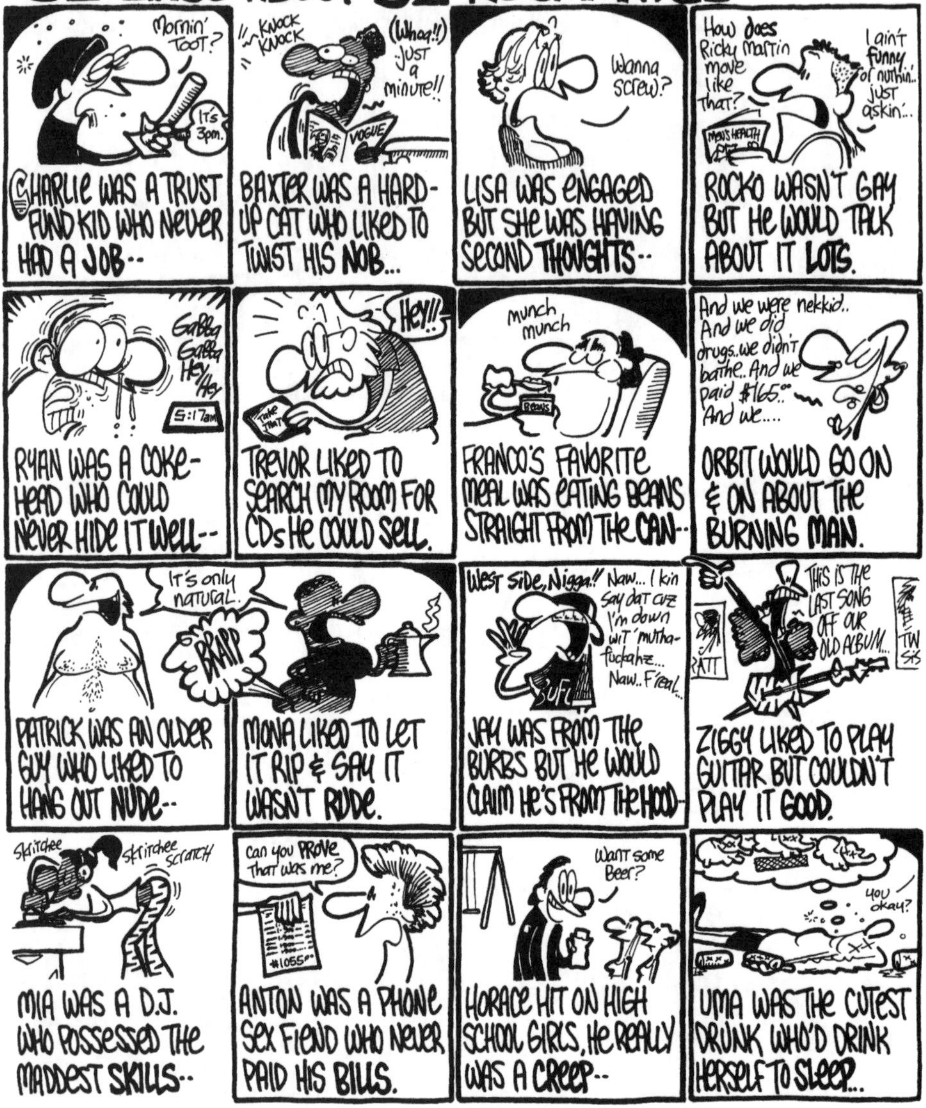
Mornin' TOOT?
It's 3pm.
CHARLIE WAS A TRUST FUND KID WHO NEVER HAD A JOB--
KNOCK KNOCK
(Whoa!!) JUST a minute!!
VOGUE
BAXTER WAS A HARD-UP CAT WHO LIKED TO TWIST HIS NOB...
Wanna screw?
LISA WAS ENGAGED BUT SHE WAS HAVING SECOND THOUGHTS--
How does Ricky Martin move like THAT?
I ain't funny of nuthin'.. just askin'..
MEN'S HEALTH
ROCKO WASN'T GAY BUT HE WOULD TALK ABOUT IT LOTS.
Gabba Gabba Hey Hey
5:17am
RYAN WAS A COKE-HEAD WHO COULD NEVER HIDE IT WELL--
HEY!!
TAKE THAT
TREVOR LIKED TO SEARCH MY ROOM FOR CDs HE COULD SELL.
munch munch
BEANS
FRANCO'S FAVORITE MEAL WAS EATING BEANS STRAIGHT FROM THE CAN--
And we were nekkid.. And we did drugs..we didn't bathe.. And we paid $165.00.. And we....
ORBIT WOULD GO ON & ON ABOUT THE BURNING MAN.
It's only natural.
BRAPP
PATRICK WAS AN OLDER GUY WHO LIKED TO HANG OUT NUDE--
MONA LIKED TO LET IT RIP & SAY IT WASN'T RUDE.
WEST SIDE, Nigga!!
Naw... I kin say dat cuz I'm down wit' mutha-fuckahz... Naw.. F'real.
SUFL
JAY WAS FROM THE BURBS BUT HE WOULD CLAIM HE'S FROM THE HOOD-
THIS IS THE LAST SONG OFF OUR OLD ALBUM...
RATT
ZIGGY LIKED TO PLAY GUITAR BUT COULDN'T PLAY IT GOOD.
skritchee skritchee scratch
MIA WAS A D.J. WHO POSSESSED THE MADDEST SKILLS--
Can you PROVE that was me?
#1055.00
ANTON WAS A PHONE SEX FIEND WHO NEVER PAID HIS BILLS.
Want some Beer?
HORACE HIT ON HIGH SCHOOL GIRLS, HE REALLY WAS A CREEP--
You okay?
UMA WAS THE CUTEST DRUNK WHO'D DRINK HERSELF TO SLEEP...

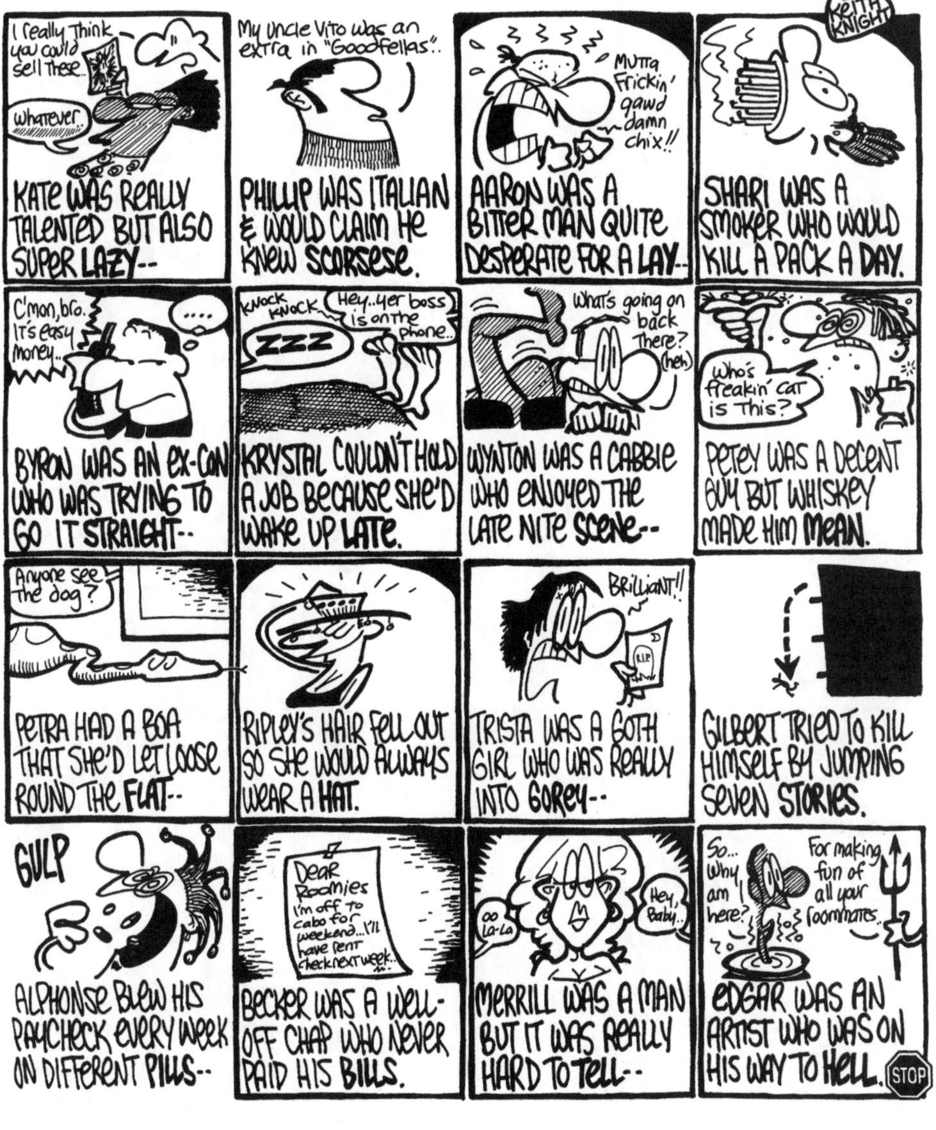
BY KEITH KNIGHT
I really Think you could sell These..
whatever..
KATE WAS REALLY TALENTED BUT ALSO SUPER LAZY--
My uncle Vito was an extra in "Goodfellas"..
PHILLIP WAS ITALIAN & WOULD CLAIM HE KNEW SCORSESE.
MUTTA Frickin' gawd damn chix!!
AARON WAS A BITTER MAN QUITE DESPERATE FOR A LAY--
SHARI WAS A SMOKER WHO WOULD KILL A PACK A DAY.
C'mon, bro. It's easy money..
....
BYRON WAS AN EX-CON WHO WAS TRYING TO GO IT STRAIGHT--
KNOCK KNOCK
Hey..yer boss is on the phone..
ZZZ
KRYSTAL COULDN'T HOLD A JOB BECAUSE SHE'D WAKE UP LATE.
What's going on back there? (heh)
WYNTON WAS A CABBIE WHO ENJOYED THE LATE NITE SCENE--
Who's freakin' cat is This?
PETEY WAS A DECENT GUY BUT WHISKEY MADE HIM MEAN.
Anyone see the dog?
PETRA HAD A BOA THAT SHE'D LET LOOSE ROUND THE FLAT--
RIPLEY'S HAIR FELL OUT SO SHE WOULD ALWAYS WEAR A HAT.
BRILLIANT!!
R.I.P.
TRISTA WAS A GOTH GIRL WHO WAS REALLY INTO GOREY--
GILBERT TRIED TO KILL HIMSELF BY JUMPING SEVEN STORIES.
GULP
ALPHONSE BLEW HIS PAYCHECK EVERY WEEK ON DIFFERENT PILLS--
Dear Roomies I'm off to cabo for weekend... I'll have rent check next week..
BECKER WAS A WELL-OFF CHAP WHO NEVER PAID HIS BILLS.
oo La-La
Hey, Baby..
MERRILL WAS A MAN BUT IT WAS REALLY HARD TO TELL--
So... Why am I here?
For making fun of all your roommates..
EDGAR WAS AN ARTIST WHO WAS ON HIS WAY TO HELL.
STOP

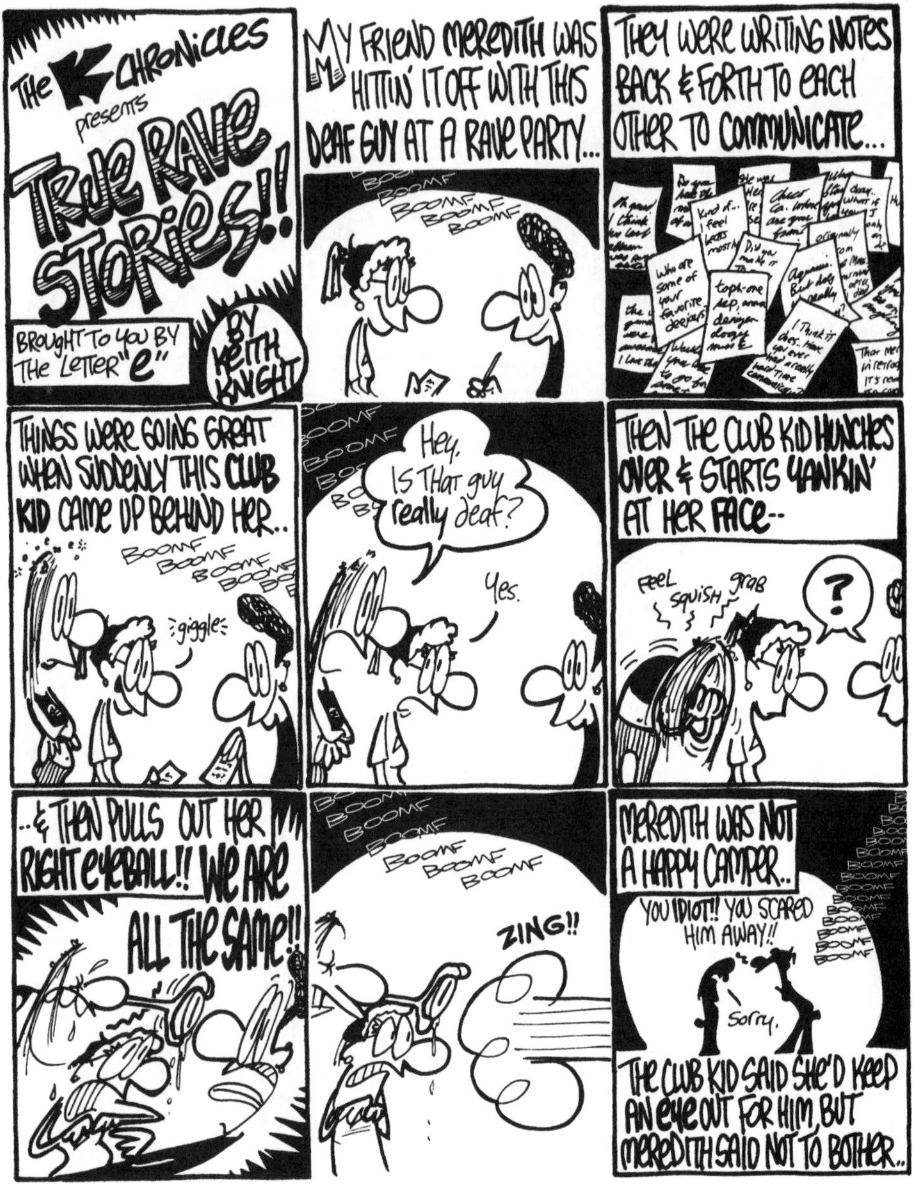
THE K CHRONICLES presents
TRUE RAVE STORIES!!
BROUGHT TO YOU BY THE LETTER "e"
BY KEITH KNIGHT
MY FRIEND MEREDITH WAS HITTIN' IT OFF WITH THIS DEAF GUY AT A RAVE PARTY...
BOOMF BOOMF BOOMF BOOMF BOOMF
THEY WERE WRITING NOTES BACK & FORTH TO EACH OTHER TO COMMUNICATE...
THINGS WERE GOING GREAT WHEN SUDDENLY THIS CLUB KID CAME UP BEHIND HER..
BOOMF BOOMF BOOMF BOOMF
giggle
Hey, IS THAT guy really deaf?
Yes.
THEN THE CLUB KID HUNCHES OVER & STARTS YANKIN' AT HER FACE--
FEEL SQUISH GRAB
?
..& THEN PULLS OUT HER RIGHT EYEBALL!! WE ARE ALL THE SAME!!
BOOMF BOOMF BOOMF BOOMF BOOMF BOOMF
ZING!!
MEREDITH WAS NOT A HAPPY CAMPER..
YOU IDIOT!! YOU SCARED HIM AWAY!!
Sorry.
THE CLUB KID SAID SHE'D KEEP AN EYE OUT FOR HIM, BUT MEREDITH SAID NOT TO BOTHER..

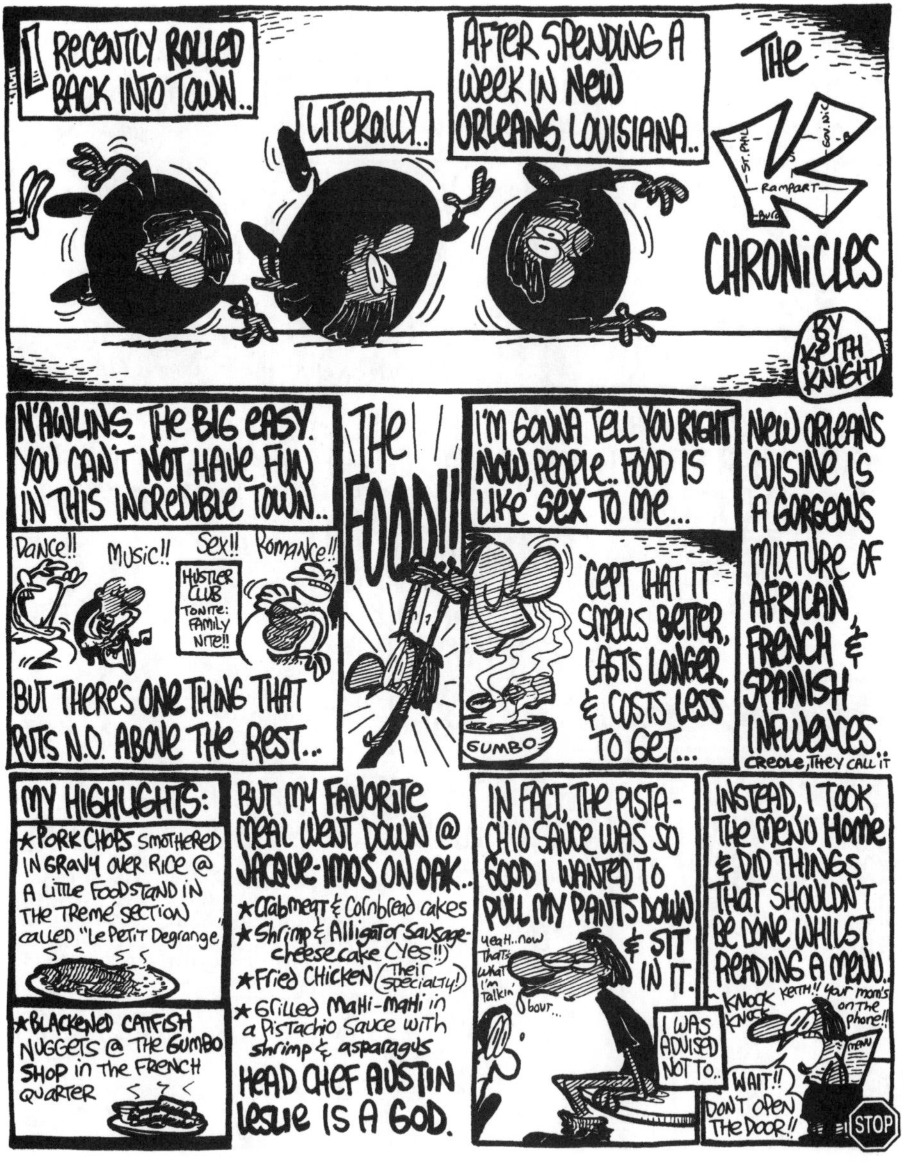
I RECENTLY ROLLED BACK INTO TOWN..
LITERALLY..
AFTER SPENDING A WEEK IN NEW ORLEANS, LOUISIANA..
THE K CHRONICLES
ST. PAUL
GOV. NIC
RAMPART
BY KEITH KNIGHT
N'AWLINS. THE BIG EASY. YOU CAN'T NOT HAVE FUN IN THIS INCREDIBLE TOWN..
Dance!!
Music!!
Sex!!
Romance!!
HUSTLER CLUB TONITE: FAMILY NITE!!
BUT THERE'S ONE THING THAT PUTS N.O. ABOVE THE REST...
THE FOOD!!
I'M GONNA TELL YOU RIGHT NOW, PEOPLE.. FOOD IS LIKE SEX TO ME...
'CEPT THAT IT SMELLS BETTER, LASTS LONGER, & COSTS LESS TO GET...
GUMBO
NEW ORLEANS CUISINE IS A GORGEOUS MIXTURE OF AFRICAN, FRENCH & SPANISH INFLUENCES..
CREOLE, THEY CALL IT
MY HIGHLIGHTS:
★PORK CHOPS SMOTHERED IN GRAVY OVER RICE @ A LITTLE FOODSTAND IN THE TREMÉ SECTION called "Le Petit Degrange"
★BLACKENED CATFISH NUGGETS @ THE GUMBO SHOP in THE FRENCH QUARTER
BUT MY FAVORITE MEAL WENT DOWN @ JACQUE-IMOS ON OAK..
★Crabmeat & Cornbread cakes
★Shrimp & Alligator Sausage-cheesecake (Yes!!)
★Fried CHICKEN (Their specialty!)
★Grilled Mahi-Mahi in a Pistachio Sauce with shrimp & asparagus
HEAD CHEF AUSTIN LESLIE IS A GOD.
IN FACT, THE PISTACHIO SAUCE WAS SO GOOD I WANTED TO PULL MY PANTS DOWN & SIT IN IT.
Yeah.. now that's what I'm talkin' 'bout..
I WAS ADVISED NOT TO..
INSTEAD, I TOOK THE MENU HOME & DID THINGS THAT SHOULDN'T BE DONE WHILST READING A MENU..
KNOCK KNOCK
KEITH!! your mom's on the phone!!
MENU
WAIT!! DON'T OPEN THE DOOR!!
STOP

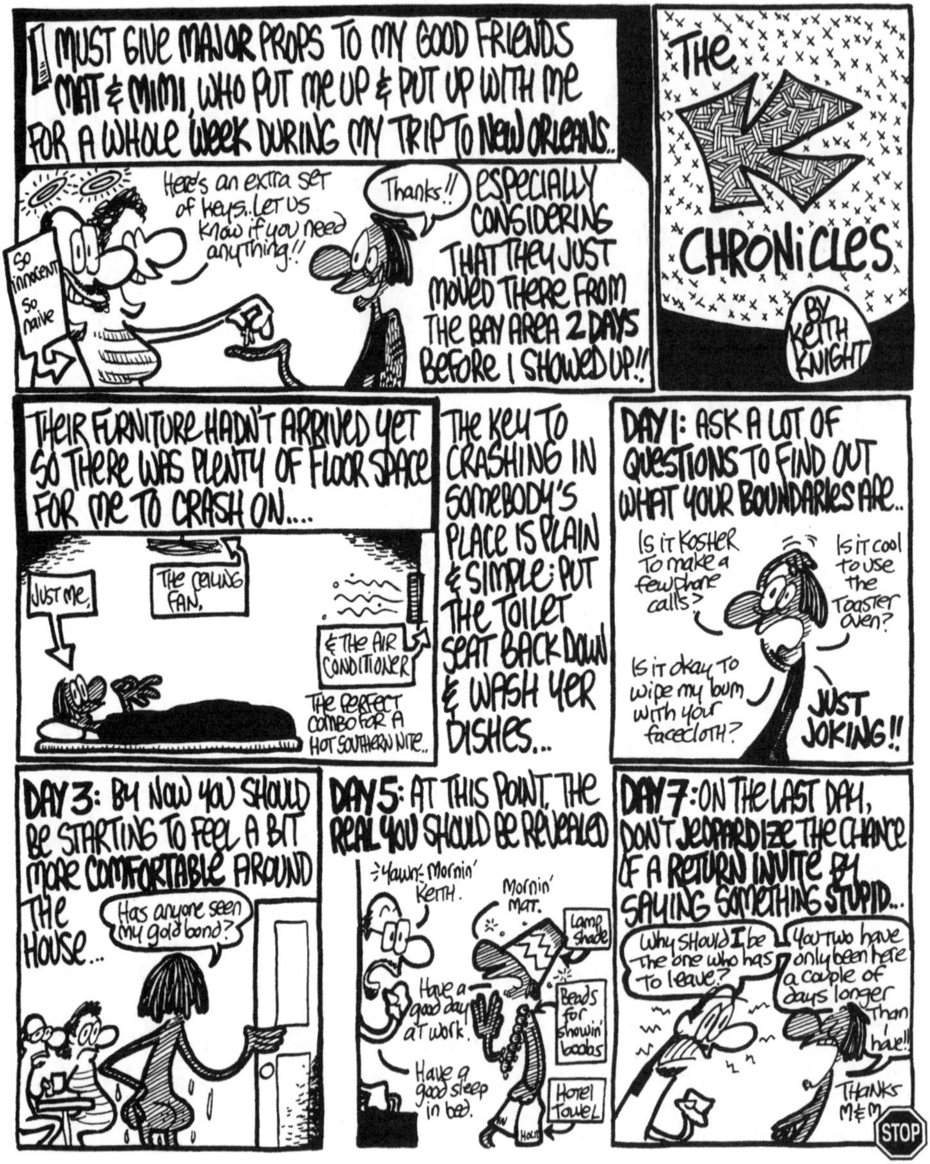
THE K CHRONICLES
BY KEITH KNIGHT
I MUST GIVE MAJOR PROPS TO MY GOOD FRIENDS MAT & MIMI, WHO PUT ME UP & PUT UP WITH ME FOR A WHOLE WEEK DURING MY TRIP TO NEW ORLEANS..
So innocent So naive
Here's an extra set of keys.. Let us know if you need anything!!
Thanks!!
ESPECIALLY CONSIDERING THAT THEY JUST MOVED THERE FROM THE BAY AREA 2 DAYS BEFORE I SHOWED UP!!
THEIR FURNITURE HADN'T ARRIVED YET SO THERE WAS PLENTY OF FLOOR SPACE FOR ME TO CRASH ON....
JUST ME,
THE CEILING FAN,
& THE AIR CONDITIONER
THE PERFECT COMBO FOR A HOT SOUTHERN NITE..
THE KEY TO CRASHING IN SOMEBODY'S PLACE IS PLAIN & SIMPLE: PUT THE TOILET SEAT BACK DOWN & WASH YER DISHES...
DAY 1: ASK A LOT OF QUESTIONS TO FIND OUT WHAT YOUR BOUNDARIES ARE..
Is it Kosher to make a few phone calls?
Is it cool to use the Toaster oven?
Is it okay to wipe my bum with your facecloth?
JUST JOKING!!
DAY 3: BY NOW YOU SHOULD BE STARTING TO FEEL A BIT MORE COMFORTABLE AROUND THE HOUSE...
Has anyone seen my gold bond?
DAY 5: AT THIS POINT, THE REAL YOU SHOULD BE REVEALED
-Yawn- Mornin' Keith.
Mornin' Mat.
Lamp Shade
Beads for showin' boobs
Hotel Towel
Have a good day at work.
Have a good sleep in bed.
DAY 7: ON THE LAST DAY, DON'T JEOPARDIZE THE CHANCE OF A RETURN INVITE BY SAYING SOMETHING STUPID...
Why should I be the one who has to leave?
You two have only been here a couple of days longer than I have!!
THANKS M&M
STOP

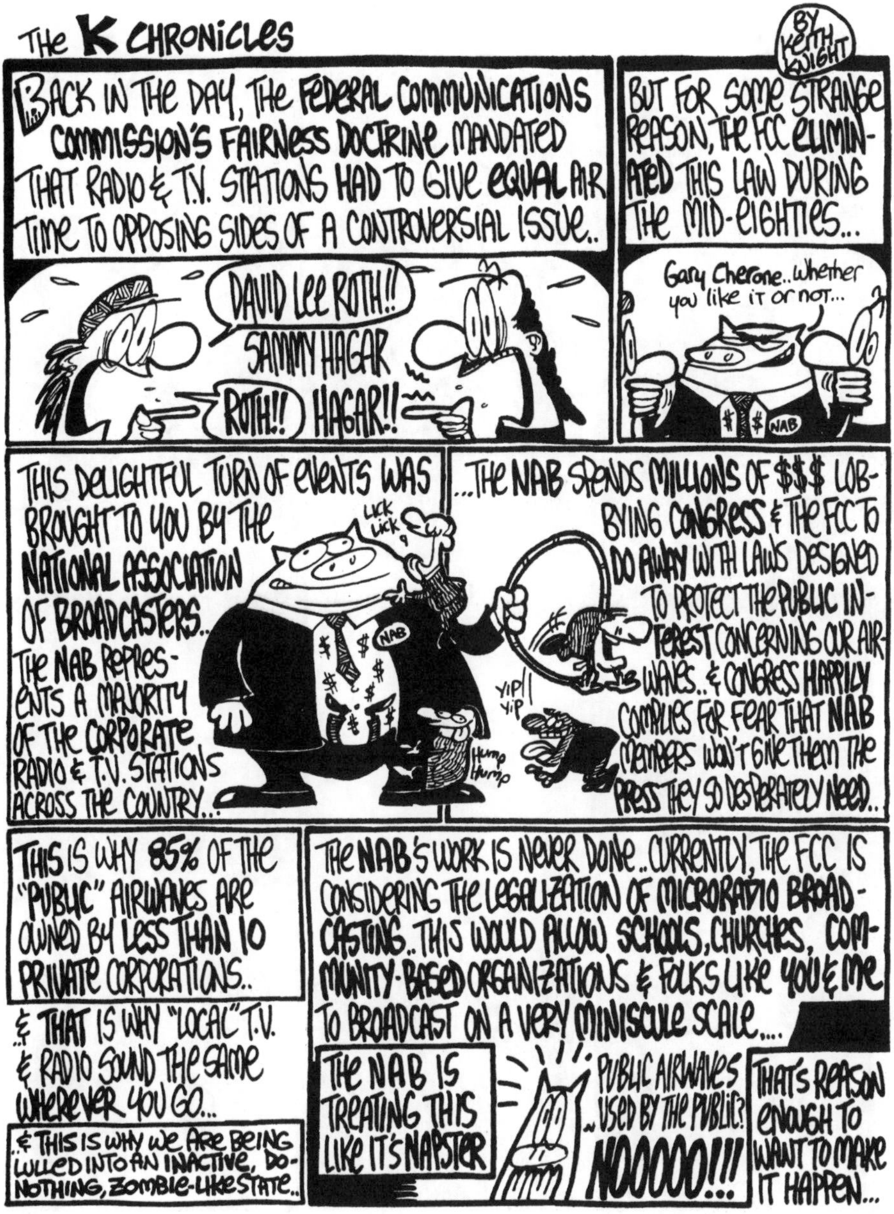
The K Chronicles
By Keith Knight
Back in the day, the Federal Communications Commission's Fairness Doctrine mandated that radio & T.V. stations had to give equal air time to opposing sides of a controversial issue..
David Lee Roth!!
Sammy Hagar
Roth!!
Hagar!!
But for some strange reason, the FCC eliminated this law during the mid-eighties...
Gary Cherone.. whether you like it or not...
NAB
This delightful turn of events was brought to you by the National Association of Broadcasters.. The NAB represents a majority of the corporate radio & T.V. stations across the country..
Lick Lick
NAB
Hump Hump
Yip Yip
...The NAB spends millions of $$$ lobbying Congress & the FCC to do away with laws designed to protect the public interest concerning our airwaves.. & Congress happily complies for fear that NAB members won't give them the press they so desperately need..
This is why 85% of the "public" airwaves are owned by less than 10 private corporations..
..& that is why "local" T.V. & radio sound the same wherever you go...
..& this is why we are being lulled into an inactive, do-nothing, zombie-like state..
The NAB's work is never done.. Currently, the FCC is considering the legalization of microradio broadcasting.. This would allow schools, churches, community-based organizations & folks like you & me to broadcast on a very miniscule scale....
The NAB is treating this like it's Napster
..Public airwaves used by the public? NOOOOO!!!...
That's reason enough to want to make it happen...

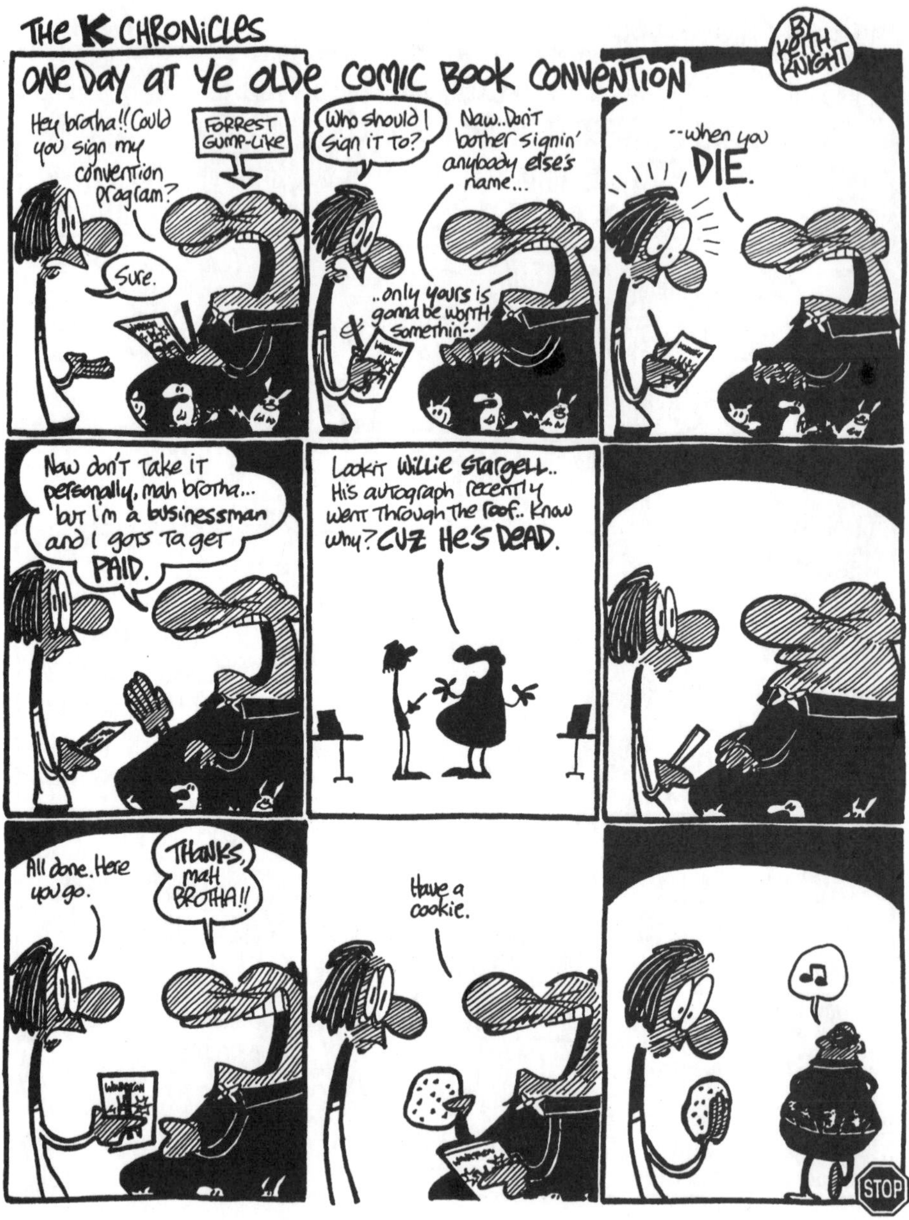
THE K CHRONICLES
BY KEITH KNIGHT
ONE DAY AT YE OLDE COMIC BOOK CONVENTION
Hey brotha!! Could you sign my convention program?
FORREST GUMP-LIKE
Sure.
Who should I sign it to?
Naw.. Don't bother signin' anybody else's name...
..only yours is gonna be worth somethin'--
--when you DIE.
Naw don't take it personally, mah brotha... but I'm a businessman and I gots ta get PAID.
Lookit Willie Stargell.. His autograph recently went through the roof.. Know why? CUZ HE'S DEAD.
All done. Here you go.
THANKS, MAH BROTHA!!
Have a cookie.
STOP

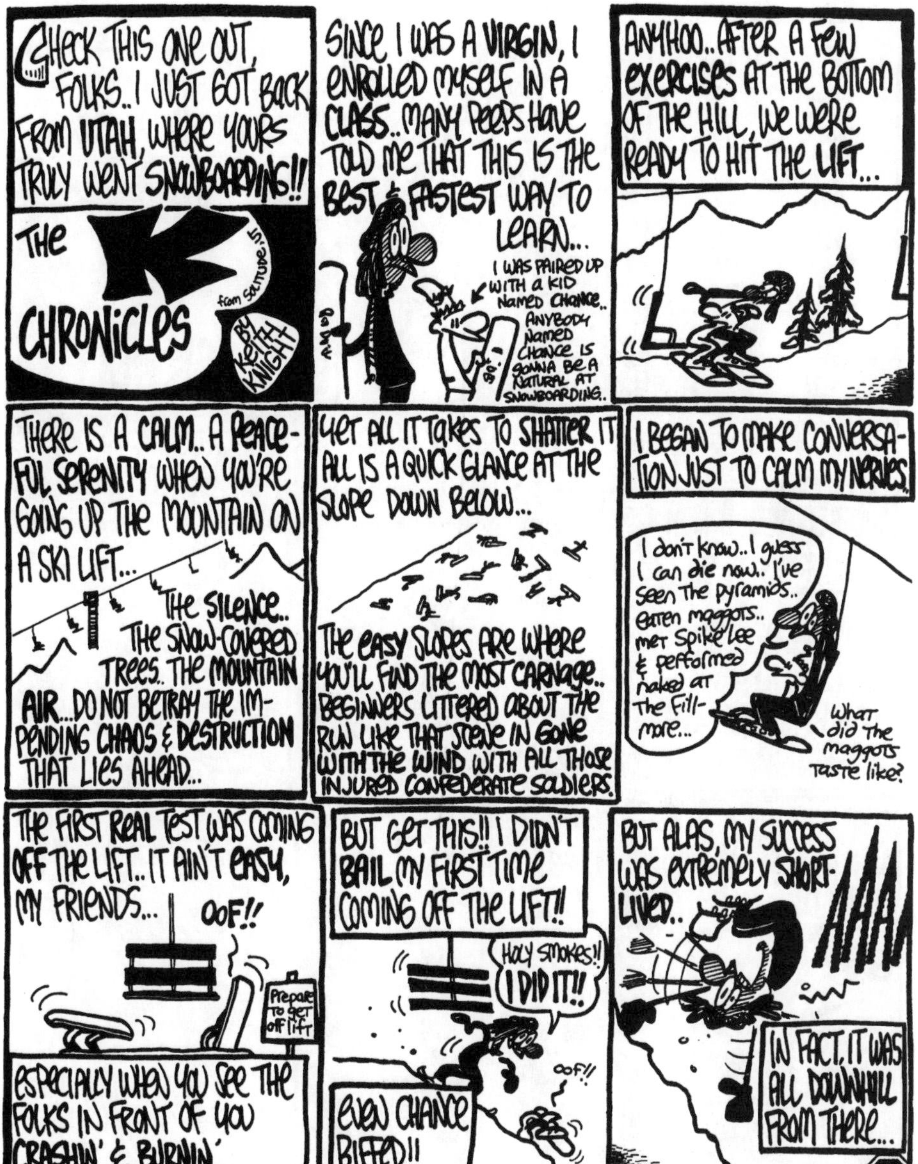
CHECK THIS ONE OUT, FOLKS.. I JUST GOT BACK FROM UTAH, WHERE YOURS TRULY WENT SNOWBOARDING!!
THE K CHRONICLES
from SOLITUDE, UT
BY KEITH KNIGHT
SINCE I WAS A VIRGIN, I ENROLLED MYSELF IN A CLASS.. MANY PEEPS HAVE TOLD ME THAT THIS IS THE BEST & FASTEST WAY TO LEARN...
I WAS PAIRED UP WITH a KID Named CHANCE..
ANYBODY Named CHANCE IS GONNA BE A NATURAL AT SNOWBOARDING..
ANYHOO.. AFTER A FEW EXERCISES AT THE BOTTOM OF THE HILL, WE WERE READY TO HIT THE LIFT...
THERE IS A CALM.. A PEACEFUL SERENITY WHEN YOU'RE GOING UP THE MOUNTAIN ON A SKI LIFT...
THE SILENCE.. THE SNOW-COVERED TREES.. THE MOUNTAIN AIR... DO NOT BETRAY THE IMPENDING CHAOS & DESTRUCTION THAT LIES AHEAD...
YET ALL IT TAKES TO SHATTER IT ALL IS A QUICK GLANCE AT THE SLOPE DOWN BELOW...
THE EASY SLOPES ARE WHERE YOU'LL FIND THE MOST CARNAGE.. BEGINNERS LITTERED ABOUT THE RUN LIKE THAT SCENE IN GONE WITH THE WIND WITH ALL THOSE INJURED CONFEDERATE SOLDIERS.
I BEGAN TO MAKE CONVERSATION JUST TO CALM MY NERVES..
I don't know.. I guess I can die now.. I've seen the pyramids.. eaten maggots.. met Spike Lee & performed naked at The Fillmore...
What did the maggots taste like?
THE FIRST REAL TEST WAS COMING OFF THE LIFT.. IT AIN'T EASY, MY FRIENDS...
OOF!!
Prepare to get off lift
ESPECIALLY WHEN YOU SEE THE FOLKS IN FRONT OF YOU CRASHIN' & BURNIN'...
BUT GET THIS!! I DIDN'T BAIL MY FIRST TIME COMING OFF THE LIFT!!
Holy Smokes!! I DID IT!!
OOF!!
EVEN CHANCE BIFFED!!
BUT ALAS, MY SUCCESS WAS EXTREMELY SHORT-LIVED...
AAA
IN FACT, IT WAS ALL DOWNHILL FROM THERE...
STOP

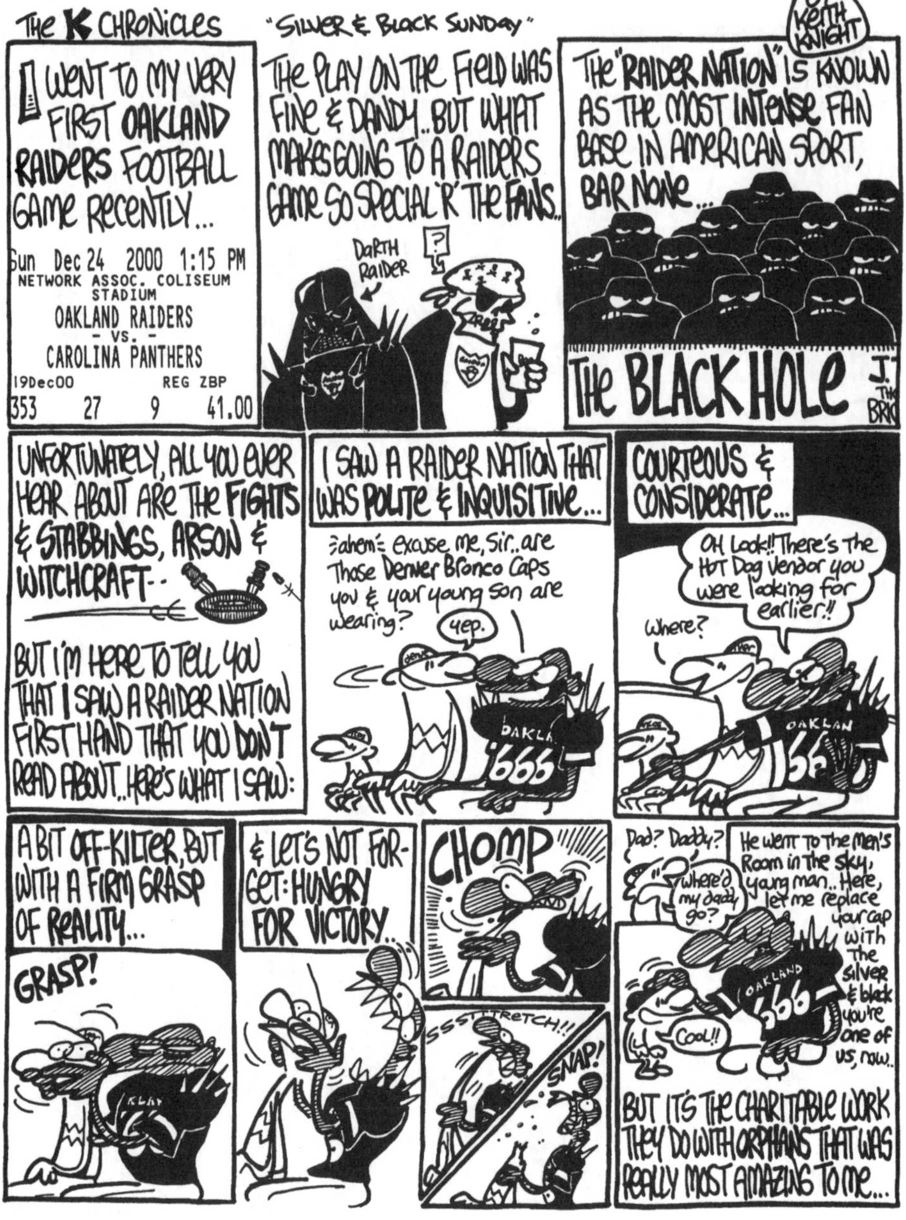
THE K CHRONICLES
"SILVER & BLACK SUNDAY"
BY KEITH KNIGHT
I WENT TO MY VERY FIRST OAKLAND RAIDERS FOOTBALL GAME RECENTLY...
Sun Dec 24 2000 1:15 PM
NETWORK ASSOC. COLISEUM STADIUM
OAKLAND RAIDERS
- VS. -
CAROLINA PANTHERS
19Dec00 REG ZBP
353 27 9 41.00
THE PLAY ON THE FIELD WAS FINE & DANDY.. BUT WHAT MAKES GOING TO A RAIDERS GAME SO SPECIAL 'R' THE FANS..
DARTH RAIDER
?
THE "RAIDER NATION" IS KNOWN AS THE MOST INTENSE FAN BASE IN AMERICAN SPORT, BAR NONE...
THE BLACK HOLE
UNFORTUNATELY, ALL YOU EVER HEAR ABOUT ARE THE FIGHTS & STABBINGS, ARSON & WITCHCRAFT--
BUT I'M HERE TO TELL YOU THAT I SAW A RAIDER NATION FIRST HAND THAT YOU DON'T READ ABOUT.. HERE'S WHAT I SAW:
I SAW A RAIDER NATION THAT WAS POLITE & INQUISITIVE...
=ahem= Excuse me, Sir.. are Those Denver Bronco Caps you & your young son are wearing?
yep.
666
COURTEOUS & CONSIDERATE...
OH Look!! There's The Hot Dog Vendor you were looking for earlier!!
Where?
A BIT OFF-KILTER, BUT WITH A FIRM GRASP OF REALITY...
GRASP!
& LET'S NOT FORGET: HUNGRY FOR VICTORY...
CHOMP
SSSTTTRETCH!!
SNAP!
Dad? Daddy?
Where'd my daddy go?
He went to the men's Room in the sky, young man.. Here, let me replace your cap with the silver & black you're one of us, now..
OAKLAND
666
Cool!!
BUT IT'S THE CHARITABLE WORK THEY DO WITH ORPHANS THAT WAS REALLY MOST AMAZING TO ME...

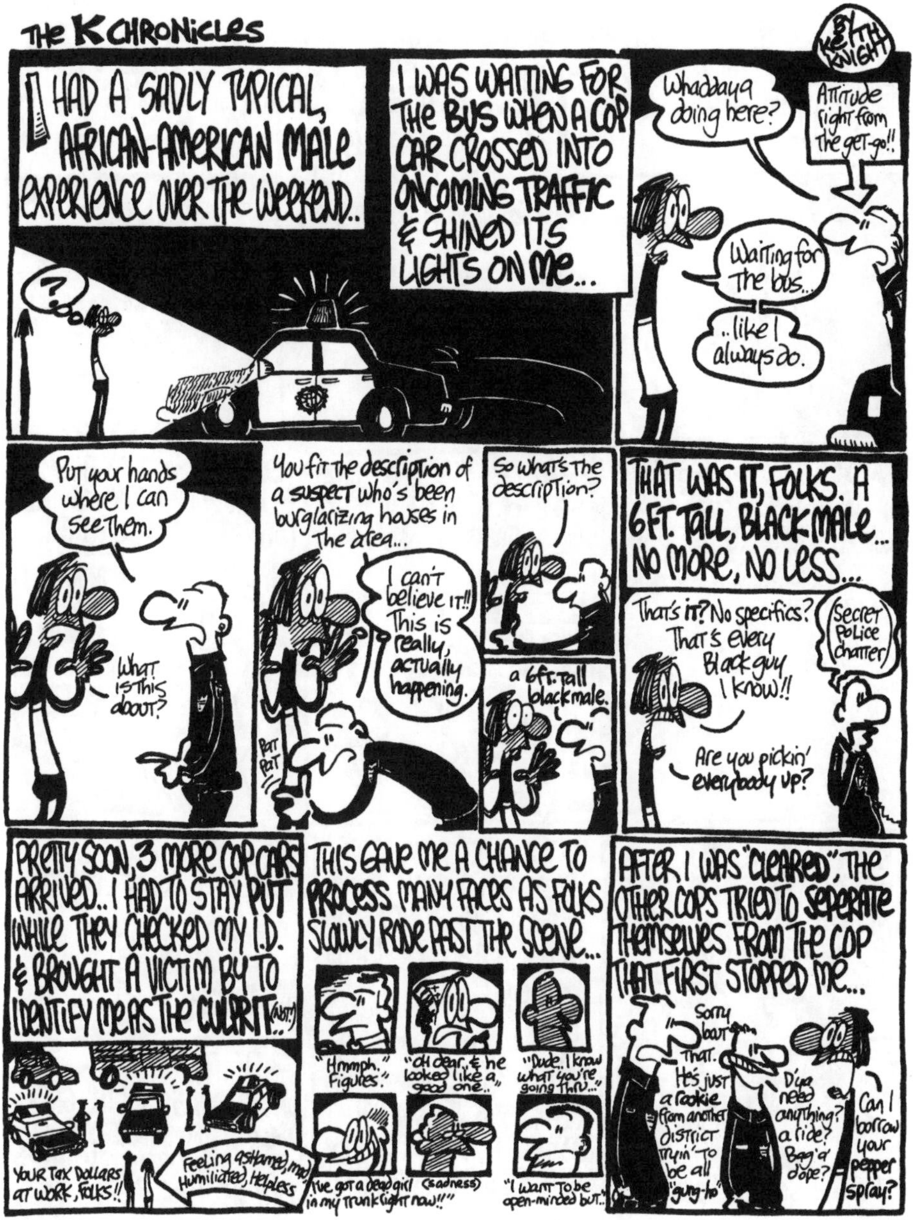
THE K CHRONICLES
BY KEITH KNIGHT
I HAD A SADLY TYPICAL, AFRICAN-AMERICAN MALE EXPERIENCE OVER THE WEEKEND..
?
I WAS WAITING FOR THE BUS WHEN A COP CAR CROSSED INTO ONCOMING TRAFFIC & SHINED ITS LIGHTS ON ME...
Whaddaya doing here?
Attitude right from the get-go!!
Waiting for the bus..
..like I always do.
Put your hands where I can see them.
What is this about?
You fit the description of a suspect who's been burglarizing houses in the area...
I can't believe it!! This is really, actually happening.
PAT PAT
So what's the description?
a 6ft. tall black male.
THAT WAS IT, FOLKS. A 6FT. TALL, BLACK MALE... NO MORE, NO LESS...
That's it? No specifics? That's every Black guy I know!!
Secret Police chatter
Are you pickin' everybody up?
PRETTY SOON, 3 MORE COP CARS ARRIVED.. I HAD TO STAY PUT WHILE THEY CHECKED MY I.D. & BROUGHT A VICTIM BY TO IDENTIFY ME AS THE CULPRIT (NOT!)..
YOUR TAX DOLLARS AT WORK, FOLKS!!
Feeling ashamed, mad, Humiliated, Helpless
THIS GAVE ME A CHANCE TO PROCESS MANY FACES AS FOLKS SLOWLY RODE PAST THE SCENE...
"Hmmph. Figures."
"Oh dear, & he looked like a good one.."
"Dude, I know what you're going thru..."
"I've got a dead girl in my trunk right now!!"
(sadness)
"I want to be open-minded but.."
AFTER I WAS "CLEARED", THE OTHER COPS TRIED TO SEPERATE THEMSELVES FROM THE COP THAT FIRST STOPPED ME...
Sorry bout that. He's just a rookie from another district tryin' to be all "gung-ho"
D'ya need anything? a ride? Bag 'a' dope?
Can I borrow your pepper spray?

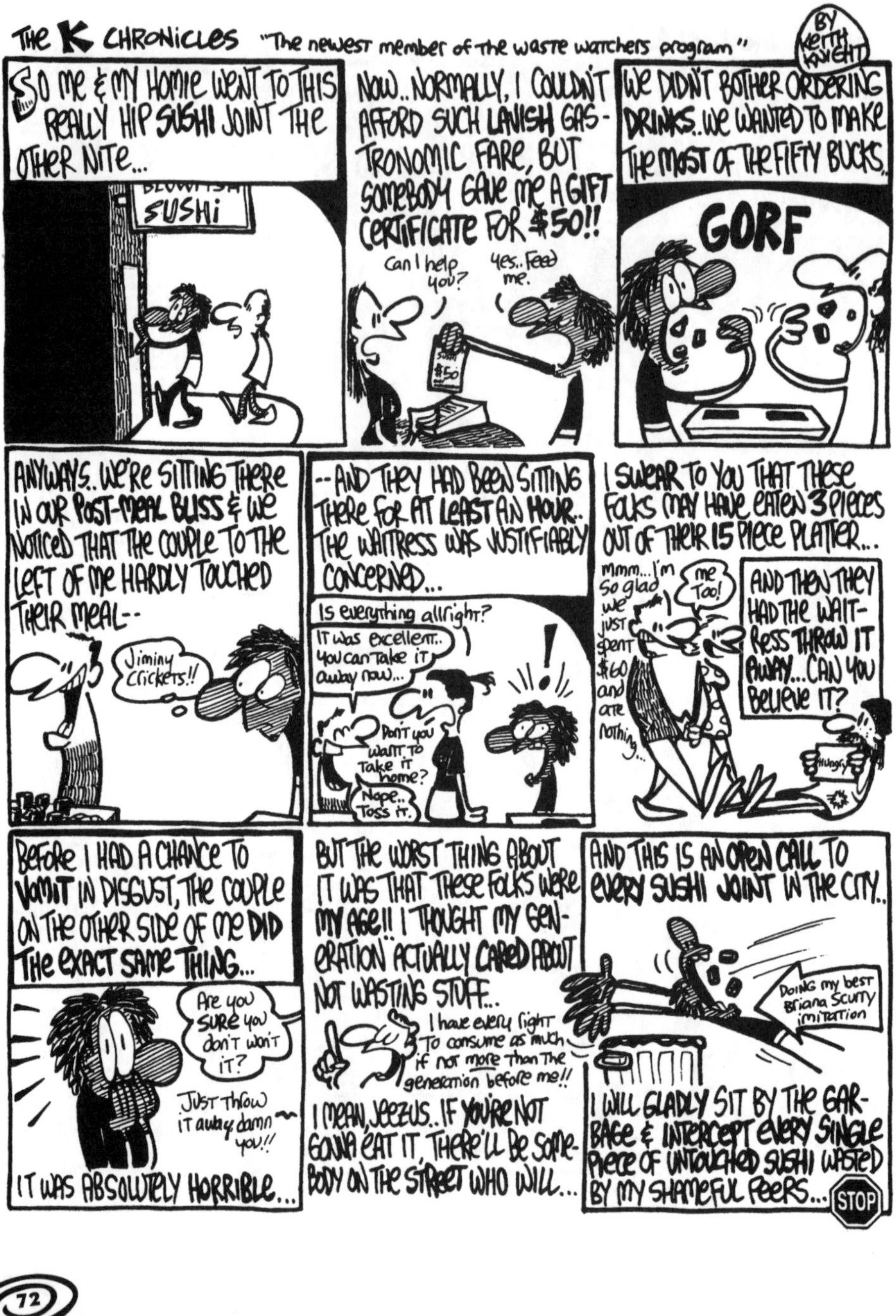
THE K CHRONICLES "The newest member of the waste watchers program"
BY KEITH KNIGHT
SO ME & MY HOMIE WENT TO THIS REALLY HIP SUSHI JOINT THE OTHER NITE...
SUSHI
NOW.. NORMALLY, I COULDN'T AFFORD SUCH LAVISH GAS-TRONOMIC FARE, BUT SOMEBODY GAVE ME A GIFT CERTIFICATE FOR $50!!
Can I help you?
Yes.. Feed me.
$50
WE DIDN'T BOTHER ORDERING DRINKS.. WE WANTED TO MAKE THE MOST OF THE FIFTY BUCKS..
GORF
ANYWAYS.. WE'RE SITTING THERE IN OUR POST-MEAL BLISS & WE NOTICED THAT THE COUPLE TO THE LEFT OF ME HARDLY TOUCHED THEIR MEAL--
Jiminy Crickets!!
--AND THEY HAD BEEN SITTING THERE FOR AT LEAST AN HOUR.. THE WAITRESS WAS JUSTIFIABLY CONCERNED...
Is everything allright?
It was excellent.. You can take it away now...
Don't you want to take it home?
Nope.. Toss it.
!
I SWEAR TO YOU THAT THESE FOLKS MAY HAVE EATEN 3 PIECES OUT OF THEIR 15 PIECE PLATTER...
mmm... I'm so glad we just spent $60 and ate nothing...
me Too!
AND THEN THEY HAD THE WAIT-RESS THROW IT AWAY... CAN YOU BELIEVE IT?
Hungry
BEFORE I HAD A CHANCE TO VOMIT IN DISGUST, THE COUPLE ON THE OTHER SIDE OF ME DID THE EXACT SAME THING...
Are you SURE you don't want it?
JUST Throw it away damn you!!
IT WAS ABSOLUTELY HORRIBLE...
BUT THE WORST THING ABOUT IT WAS THAT THESE FOLKS WERE MY AGE!! I THOUGHT MY GEN-ERATION ACTUALLY CARED ABOUT NOT WASTING STUFF...
I have every right to consume as much if not more than the generation before me!!
I MEAN, JEEZUS.. IF YOU'RE NOT GONNA EAT IT, THERE'LL BE SOME-BODY ON THE STREET WHO WILL...
AND THIS IS AN OPEN CALL TO EVERY SUSHI JOINT IN THE CITY..
Doing my best Briana Scurry imitation
I WILL GLADLY SIT BY THE GAR-BAGE & INTERCEPT EVERY SINGLE PIECE OF UNTOUCHED SUSHI WASTED BY MY SHAMEFUL PEERS...
STOP

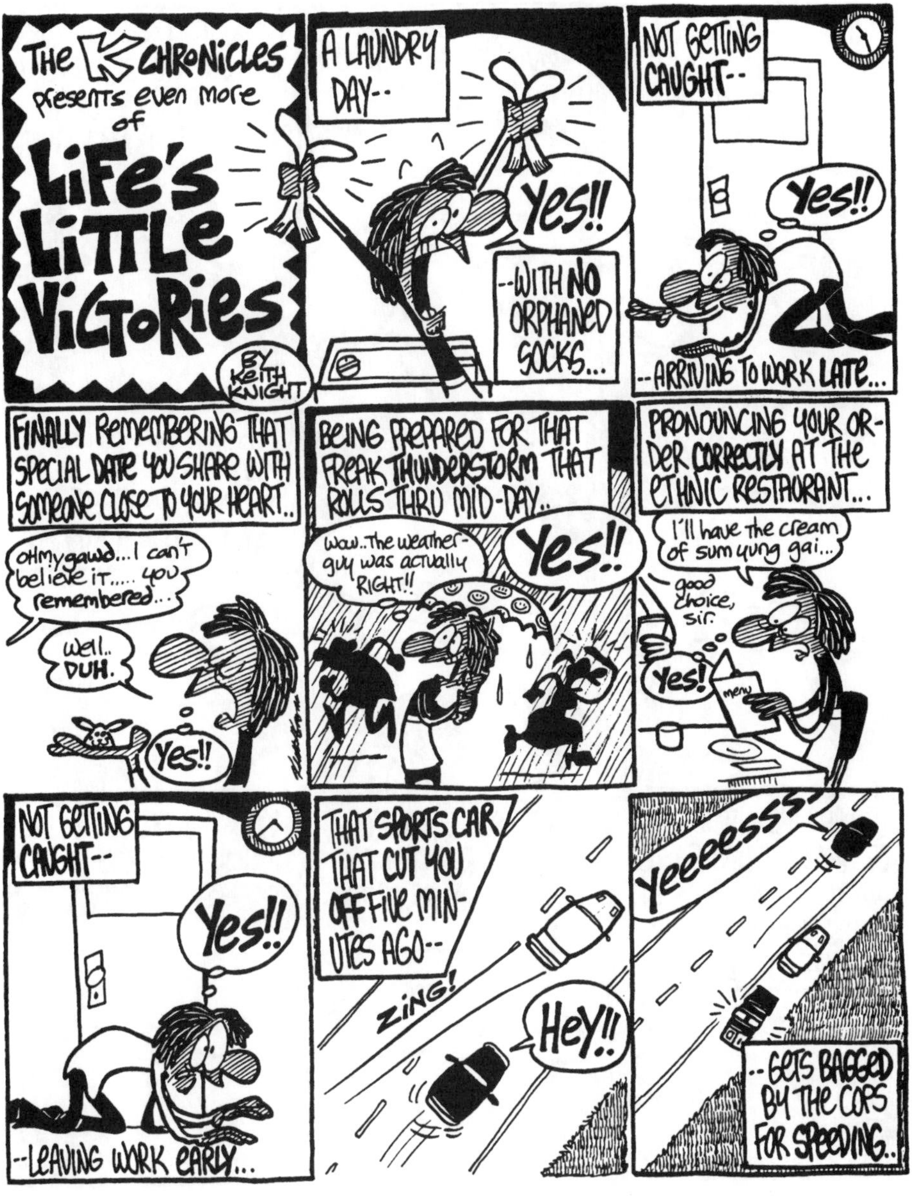
THE K CHRONICLES presents even more of
LIFE'S LITTLE VICTORIES
BY KEITH KNIGHT
A LAUNDRY DAY--
Yes!!
--WITH NO ORPHANED SOCKS...
NOT GETTING CAUGHT--
Yes!!
--ARRIVING TO WORK LATE...
FINALLY REMEMBERING THAT SPECIAL DATE YOU SHARE WITH SOMEONE CLOSE TO YOUR HEART..
OHmygawd...I can't believe it..... you remembered...
Well.. DUH.
Yes!!
BEING PREPARED FOR THAT FREAK THUNDERSTORM THAT ROLLS THRU MID-DAY..
Wow..The weather-guy was actually RIGHT!!
Yes!!
PRONOUNCING YOUR ORDER CORRECTLY AT THE ETHNIC RESTAURANT...
I'll have the cream of sum yung gai...
good choice, sir.
Yes!
menu
NOT GETTING CAUGHT--
Yes!!
--LEAVING WORK EARLY...
THAT SPORTS CAR THAT CUT YOU OFF FIVE MINUTES AGO--
ZING!
Hey!!
Yeeeesss!
--GETS BAGGED BY THE COPS FOR SPEEDING..

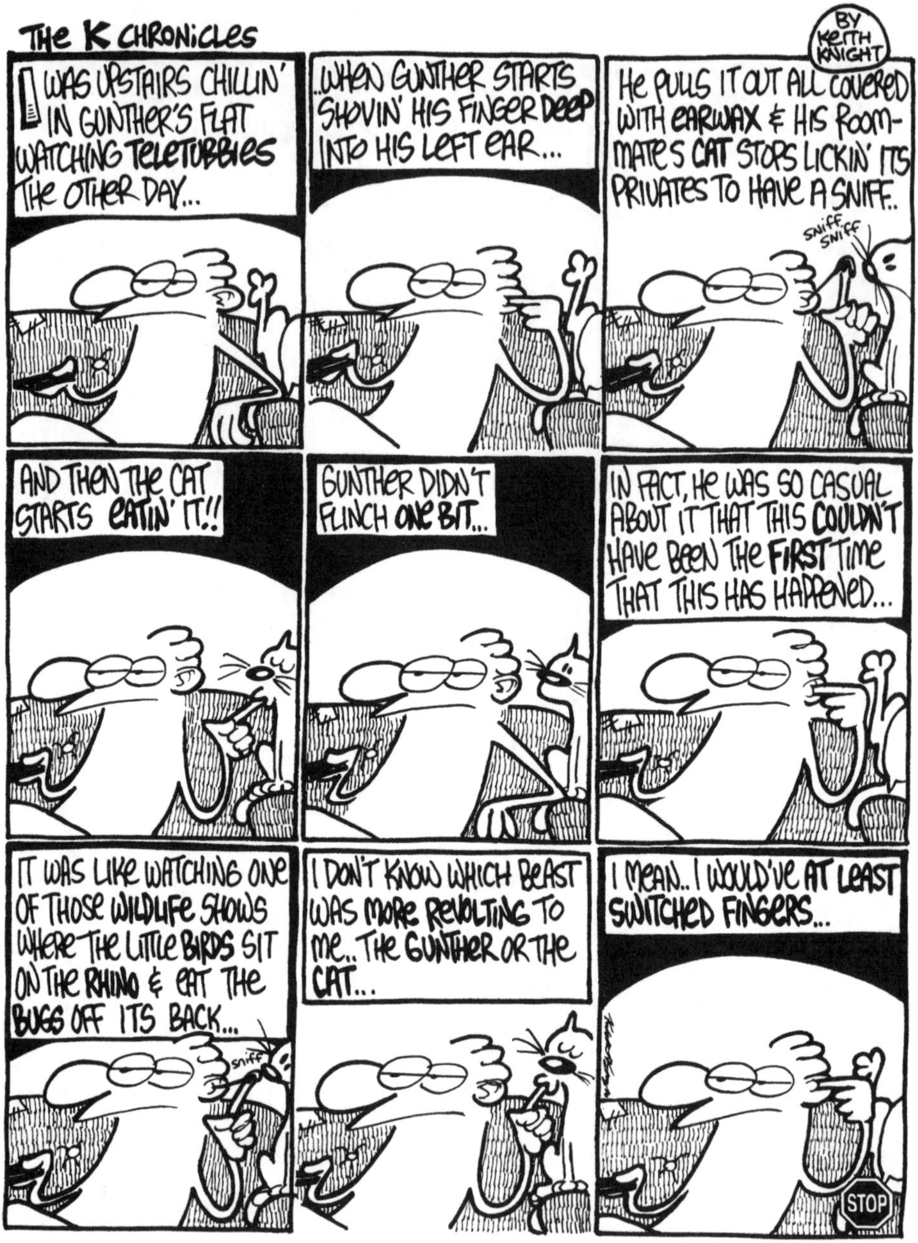
THE K CHRONICLES
BY KEITH KNIGHT
I WAS UPSTAIRS CHILLIN' IN GUNTHER'S FLAT WATCHING TELETUBBIES THE OTHER DAY...
...WHEN GUNTHER STARTS SHOVIN' HIS FINGER DEEP INTO HIS LEFT EAR...
HE PULLS IT OUT ALL COVERED WITH EARWAX & HIS ROOM-MATE'S CAT STOPS LICKIN' ITS PRIVATES TO HAVE A SNIFF..
SNIFF SNIFF
AND THEN THE CAT STARTS EATIN' IT!!
GUNTHER DIDN'T FLINCH ONE BIT...
IN FACT, HE WAS SO CASUAL ABOUT IT THAT THIS COULDN'T HAVE BEEN THE FIRST TIME THAT THIS HAS HAPPENED...
IT WAS LIKE WATCHING ONE OF THOSE WILDLIFE SHOWS WHERE THE LITTLE BIRDS SIT ON THE RHINO & EAT THE BUGS OFF ITS BACK...
SNIFF
I DON'T KNOW WHICH BEAST WAS MORE REVOLTING TO ME.. THE GUNTHER OR THE CAT...
I MEAN.. I WOULD'VE AT LEAST SWITCHED FINGERS...
STOP

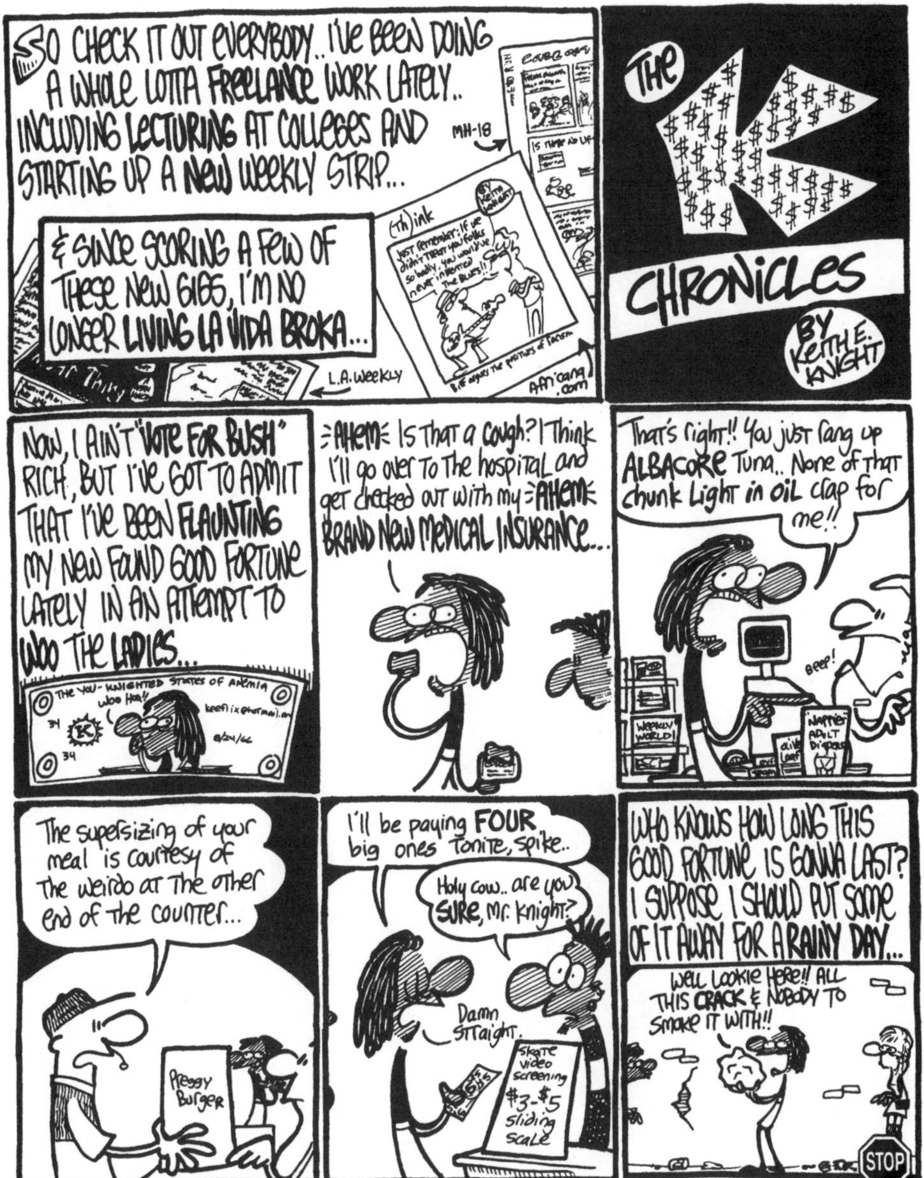

SO CHECK IT OUT EVERYBODY.. I'VE BEEN DOING A WHOLE LOTTA FREELANCE WORK LATELY.. INCLUDING LECTURING AT COLLEGES AND STARTING UP A NEW WEEKLY STRIP...
& SINCE SCORING A FEW OF THESE NEW GIGS, I'M NO LONGER LIVING LA VIDA BROKA...
MH-18
(th)ink
BY KEITH KNIGHT
JUST REMEMBER: IF WE DIDN'T TREAT YOU FOLKS SO BADLY, YOU WOULD'VE NEVER INVENTED THE BLUES!!
L.A. WEEKLY
Afri'cana .com
THE K CHRONICLES
BY KEITH E. KNIGHT
NOW, I AIN'T "VOTE FOR BUSH" RICH, BUT I'VE GOT TO ADMIT THAT I'VE BEEN FLAUNTING MY NEW FOUND GOOD FORTUNE LATELY IN AN ATTEMPT TO WOO THE LADIES...
THE YOU-KNIGHTED STATES OF ANEMIA
WOO HOO!!
keeflix@hotmail.com
=AHEM= IS THAT A COUGH? I THINK I'LL GO OVER TO THE HOSPITAL AND GET CHECKED OUT WITH MY =AHEM= BRAND NEW MEDICAL INSURANCE...
THAT'S RIGHT!! YOU JUST RANG UP ALBACORE TUNA.. NONE OF THAT CHUNK LIGHT IN OIL CRAP FOR ME!!
BEEP!
WEEKLY WORLD
Nappier ADULT Diapers
THE SUPERSIZING OF YOUR MEAL IS COURTESY OF THE WEIRDO AT THE OTHER END OF THE COUNTER...
PREGGY BURGER
I'LL BE PAYING FOUR BIG ONES TONITE, SPIKE..
HOLY COW.. ARE YOU SURE, MR. KNIGHT?
DAMN STRAIGHT.
SKATE VIDEO SCREENING $3-$5 SLIDING SCALE
WHO KNOWS HOW LONG THIS GOOD FORTUNE IS GONNA LAST? I SUPPOSE I SHOULD PUT SOME OF IT AWAY FOR A RAINY DAY...
WELL LOOKIE HERE!! ALL THIS CRACK & NOBODY TO SMOKE IT WITH!!
STOP

Sept. 11th, 2001

(The only Time I've ever missed a deadline)

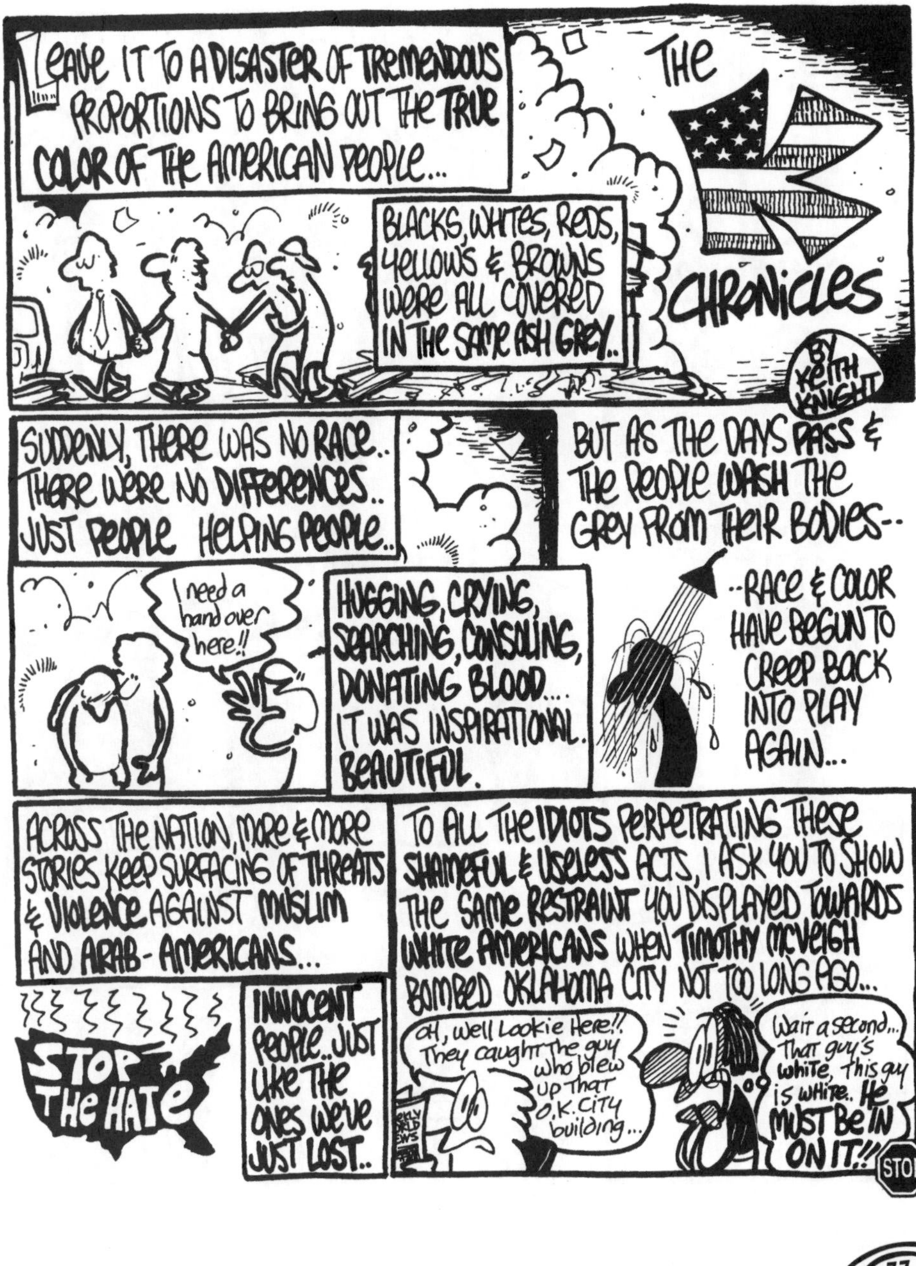

Leave it to a DISASTER of TREMENDOUS PROPORTIONS to bring out the TRUE COLOR of the American people...
THE
CHRONICLES
BY KEITH KNIGHT
BLACKS, WHITES, REDS, YELLOWS & BROWNS WERE ALL COVERED IN THE SAME ASH GREY..
SUDDENLY, THERE WAS NO RACE.. THERE WERE NO DIFFERENCES.. JUST PEOPLE HELPING PEOPLE..
I need a hand over here!!
HUGGING, CRYING, SEARCHING, CONSOLING, DONATING BLOOD.... IT WAS INSPIRATIONAL. BEAUTIFUL.
BUT AS THE DAYS PASS & THE PEOPLE WASH THE GREY FROM THEIR BODIES--
--RACE & COLOR HAVE BEGUN TO CREEP BACK INTO PLAY AGAIN...
ACROSS THE NATION, MORE & MORE STORIES KEEP SURFACING OF THREATS & VIOLENCE AGAINST MUSLIM AND ARAB-AMERICANS...
STOP THE HATE
INNOCENT PEOPLE.. JUST LIKE THE ONES WE'VE JUST LOST..
TO ALL THE IDIOTS PERPETRATING THESE SHAMEFUL & USELESS ACTS, I ASK YOU TO SHOW THE SAME RESTRAINT YOU DISPLAYED TOWARDS WHITE AMERICANS WHEN TIMOTHY MCVEIGH BOMBED OKLAHOMA CITY NOT TOO LONG AGO...
OH, Well Lookie Here!! They caught the guy who blew up that O.K. City building...
Wait a second... That guy's white, this guy is white.. HE MUST BE IN ON IT!!
STOP

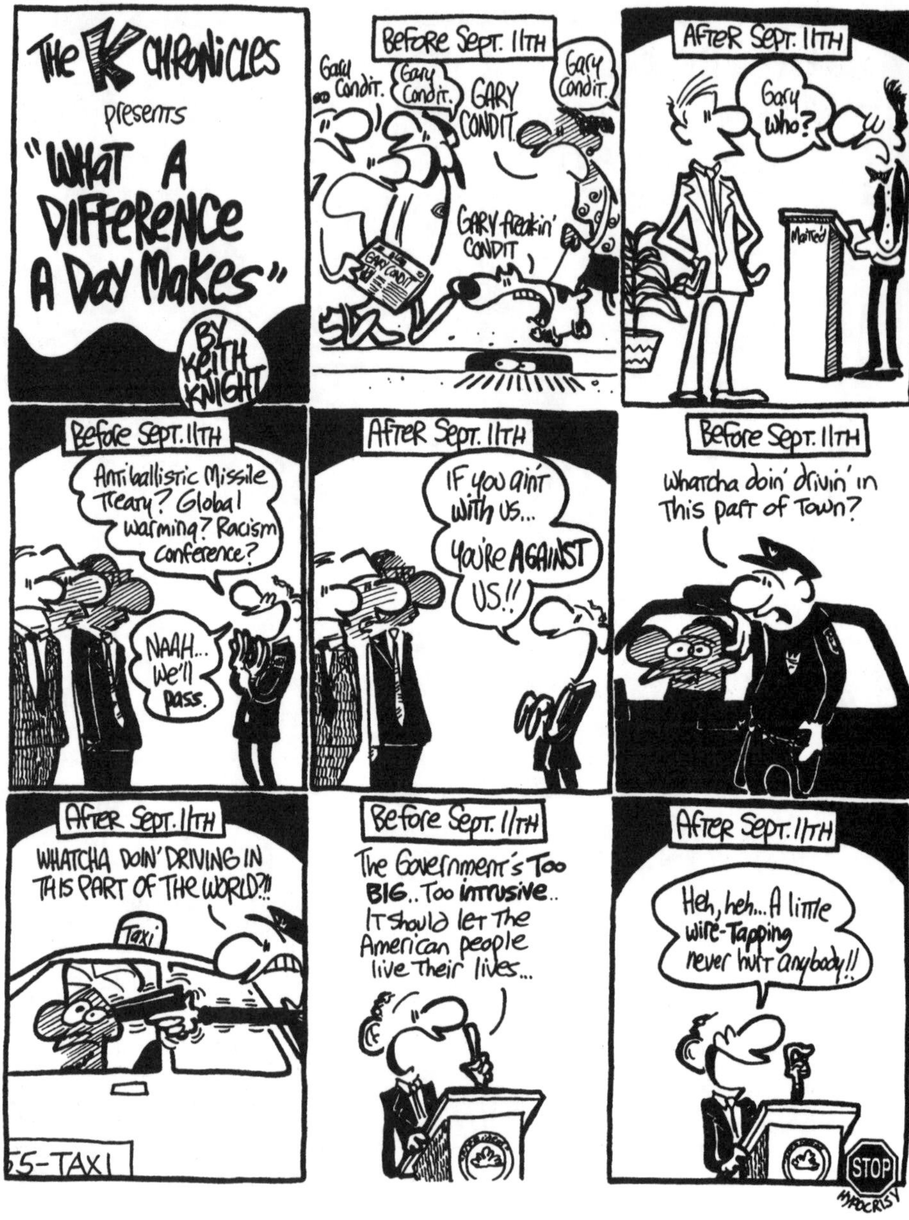

The K Chronicles presents
"What a Difference a Day Makes"
By Keith Knight
Before Sept. 11th
Gary Condit.
Gary Condit.
GARY CONDIT.
Gary Condit.
GARY CONDIT
Gary-freakin' CONDIT
After Sept. 11th
Gary who?
Maitre'd
Before Sept. 11th
Antiballistic Missile Treaty? Global warming? Racism conference?
NAAH... we'll pass.
After Sept. 11th
IF you ain't with us... You're AGAINST US!!
Before Sept. 11th
Whatcha doin' drivin' in This part of Town?
After Sept. 11th
WHATCHA DOIN' DRIVING IN THIS PART OF THE WORLD?!!
Taxi
55-TAXI
Before Sept. 11th
The Government's Too BIG.. Too intrusive.. It should let The American people live Their lives...
After Sept. 11th
Heh, heh... A little wire-Tapping never hurt anybody!!
STOP
HYPOCRISY

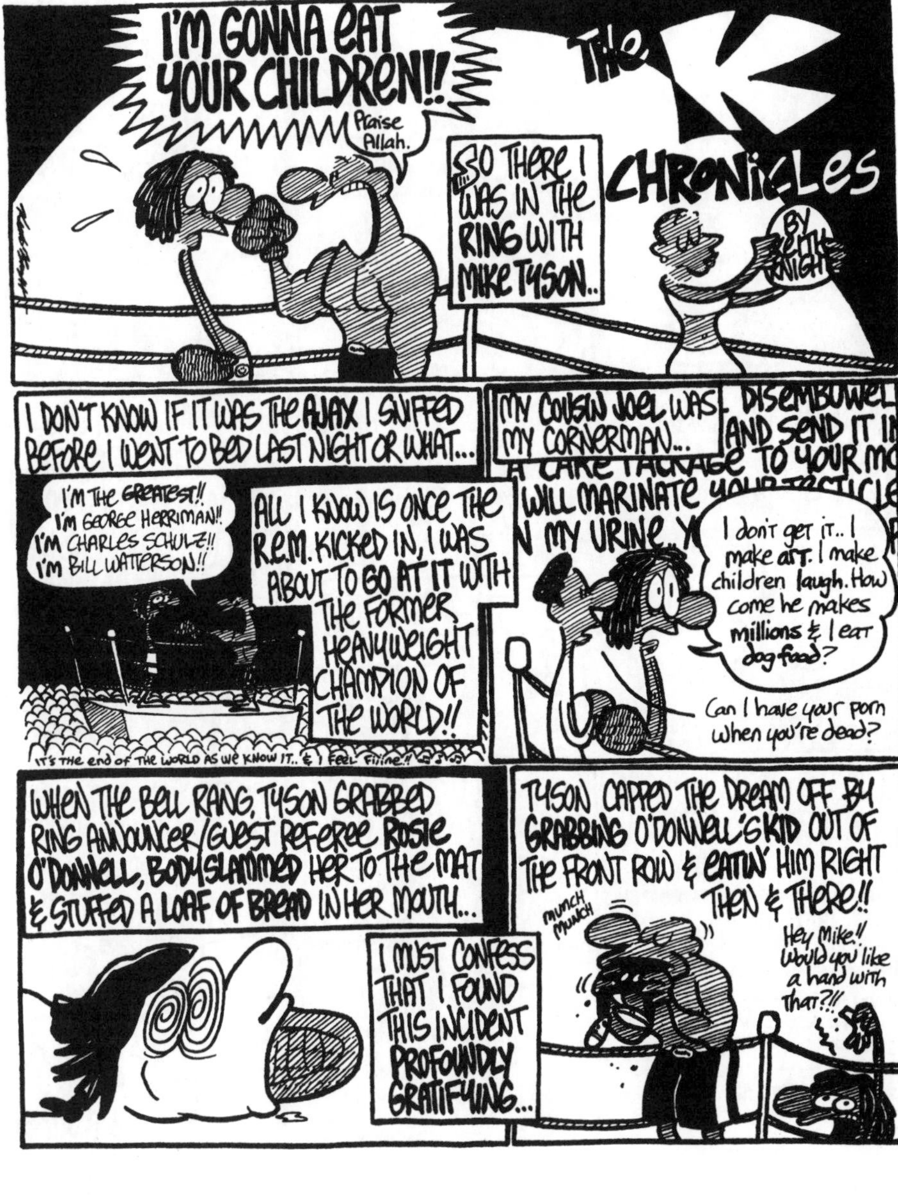
I'M GONNA EAT YOUR CHILDREN!!
Praise Allah.
THE K CHRONICLES
BY KEITH KNIGHT
SO THERE I WAS IN THE RING WITH MIKE TYSON..
I DON'T KNOW IF IT WAS THE AJAX I SNIFFED BEFORE I WENT TO BED LAST NIGHT OR WHAT...
I'M THE GREATEST!! I'M GEORGE HERRIMAN!! I'M CHARLES SCHULZ!! I'M BILL WATTERSON!!
ALL I KNOW IS ONCE THE R.E.M. KICKED IN, I WAS ABOUT TO GO AT IT WITH THE FORMER HEAVYWEIGHT CHAMPION OF THE WORLD!!
IT'S THE END OF THE WORLD AS WE KNOW IT.. & I FEEL FIIINE!!
MY COUSIN JOEL WAS MY CORNERMAN...
DISEMBOWEL
AND SEND IT I
TO YOUR M
WILL MARINATE
N MY URINE..
I don't get it.. I make art. I make children laugh. How come he makes millions & I eat dog food?
Can I have your porn when you're dead?
WHEN THE BELL RANG, TYSON GRABBED RING ANNOUNCER/GUEST REFEREE ROSIE O'DONNELL, BODYSLAMMED HER TO THE MAT & STUFFED A LOAF OF BREAD IN HER MOUTH...
I MUST CONFESS THAT I FOUND THIS INCIDENT PROFOUNDLY GRATIFYING...
TYSON CAPPED THE DREAM OFF BY GRABBING O'DONNELL'S KID OUT OF THE FRONT ROW & EATIN' HIM RIGHT THEN & THERE!!
MUNCH MUNCH
Hey Mike!! Would you like a hand with that?!!

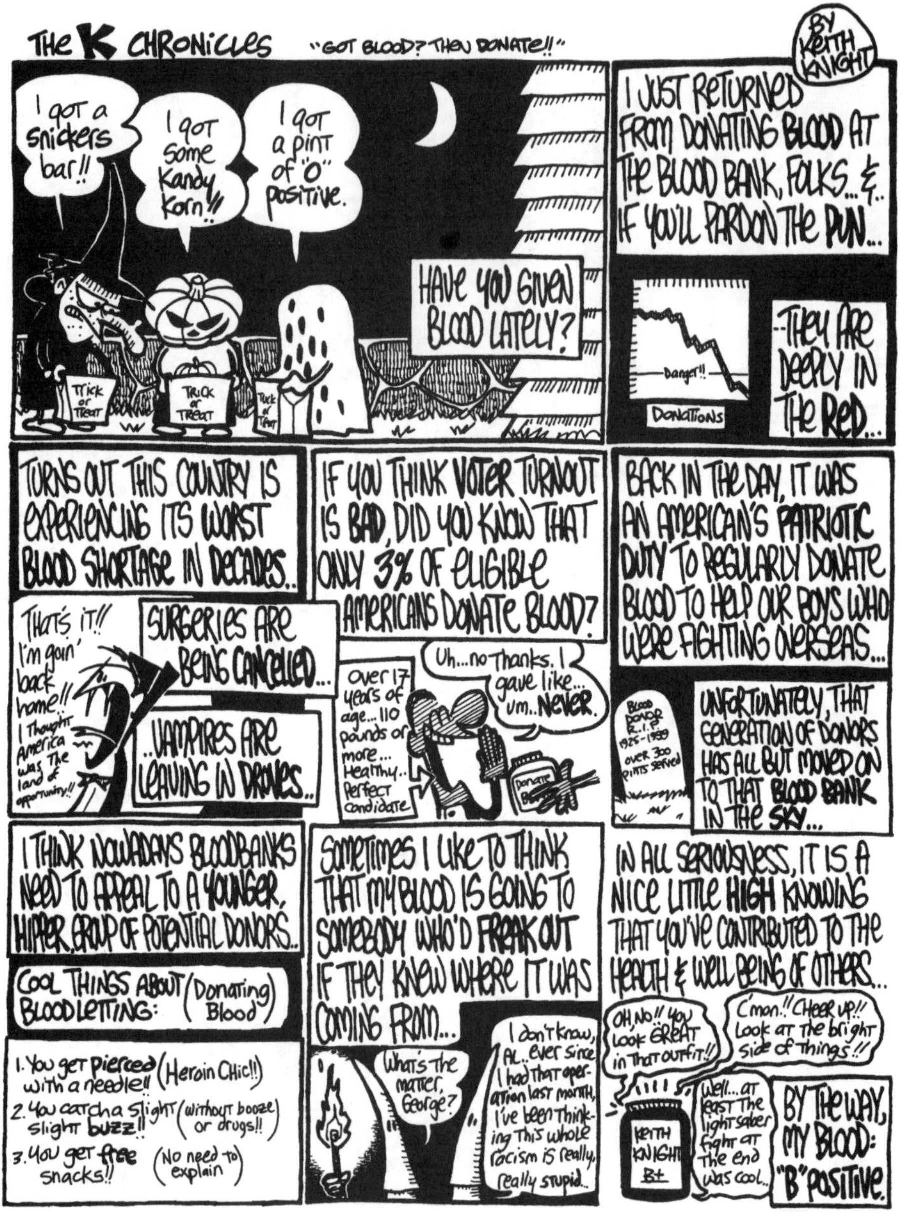
THE K CHRONICLES
"GOT BLOOD? THEN DONATE!!"
BY KEITH KNIGHT
I got a snickers bar!!
I got some Kandy Korn!!
I got a pint of "O" positive.
HAVE YOU GIVEN BLOOD LATELY?
TRICK or TREAT
TRICK or TREAT
TRICK or TREAT
I JUST RETURNED FROM DONATING BLOOD AT THE BLOOD BANK, FOLKS... & IF YOU'LL PARDON THE PUN...
Danger!!
DONATIONS
...THEY ARE DEEPLY IN THE RED...
TURNS OUT THIS COUNTRY IS EXPERIENCING ITS WORST BLOOD SHORTAGE IN DECADES..
IF YOU THINK VOTER TURNOUT IS BAD, DID YOU KNOW THAT ONLY 3% OF ELIGIBLE AMERICANS DONATE BLOOD?
BACK IN THE DAY, IT WAS AN AMERICAN'S PATRIOTIC DUTY TO REGULARLY DONATE BLOOD TO HELP OUR BOYS WHO WERE FIGHTING OVERSEAS...
That's it!! I'm goin' back home!! I thought America was the land of opportunity!!
SURGERIES ARE BEING CANCELLED...
..VAMPIRES ARE LEAVING IN DROVES..
Over 17 years of age... 110 pounds or more... Healthy.. Perfect candidate
Uh...no thanks. I gave like... um.. NEVER.
Donate
BLOOD DONOR R.I.P. 1925-1999 over 300 pints served
UNFORTUNATELY, THAT GENERATION OF DONORS HAS ALL BUT MOVED ON TO THAT BLOOD BANK IN THE SKY...
I THINK NOWADAYS BLOODBANKS NEED TO APPEAL TO A YOUNGER, HIPPER GROUP OF POTENTIAL DONORS..
COOL THINGS ABOUT BLOODLETTING: (Donating Blood)
1. You get pierced with a needle!! (Heroin CHic!!)
2. You catch a slight slight buzz!! (without booze or drugs!!)
3. You get free snacks!! (No need to explain)
SOMETIMES I LIKE TO THINK THAT MY BLOOD IS GOING TO SOMEBODY WHO'D FREAK OUT IF THEY KNEW WHERE IT WAS COMING FROM...
What's the matter, George?
I don't know, AL.. ever since I had that operation last month, I've been thinking this whole racism is really, really stupid..
IN ALL SERIOUSNESS, IT IS A NICE LITTLE HIGH KNOWING THAT YOU'VE CONTRIBUTED TO THE HEALTH & WELL BEING OF OTHERS...
OH, NO!! YOU LOOK GREAT in THAT OUTFIT!!
C'mon!! CHEER UP!! Look at the bright side of things!!
KEITH KNIGHT B+
Well... at least the light saber fight at the end was cool..
BY THE WAY, MY BLOOD: "B" POSITIVE.

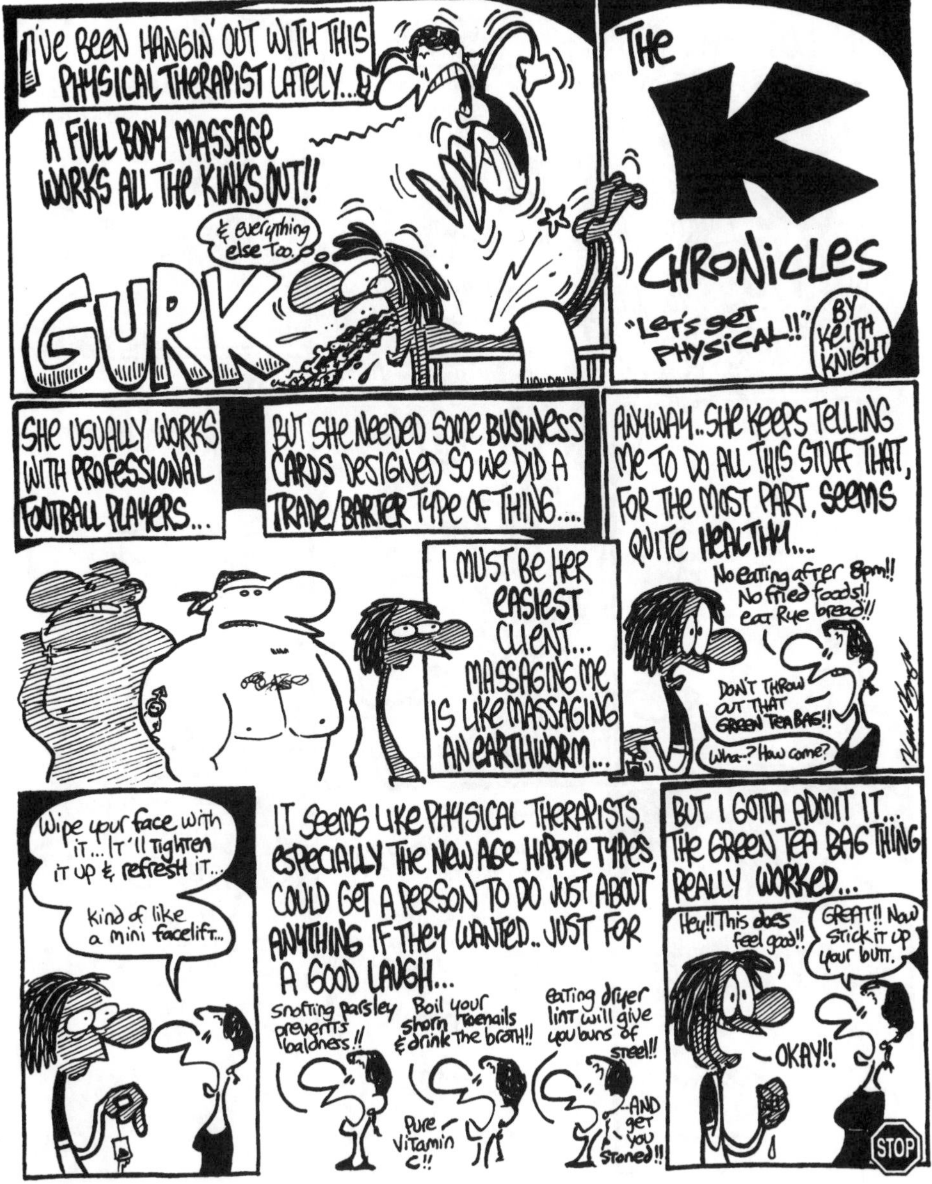
I'VE BEEN HANGIN' OUT WITH THIS PHYSICAL THERAPIST LATELY...
A FULL BODY MASSAGE WORKS ALL THE KINKS OUT!!
& everything else too.
GURK
THE K CHRONICLES
"LET'S GET PHYSICAL!!"
BY KEITH KNIGHT
SHE USUALLY WORKS WITH PROFESSIONAL FOOTBALL PLAYERS...
BUT SHE NEEDED SOME BUSINESS CARDS DESIGNED SO WE DID A TRADE/BARTER TYPE OF THING....
I MUST BE HER EASIEST CLIENT... MASSAGING ME IS LIKE MASSAGING AN EARTHWORM...
ANYWAY.. SHE KEEPS TELLING ME TO DO ALL THIS STUFF THAT, FOR THE MOST PART, SEEMS QUITE HEALTHY....
No eating after 8pm!! No fried foods!! eat Rye bread!!
DON'T THROW OUT THAT GREEN TEA BAG!!
Wha-? How come?
Wipe your face with it... It'll tighten it up & refresh it...
Kind of like a mini facelift...
IT SEEMS LIKE PHYSICAL THERAPISTS, ESPECIALLY THE NEW AGE HIPPIE TYPES, COULD GET A PERSON TO DO JUST ABOUT ANYTHING IF THEY WANTED.. JUST FOR A GOOD LAUGH...
Snorting parsley prevents baldness!!
Boil your shorn toenails & drink the broth!!
Pure Vitamin C!!
Eating dryer lint will give you buns of steel!!
AND get you stoned!!
BUT I GOTTA ADMIT IT... THE GREEN TEA BAG THING REALLY WORKED...
Hey!! This does feel good!!
GREAT!! Now stick it up your butt.
OKAY!!
STOP

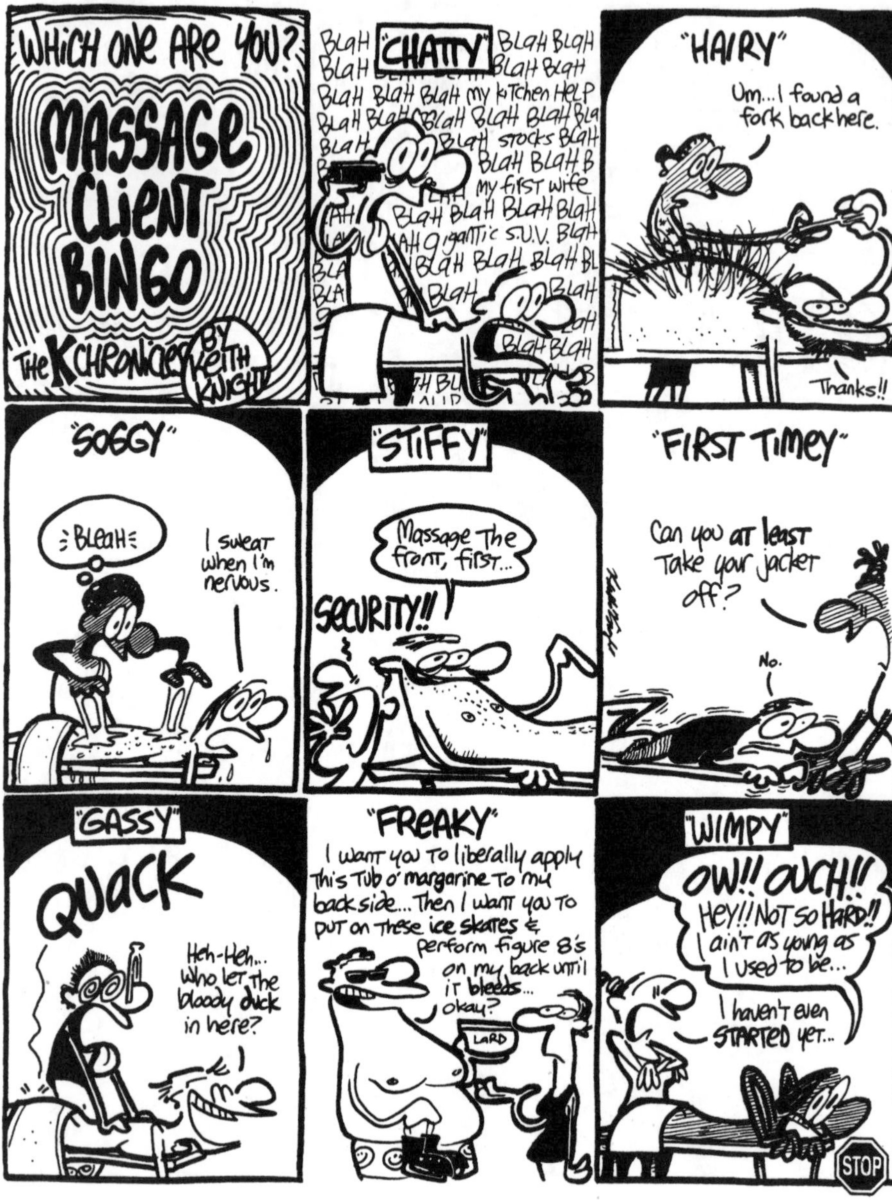
WHICH ONE ARE YOU?
MASSAGE CLIENT BINGO
THE K CHRONICLES BY KEITH KNIGHT
"CHATTY"
BLAH BLAH BLAH BLAH BLAH BLAH
BLAH BLAH BLAH my kitchen HELP
BLAH BLAH BLAH BLAH BLAH BLA
BLAH BLAH stocks BLAH
BLAH BLAH B
my first wife
BLAH BLAH BLAH BLAH
gigantic S.U.V. BLAH
BLAH BLAH BLAH BL
BLAH BLAH BLAH BLAH BLAH BLAH
"HAIRY"
Um... I found a fork back here.
Thanks!!
"SOGGY"
BLEAH
I sweat when I'm nervous.
"STIFFY"
Massage the front, first...
SECURITY!!
"FIRST TIMEY"
Can you at least take your jacket off?
No.
"GASSY"
QUACK
Heh-Heh... Who let the bloody duck in here?
"FREAKY"
I want you to liberally apply this tub o' margarine to my backside... Then I want you to put on these ice skates & perform figure 8's on my back until it bleeds... okay?
LARD
"WIMPY"
OW!! OUCH!! HEY!! NOT SO HARD!! I ain't as young as I used to be...
I haven't even STARTED yet...
STOP

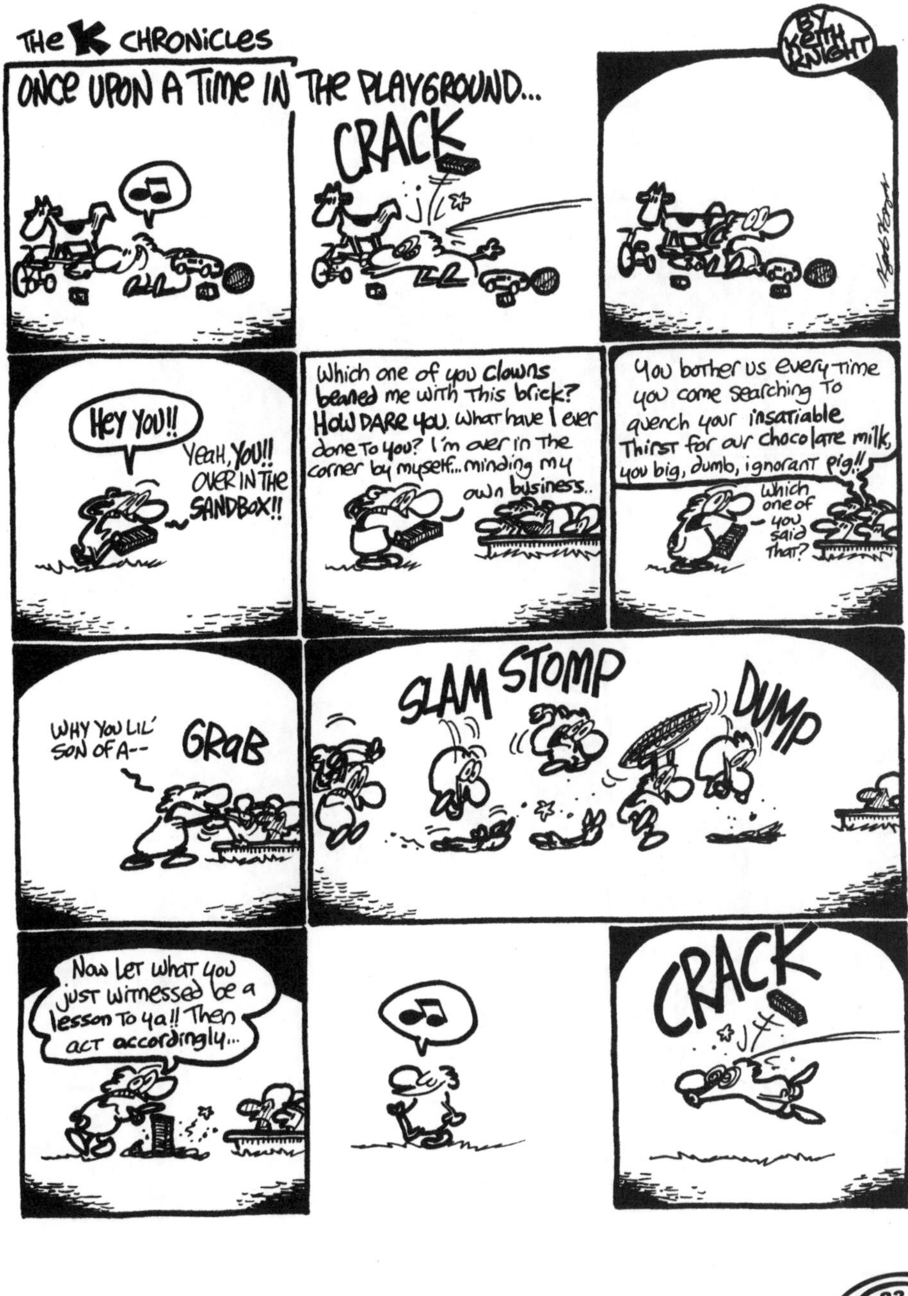
THE K CHRONICLES
BY KEITH KNIGHT
ONCE UPON A TIME IN THE PLAYGROUND...
CRACK
HEY YOU!!
YEAH, YOU!! OVER IN THE SANDBOX!!
Which one of you clowns beaned me with this brick? HOW DARE YOU. What have I ever done to you? I'm over in the corner by myself... minding my own business..
You bother us every time you come searching to quench your insatiable thirst for our chocolate milk, you big, dumb, ignorant pig!!
Which one of you said that?
WHY YOU LIL' SON OF A--
GRAB
SLAM
STOMP
DUMP
Now let what you just witnessed be a lesson to ya!! Then act accordingly...
CRACK

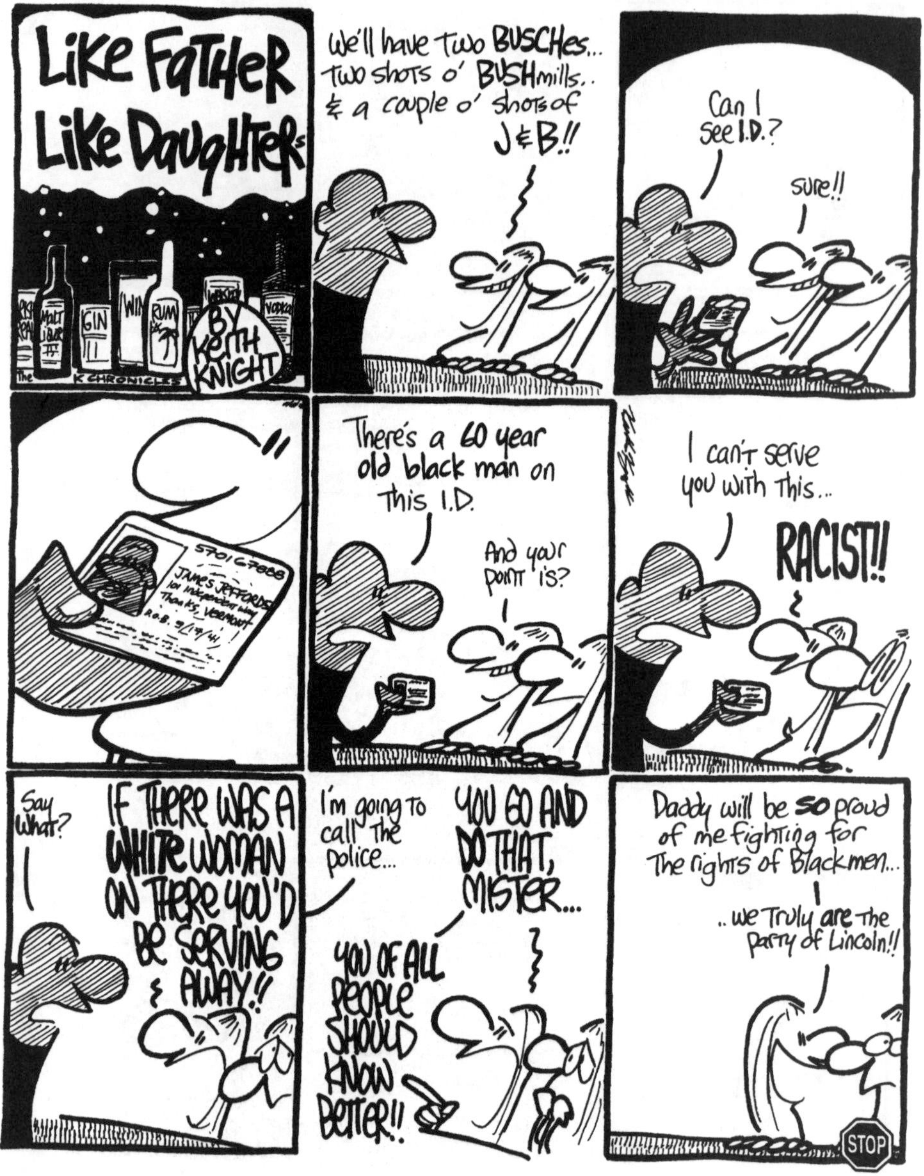

LIKE FATHER LIKE DAUGHTERs
BY KEITH KNIGHT
The K CHRONICLES
We'll have two BUSCHes... two shots o' BUSHmills.. & a couple o' shots of J&B!!
Can I see I.D.?
sure!!
There's a 60 year old black man on this I.D.
And your point is?
I can't serve you with this...
RACIST!!
Say What?
IF THERE WAS A WHITE WOMAN ON THERE YOU'D BE SERVING AWAY!!
I'm going to call the police...
YOU GO AND DO THAT, MISTER...
YOU OF ALL PEOPLE SHOULD KNOW BETTER!!
Daddy will be SO proud of me fighting for the rights of Blackmen...
..we truly are the party of Lincoln!!
STOP

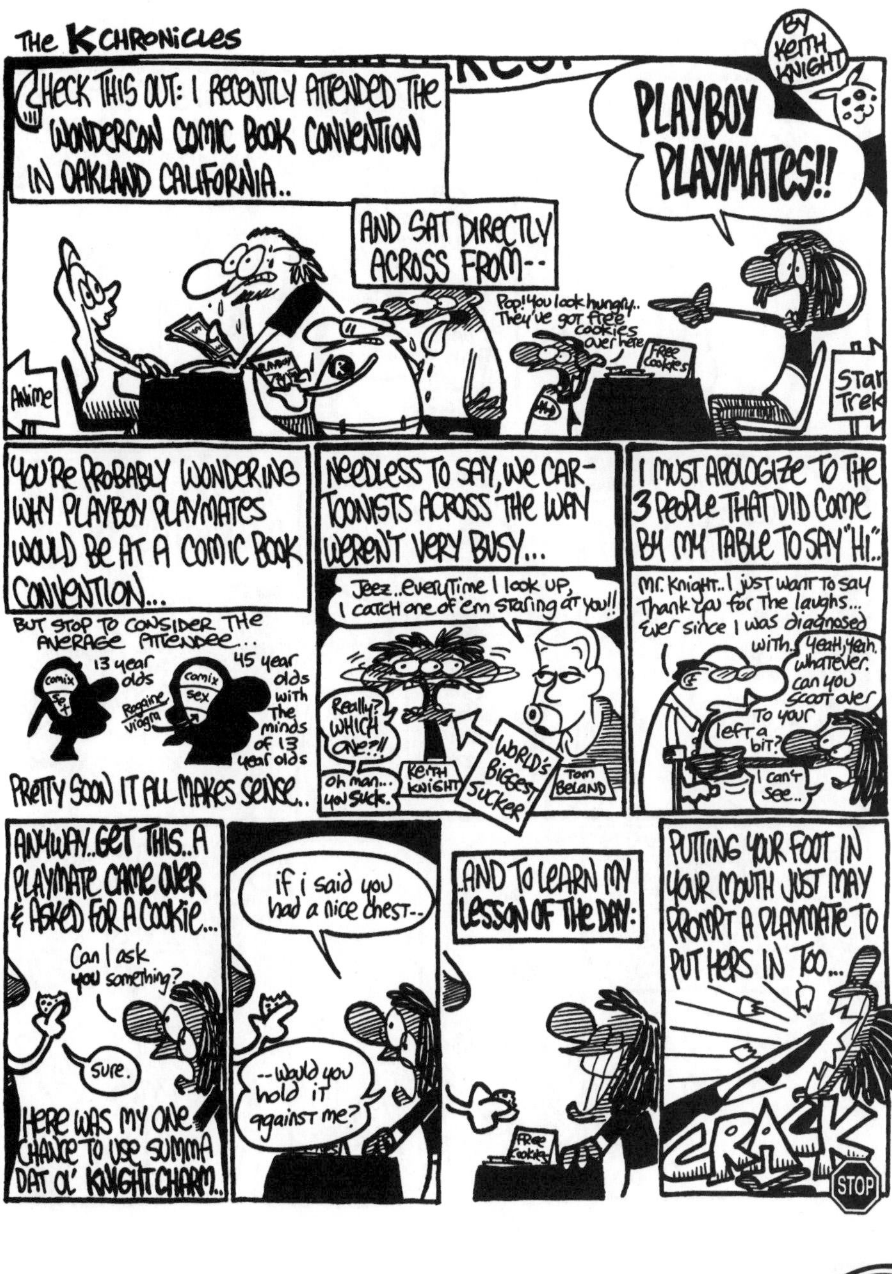
THE K CHRONICLES
BY KEITH KNIGHT
CHECK THIS OUT: I RECENTLY ATTENDED THE WONDERCON COMIC BOOK CONVENTION IN OAKLAND CALIFORNIA..
AND SAT DIRECTLY ACROSS FROM--
PLAYBOY PLAYMATES!!
Pop! You look hungry.. They've got free cookies over here
Free cookies
Anime
Star Trek
YOU'RE PROBABLY WONDERING WHY PLAYBOY PLAYMATES WOULD BE AT A COMIC BOOK CONVENTION...
BUT STOP TO CONSIDER THE AVERAGE ATTENDEE...
13 year olds
comix
sex
45 year olds with the minds of 13 year olds
comix
sex
Rogaine
viagra
PRETTY SOON IT ALL MAKES SENSE..
NEEDLESS TO SAY, WE CAR-TOONISTS ACROSS THE WAY WEREN'T VERY BUSY...
Jeez.. everytime I look up, I catch one of 'em staring at you!!
Really? WHICH ONE?!!
Oh man... you suck.
WORLD'S BIGGEST SUCKER
KEITH KNIGHT
TOM BELAND
I MUST APOLOGIZE TO THE 3 PEOPLE THAT DID COME BY MY TABLE TO SAY "HI."
Mr. Knight.. I just want to say Thank you for the laughs... Ever since I was diagnosed with..
Yeah, yeah. whatever. can you scoot over to your left a bit?
I can't see..
ANYWAY..GET THIS..A PLAYMATE CAME OVER & ASKED FOR A COOKIE...
Can I ask you something?
Sure.
HERE WAS MY ONE CHANCE TO USE SUMMA DAT OL' KNIGHT CHARM..
if i said you had a nice chest--
--would you hold it against me?
..AND TO LEARN MY LESSON OF THE DAY:
Free cookies
PUTTING YOUR FOOT IN YOUR MOUTH JUST MAY PROMPT A PLAYMATE TO PUT HERS IN TOO...
CRACK
STOP

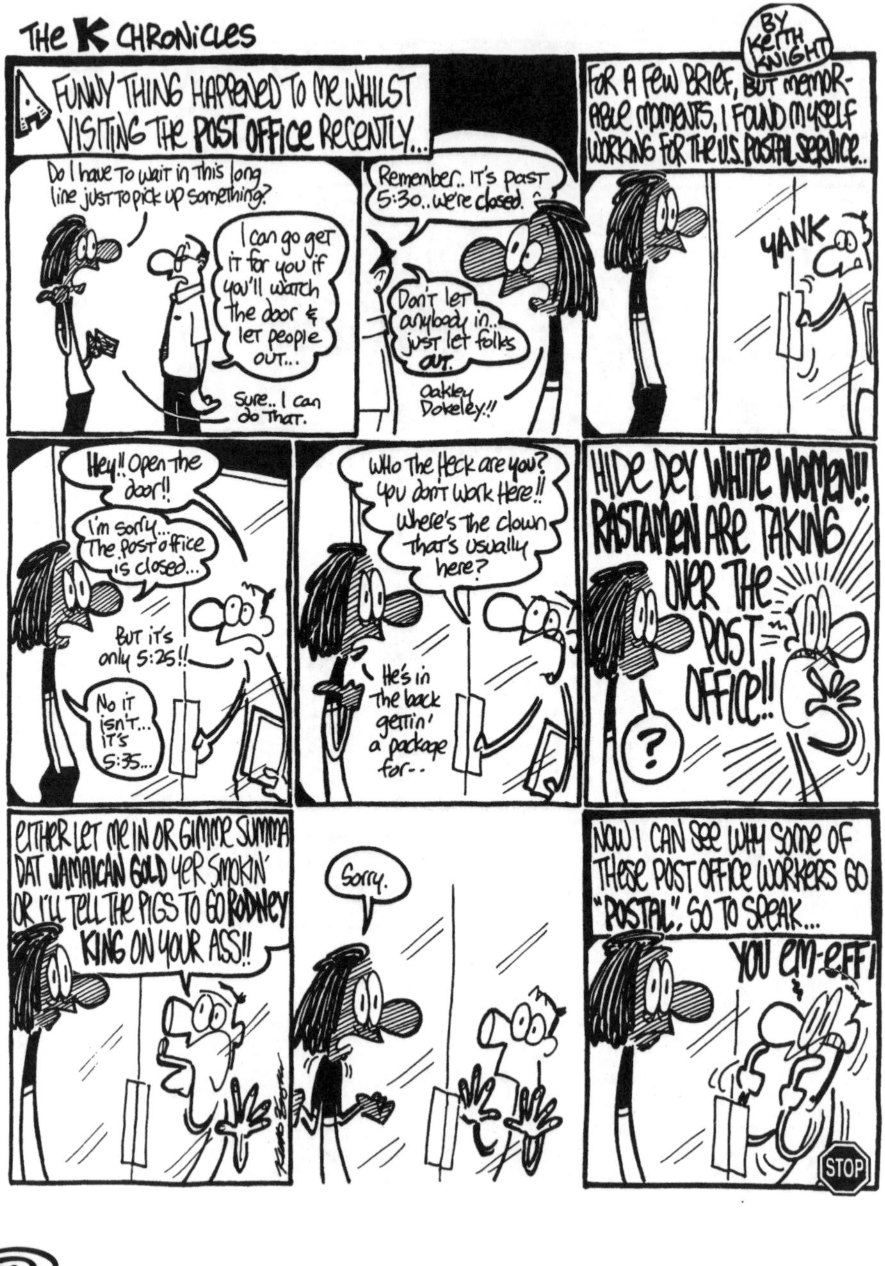
THE K CHRONICLES
BY KEITH KNIGHT
A FUNNY THING HAPPENED TO ME WHILST VISITING THE POST OFFICE RECENTLY...
Do I have to wait in this long line just to pick up something?
I can go get it for you if you'll watch the door & let people out...
Sure.. I can do that.
Remember.. IT'S past 5:30.. we're closed.
Don't let anybody in.. just let folks OUT.
Oakley Dokeley!!
FOR A FEW BRIEF, BUT MEMORABLE MOMENTS, I FOUND MYSELF WORKING FOR THE U.S. POSTAL SERVICE..
YANK
Hey!! Open the door!!
I'm sorry... The post office is closed...
But it's only 5:25!!
No it isn't... it's 5:35...
Who the Heck are you? You don't work Here!! Where's the clown that's usually here?
He's in the back gettin' a package for--
HIDE DEY WHITE WOMEN!! RASTAMEN ARE TAKING OVER THE POST OFFICE!!
?
EITHER LET ME IN OR GIMME SUMMA DAT JAMAICAN GOLD YER SMOKIN' OR I'LL TELL THE PIGS TO GO RODNEY KING ON YOUR ASS!!
Sorry.
NOW I CAN SEE WHY SOME OF THESE POST OFFICE WORKERS GO "POSTAL", SO TO SPEAK...
YOU EM-EFF!
STOP

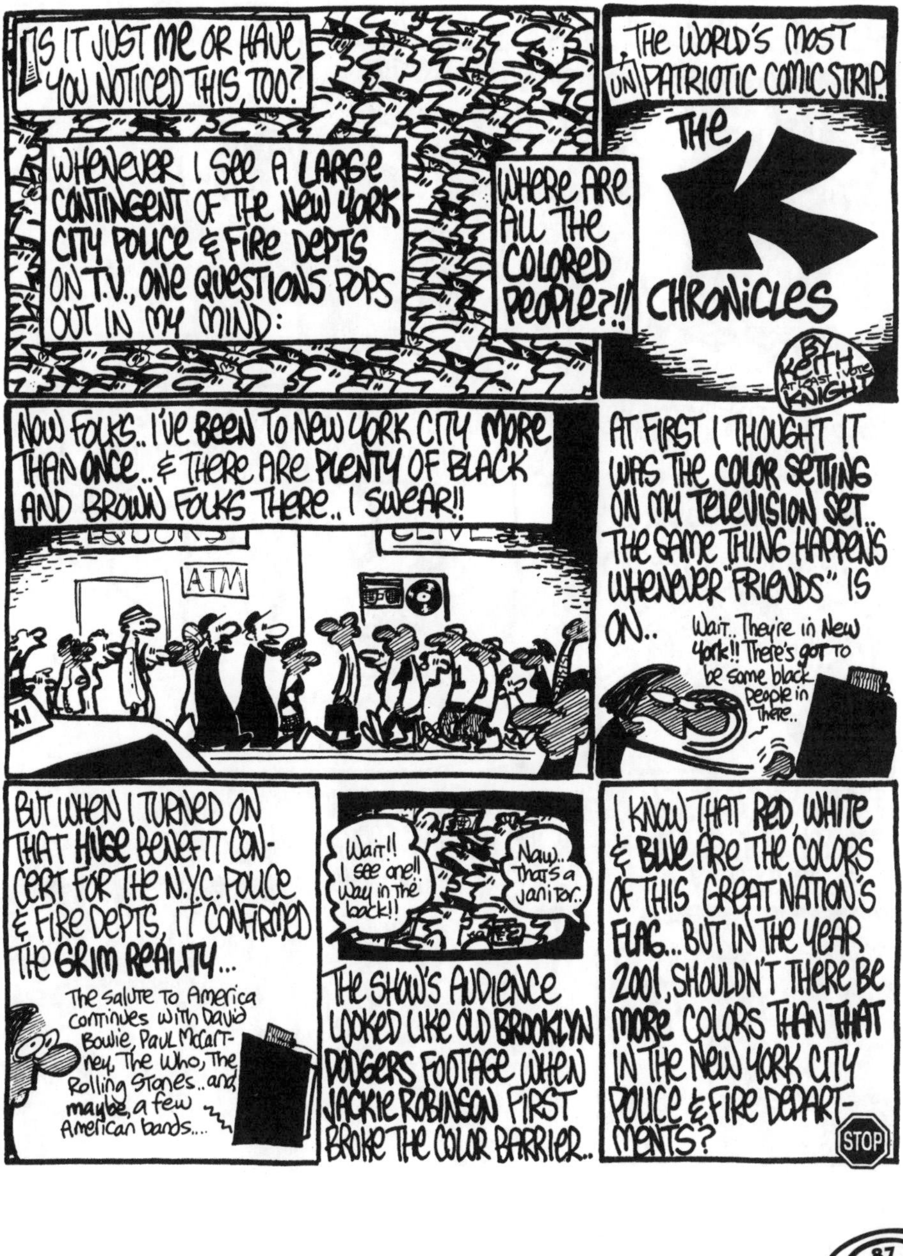
IS IT JUST ME OR HAVE YOU NOTICED THIS, TOO?
WHENEVER I SEE A LARGE CONTINGENT OF THE NEW YORK CITY POLICE & FIRE DEPTS ON T.V., ONE QUESTIONS POPS OUT IN MY MIND:
WHERE ARE ALL THE COLORED PEOPLE?!!
THE WORLD'S MOST UN PATRIOTIC COMIC STRIP.
THE K CHRONICLES
BY KEITH KNIGHT
AT LEAST I VOTE
NOW FOLKS.. I'VE BEEN TO NEW YORK CITY MORE THAN ONCE.. & THERE ARE PLENTY OF BLACK AND BROWN FOLKS THERE.. I SWEAR!!
ATM
AT FIRST I THOUGHT IT WAS THE COLOR SETTING ON MY TELEVISION SET.. THE SAME THING HAPPENS WHENEVER "FRIENDS" IS ON..
Wait.. They're in New York!! There's got to be some black people in there..
BUT WHEN I TURNED ON THAT HUGE BENEFIT CON-CERT FOR THE N.Y.C. POLICE & FIRE DEPTS, IT CONFIRMED THE GRIM REALITY...
The salute to America continues with David Bowie, Paul McCart-ney, The Who, The Rolling Stones.. and, maybe, a few American bands....
Wait!! I see one!! Way in the back!!
Naw.. That's a janitor..
THE SHOW'S AUDIENCE LOOKED LIKE OLD BROOKLYN DODGERS FOOTAGE WHEN JACKIE ROBINSON FIRST BROKE THE COLOR BARRIER..
I KNOW THAT RED, WHITE & BLUE ARE THE COLORS OF THIS GREAT NATION'S FLAG... BUT IN THE YEAR 2001, SHOULDN'T THERE BE MORE COLORS THAN THAT IN THE NEW YORK CITY POLICE & FIRE DEPART-MENTS?
STOP

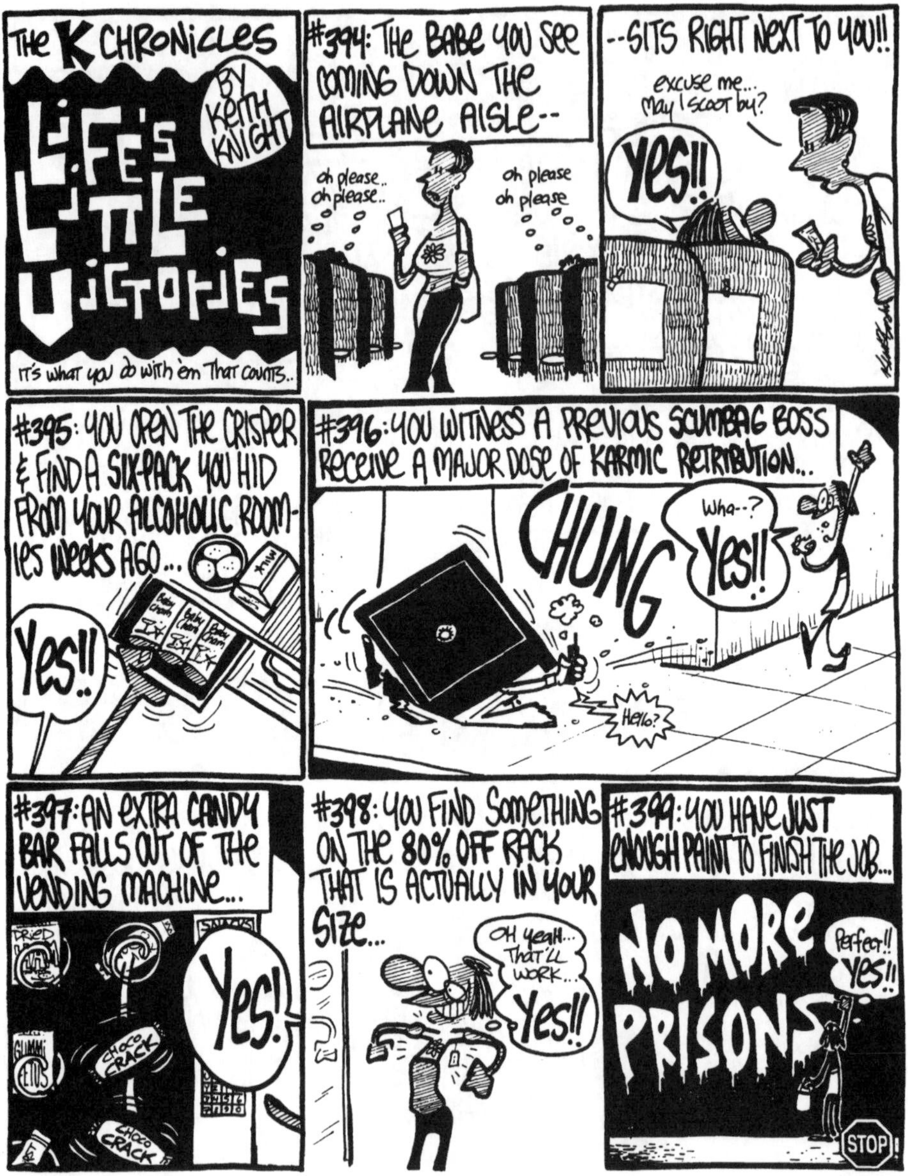

THE K CHRONICLES
BY KEITH KNIGHT
LIFE'S LITTLE VICTORIES
IT'S WHAT YOU DO WITH 'EM THAT COUNTS..
#394: THE BABE YOU SEE COMING DOWN THE AIRPLANE AISLE--
oh please.. oh please..
oh please oh please
--SITS RIGHT NEXT TO YOU!!
excuse me... May I scoot by?
YES!!
#395: YOU OPEN THE CRISPER & FIND A SIX-PACK YOU HID FROM YOUR ALCOHOLIC ROOM-IES WEEKS AGO...
MILK
Baby Cham
Yes!!
#396: YOU WITNESS A PREVIOUS SCUMBAG BOSS RECEIVE A MAJOR DOSE OF KARMIC RETRIBUTION...
CHUNG
Wha--?
Yes!!
Hello?
#397: AN EXTRA CANDY BAR FALLS OUT OF THE VENDING MACHINE...
DRIED
GUMMI FETUS
CHOCO CRACK
CHOCO CRACK
Yes!
#398: YOU FIND SOMETHING ON THE 80% OFF RACK THAT IS ACTUALLY IN YOUR SIZE...
OH YEAH... THAT'LL WORK...
Yes!!
#399: YOU HAVE JUST ENOUGH PAINT TO FINISH THE JOB...
NO MORE PRISONS
Perfect!! Yes!!
STOP!

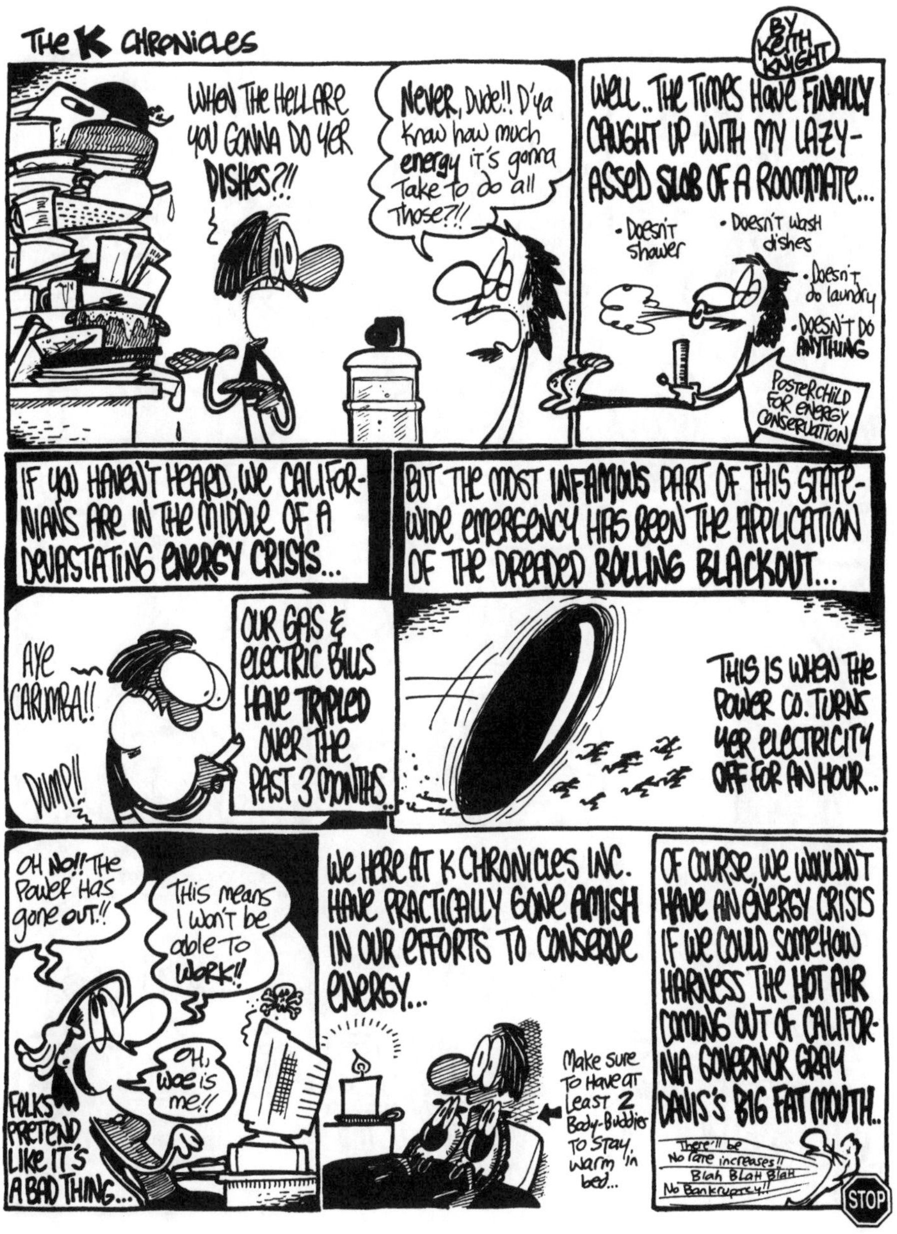
THE K CHRONICLES
BY KEITH KNIGHT
WHEN THE HELL ARE YOU GONNA DO YER DISHES?!!
Never, Dude!! D'ya know how much energy it's gonna take to do all those?!!
WELL.. THE TIMES HAVE FINALLY CAUGHT UP WITH MY LAZY-ASSED SLOB OF A ROOMMATE...
• Doesn't shower
• Doesn't wash dishes
• Doesn't do laundry
• Doesn't do ANYTHING
POSTERCHILD FOR ENERGY CONSERVATION
IF YOU HAVEN'T HEARD, WE CALIFORNIANS ARE IN THE MIDDLE OF A DEVASTATING ENERGY CRISIS...
AYE CARUMBA!!
DUMP!!
OUR GAS & ELECTRIC BILLS HAVE TRIPLED OVER THE PAST 3 MONTHS..
BUT THE MOST INFAMOUS PART OF THIS STATEWIDE EMERGENCY HAS BEEN THE APPLICATION OF THE DREADED ROLLING BLACKOUT...
THIS IS WHEN THE POWER CO. TURNS YER ELECTRICITY OFF FOR AN HOUR..
OH NO!! The Power Has gone OUT!!
THIS means I won't be able to WORK!!
OH, Woe is me!!
FOLKS PRETEND LIKE IT'S A BAD THING...
WE HERE AT K CHRONICLES INC. HAVE PRACTICALLY GONE AMISH IN OUR EFFORTS TO CONSERVE ENERGY...
Make sure to have at least 2 Body-Buddies to stay warm in bed...
OF COURSE, WE WOULDN'T HAVE AN ENERGY CRISIS IF WE COULD SOMEHOW HARNESS THE HOT AIR COMING OUT OF CALIFORNIA GOVERNOR GRAY DAVIS'S BIG FAT MOUTH..
There'll be No rate increases!!
Blah Blah Blah
No Bankruptcy!!
STOP

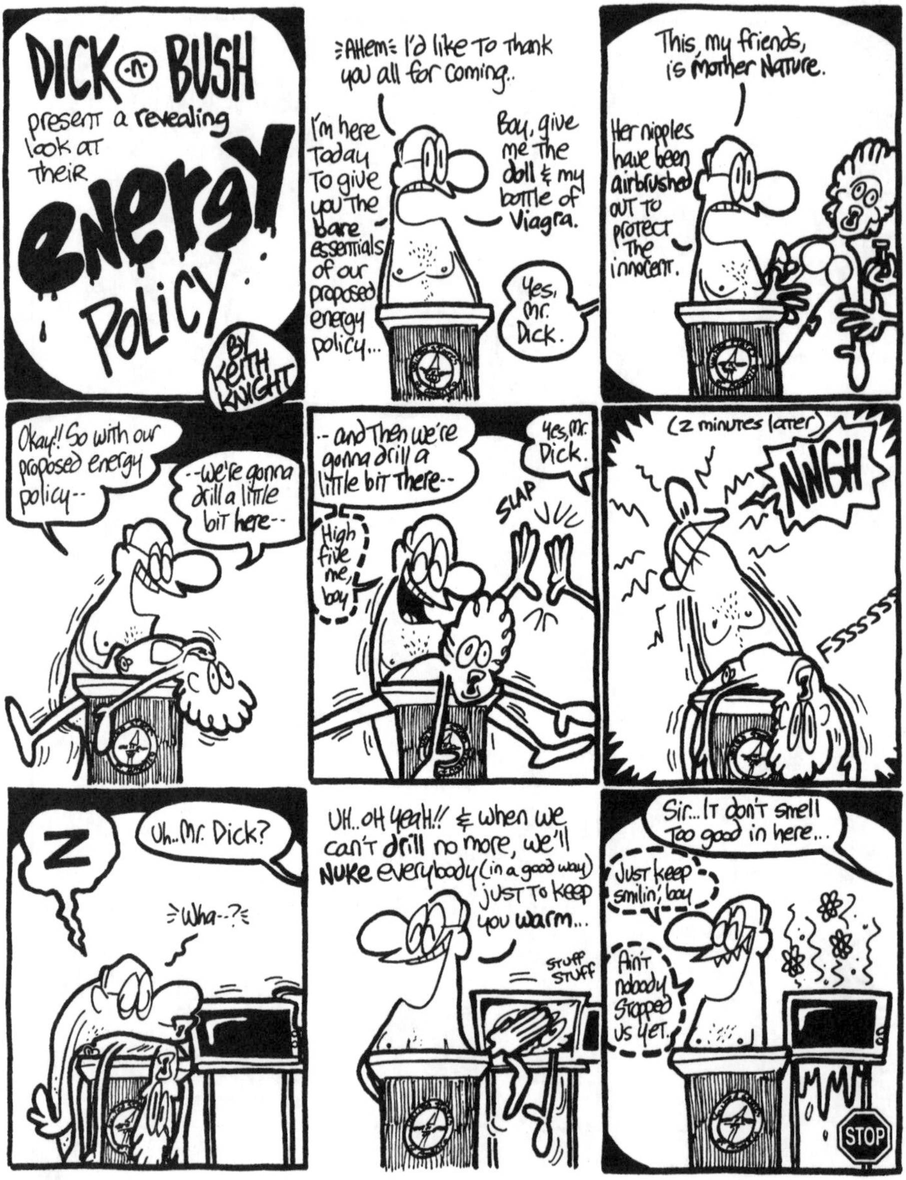
DICK -n- BUSH
present a revealing look at their
energy POLICY
BY KEITH KNIGHT
=AHEM= I'd like to thank you all for coming..
I'm here today to give you the bare essentials of our proposed energy policy...
Boy, give me the doll & my bottle of Viagra.
Yes, Mr. Dick.
This, my friends, is Mother Nature.
Her nipples have been airbrushed out to protect the innocent.
Okay!! So with our proposed energy policy--
--we're gonna drill a little bit here--
--and then we're gonna drill a little bit there--
Yes, Mr. Dick.
High five me, boy!
SLAP
(2 minutes later)
NNGH
FSSSSSS
Z
Uh..Mr. Dick?
=Wha--?=
UH..OH YEAH!! & when we can't drill no more, we'll NUKE everybody (in a good way) JUST to keep you warm...
STUFF STUFF
Sir... It don't smell too good in here...
Just keep smilin', boy
Ain't nobody stopped us yet.
STOP

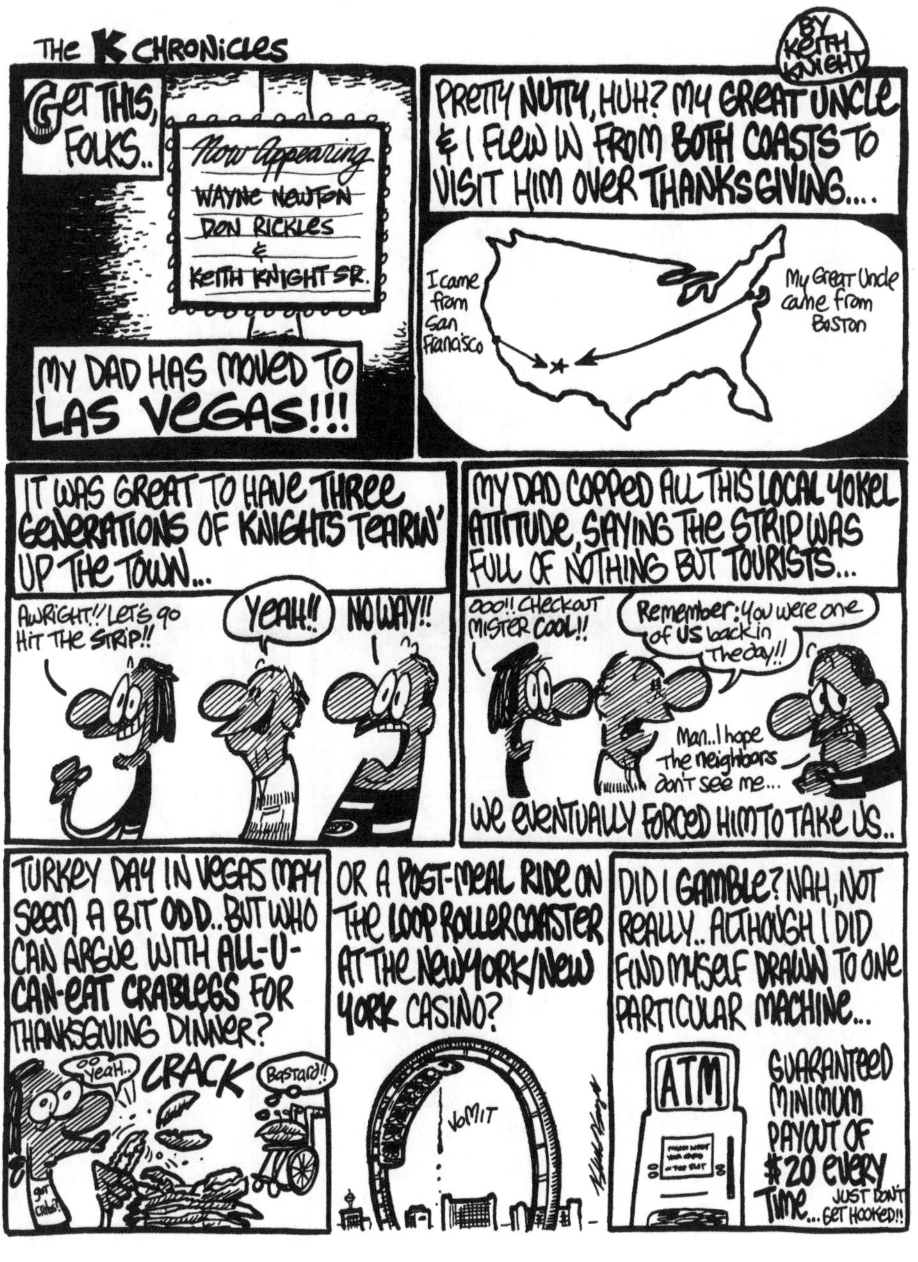
THE K CHRONICLES
BY KEITH KNIGHT
GET THIS, FOLKS..
Now Appearing
WAYNE NEWTON
DON RICKLES
&
KEITH KNIGHT SR.
MY DAD HAS MOVED TO LAS VEGAS!!!
PRETTY NUTTY, HUH? MY GREAT UNCLE & I FLEW IN FROM BOTH COASTS TO VISIT HIM OVER THANKSGIVING....
I came from San Francisco
My Great Uncle came from Boston
IT WAS GREAT TO HAVE THREE GENERATIONS OF KNIGHTS TEARIN' UP THE TOWN...
AWRIGHT!! LET'S GO HIT THE STRIP!!
YEAH!!
NO WAY!!
MY DAD COPPED ALL THIS LOCAL YOKEL ATTITUDE, SAYING THE STRIP WAS FULL OF NOTHING BUT TOURISTS...
OOO!! CHECK OUT MISTER COOL!!
Remember: You were one of US back in The day!!
Man.. I hope The neighbors don't see me...
WE EVENTUALLY FORCED HIM TO TAKE US..
TURKEY DAY IN VEGAS MAY SEEM A BIT ODD.. BUT WHO CAN ARGUE WITH ALL-U-CAN-EAT CRABLEGS FOR THANKSGIVING DINNER?
OO YEAH..
CRACK
Bastard!!
got crabs?
OR A POST-MEAL RIDE ON THE LOOP ROLLER COASTER AT THE NEW YORK/NEW YORK CASINO?
VOMIT
DID I GAMBLE? NAH, NOT REALLY.. ALTHOUGH I DID FIND MYSELF DRAWN TO ONE PARTICULAR MACHINE...
ATM
GUARANTEED MINIMUM PAYOUT OF $20 EVERY TIME...
JUST DON'T GET HOOKED!!

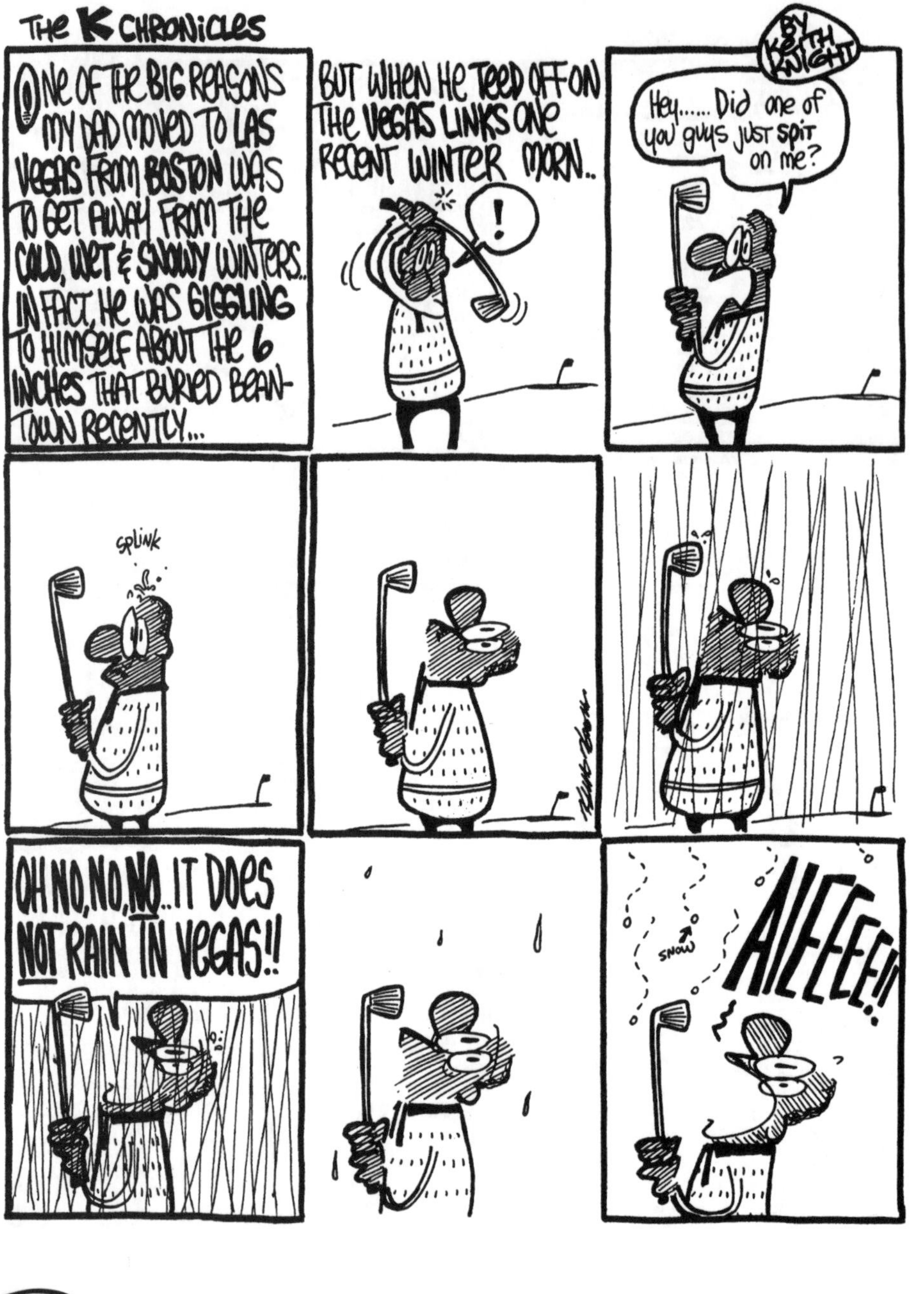
THE K CHRONICLES
BY KEITH KNIGHT
ONE OF THE BIG REASONS MY DAD MOVED TO LAS VEGAS FROM BOSTON WAS TO GET AWAY FROM THE COLD, WET & SNOWY WINTERS.. IN FACT, HE WAS GIGGLING TO HIMSELF ABOUT THE 6 INCHES THAT BURIED BEAN-TOWN RECENTLY...
BUT WHEN HE TEED OFF ON THE VEGAS LINKS ONE RECENT WINTER MORN..
!
Hey...... Did one of you guys just spit on me?
SPLINK
OH NO, NO, NO.. IT DOES NOT RAIN IN VEGAS!!
SNOW
AIEEEE!!

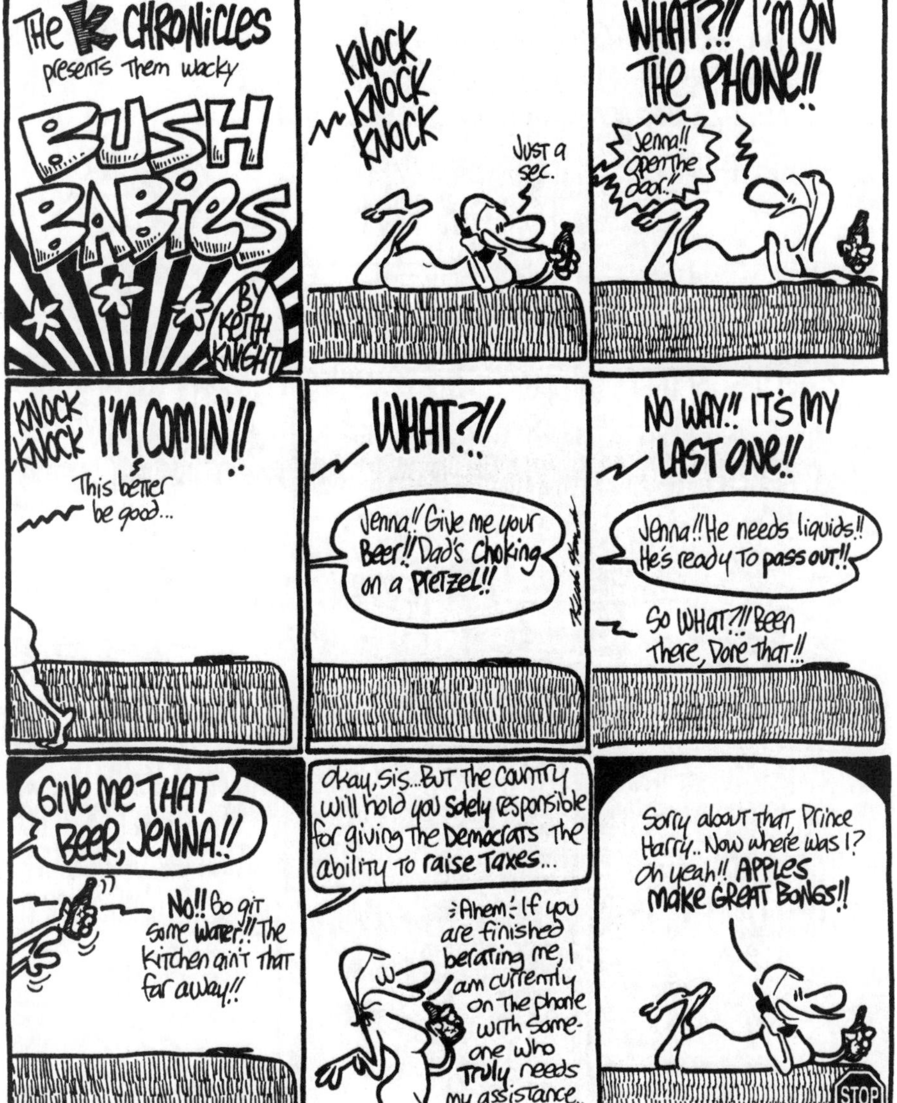
The K Chronicles presents them wacky
BUSH BABIES
By Keith Knight
KNOCK KNOCK KNOCK
Just a sec.
WHAT?!! I'M ON THE PHONE!!
Jenna!! Open the door!!
KNOCK KNOCK
I'M COMIN'!!
This better be good...
WHAT?!!
Jenna!! Give me your Beer!! Dad's choking on a pretzel!!
NO WAY!! IT'S MY LAST ONE!!
Jenna!! He needs liquids!! He's ready to pass out!!
So WHAT?!! Been there, Done that!!
GIVE ME THAT BEER, JENNA!!
No!! Go git some water!! The kitchen ain't that far away!!
Okay, Sis...But the country will hold you solely responsible for giving the Democrats the ability to raise taxes...
Ahem If you are finished berating me, I am currently on the phone with someone who truly needs my assistance..
Sorry about that, Prince Harry.. Now where was I? Oh yeah!! APPLES make GREAT BONGS!!
STOP

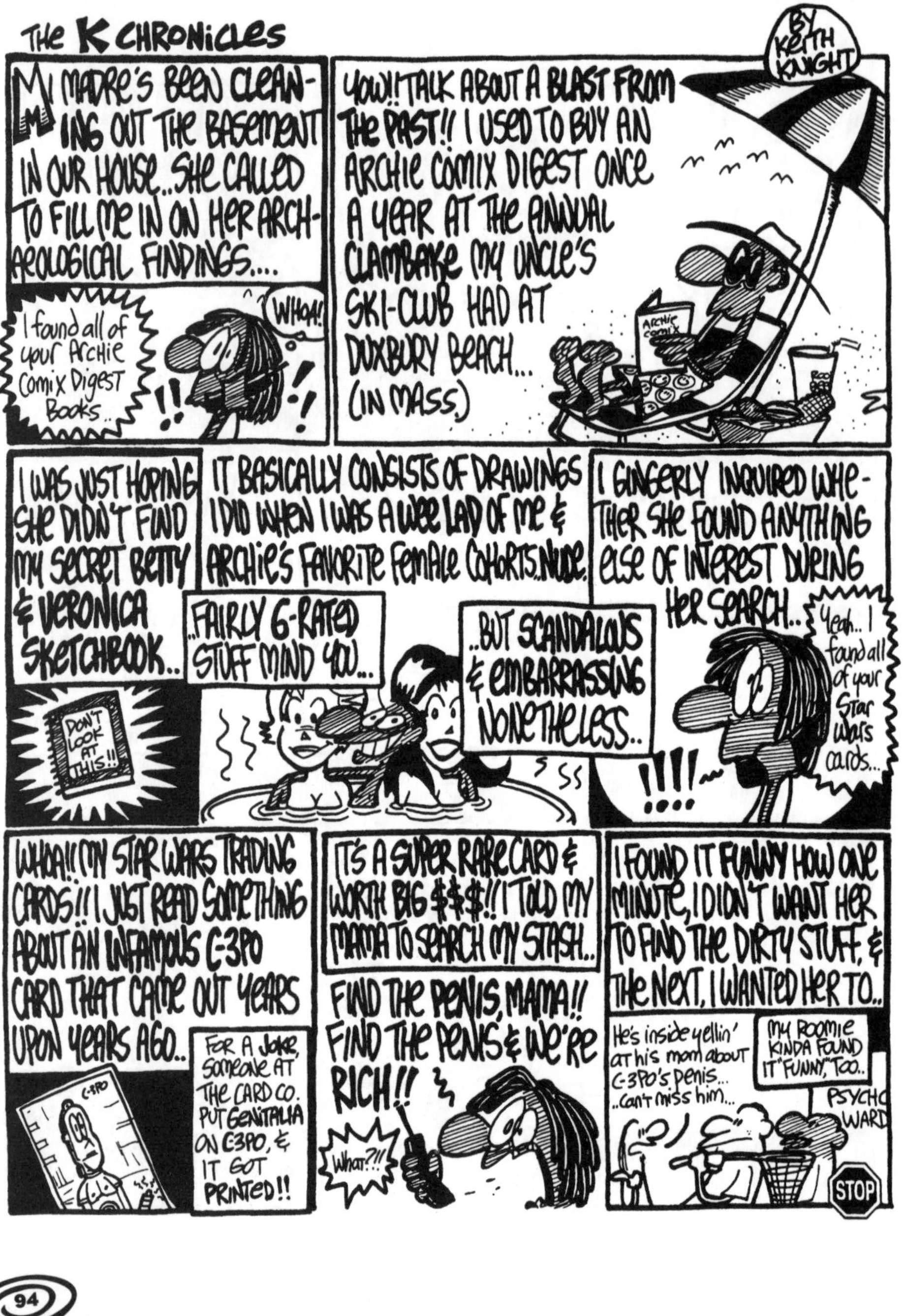
THE K CHRONICLES
BY KEITH KNIGHT
MI MADRE'S BEEN CLEANING OUT THE BASEMENT IN OUR HOUSE... SHE CALLED TO FILL ME IN ON HER ARCHAEOLOGICAL FINDINGS....
I found all of your Archie Comix Digest Books..
WHOA!!
YOW!! TALK ABOUT A BLAST FROM THE PAST!! I USED TO BUY AN ARCHIE COMIX DIGEST ONCE A YEAR AT THE ANNUAL CLAMBAKE MY UNCLE'S SKI-CLUB HAD AT DUXBURY BEACH... (IN MASS.)
ARCHIE COMIX
I WAS JUST HOPING SHE DIDN'T FIND MY SECRET BETTY & VERONICA SKETCHBOOK..
DON'T LOOK AT THIS!!
IT BASICALLY CONSISTS OF DRAWINGS I DID WHEN I WAS A WEE LAD OF ME & ARCHIE'S FAVORITE FEMALE COHORTS..NUDE.
..FAIRLY G-RATED STUFF MIND YOU...
..BUT SCANDALOUS & EMBARRASSING NONETHELESS..
I GINGERLY INQUIRED WHETHER SHE FOUND ANYTHING ELSE OF INTEREST DURING HER SEARCH..
Yeah.. I found all of your Star Wars cards...
WHOA!! MY STAR WARS TRADING CARDS!! I JUST READ SOMETHING ABOUT AN INFAMOUS C-3PO CARD THAT CAME OUT YEARS UPON YEARS AGO..
C-3PO
FOR A JOKE, SOMEONE AT THE CARD CO. PUT GENITALIA ON C-3PO, & IT GOT PRINTED!!
IT'S A SUPER RARE CARD & WORTH BIG $$$!! I TOLD MY MAMA TO SEARCH MY STASH..
FIND THE PENIS, MAMA!! FIND THE PENIS & WE'RE RICH!!
What?!!
I FOUND IT FUNNY HOW ONE MINUTE, I DIDN'T WANT HER TO FIND THE DIRTY STUFF, & THE NEXT, I WANTED HER TO..
He's inside yellin' at his mom about C-3PO's penis... ..Can't miss him...
MY ROOMIE KINDA FOUND IT "FUNNY," TOO..
PSYCHO WARD
STOP

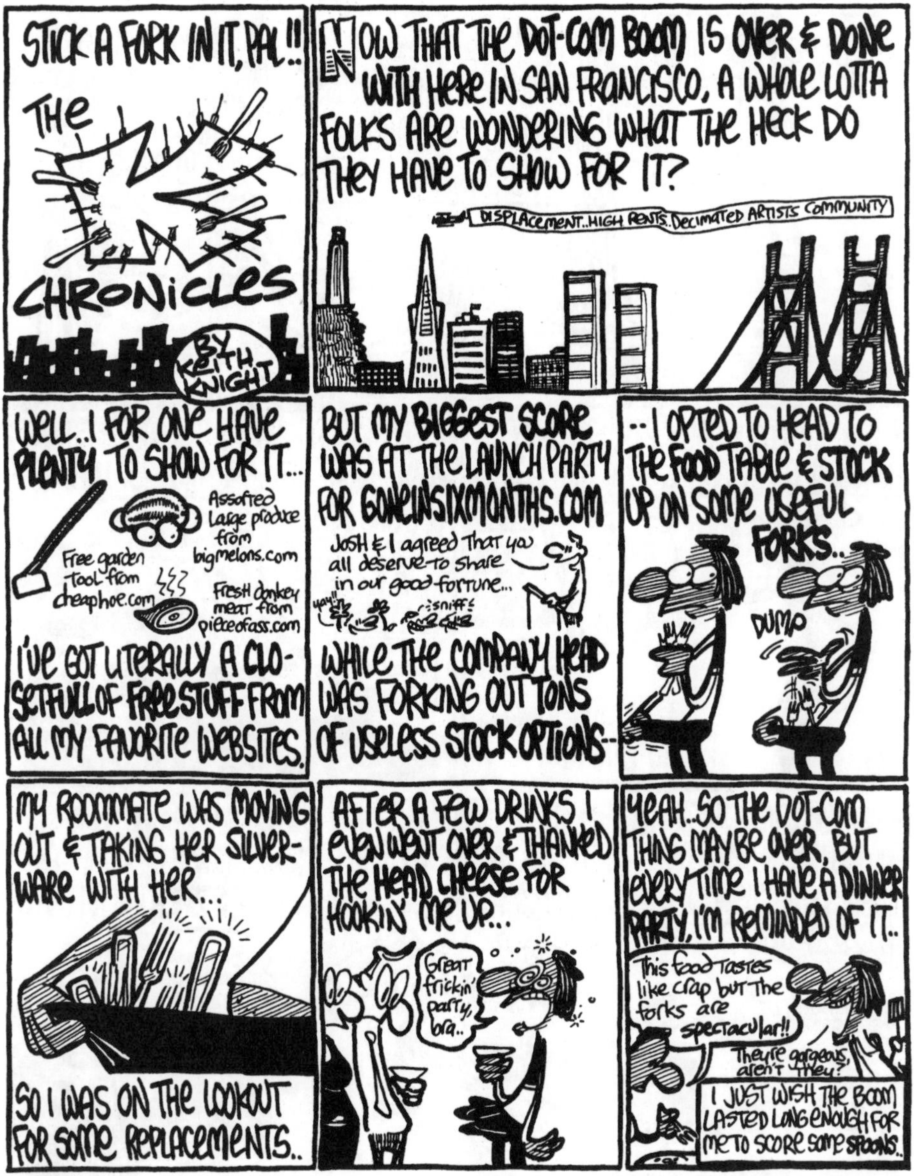

STICK A FORK IN IT, PAL!!..
THE K CHRONICLES
BY KEITH KNIGHT
NOW THAT THE DOT-COM BOOM IS OVER & DONE WITH HERE IN SAN FRANCISCO, A WHOLE LOTTA FOLKS ARE WONDERING WHAT THE HECK DO THEY HAVE TO SHOW FOR IT?
DISPLACEMENT..HIGH RENTS..DECIMATED ARTISTS COMMUNITY
WELL..I FOR ONE HAVE PLENTY TO SHOW FOR IT...
Free garden tool from cheaphoe.com
Assorted Large produce from bigmelons.com
Fresh donkey meat from pieceofass.com
I'VE GOT LITERALLY A CLOSETFULL OF FREE STUFF FROM ALL MY FAVORITE WEBSITES.
BUT MY BIGGEST SCORE WAS AT THE LAUNCH PARTY FOR GONEINSIXMONTHS.COM
Josh & I agreed that you all deserve to share in our good fortune...
yay!!
sniff
WHILE THE COMPANY HEAD WAS FORKING OUT TONS OF USELESS STOCK OPTIONS--
..I OPTED TO HEAD TO THE FOOD TABLE & STOCK UP ON SOME USEFUL FORKS..
DUMP
MY ROOMMATE WAS MOVING OUT & TAKING HER SILVERWARE WITH HER...
SO I WAS ON THE LOOKOUT FOR SOME REPLACEMENTS..
AFTER A FEW DRINKS I EVEN WENT OVER & THANKED THE HEAD CHEESE FOR HOOKIN' ME UP...
Great frickin' party, bra..
YEAH..SO THE DOT-COM THING MAY BE OVER, BUT EVERY TIME I HAVE A DINNER PARTY, I'M REMINDED OF IT..
This food tastes like crap but the forks are spectacular!!
They're gorgeous, aren't they?
I JUST WISH THE BOOM LASTED LONG ENOUGH FOR ME TO SCORE SOME SPOONS..

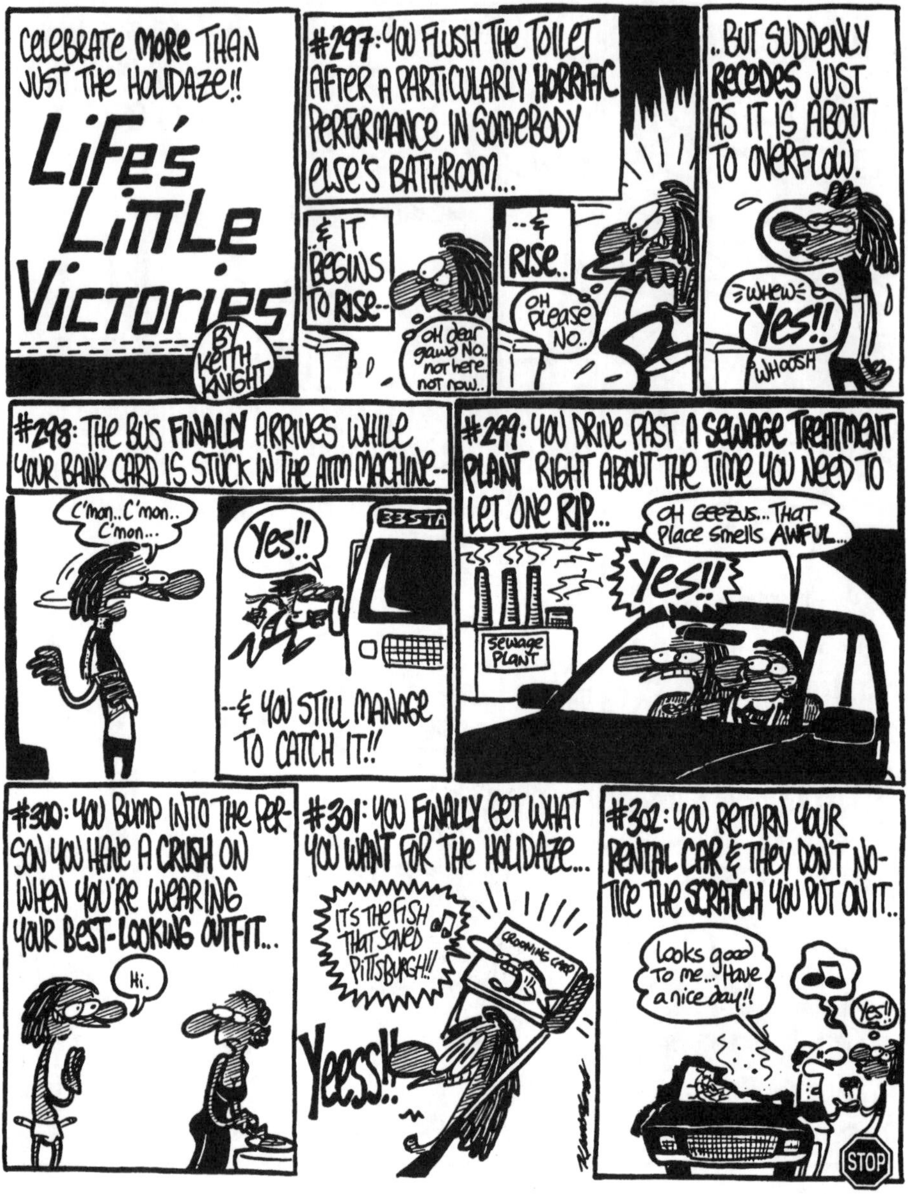
CELEBRATE MORE THAN JUST THE HOLIDAZE!!
Life's Little Victories
BY KEITH KNIGHT
#297: YOU FLUSH THE TOILET AFTER A PARTICULARLY HORRIFIC PERFORMANCE IN SOMEBODY ELSE'S BATHROOM...
..& IT BEGINS TO RISE--
OH dear gawd NO.. not here.. not now..
--& RISE..
OH please NO..
..BUT SUDDENLY RECEDES JUST AS IT IS ABOUT TO OVERFLOW.
WHEW
YES!!
WHOOSH
#298: THE BUS FINALLY ARRIVES WHILE YOUR BANK CARD IS STUCK IN THE ATM MACHINE--
C'mon..C'mon.. C'mon...
Yes!!..
33 STA
--& YOU STILL MANAGE TO CATCH IT!!
#299: YOU DRIVE PAST A SEWAGE TREATMENT PLANT RIGHT ABOUT THE TIME YOU NEED TO LET ONE RIP...
OH GEEZUS... THAT place smells AWFUL...
Yes!!
SEWAGE PLANT
#300: YOU BUMP INTO THE PERSON YOU HAVE A CRUSH ON WHEN YOU'RE WEARING YOUR BEST-LOOKING OUTFIT...
Hi.
#301: YOU FINALLY GET WHAT YOU WANT FOR THE HOLIDAZE...
IT'S THE FISH THAT SAVED PITTSBURGH!!
GROOMING CARD
YEESS!!..
#302: YOU RETURN YOUR RENTAL CAR & THEY DON'T NOTICE THE SCRATCH YOU PUT ON IT..
Looks good to me... Have a nice day!!
Yes!!
STOP

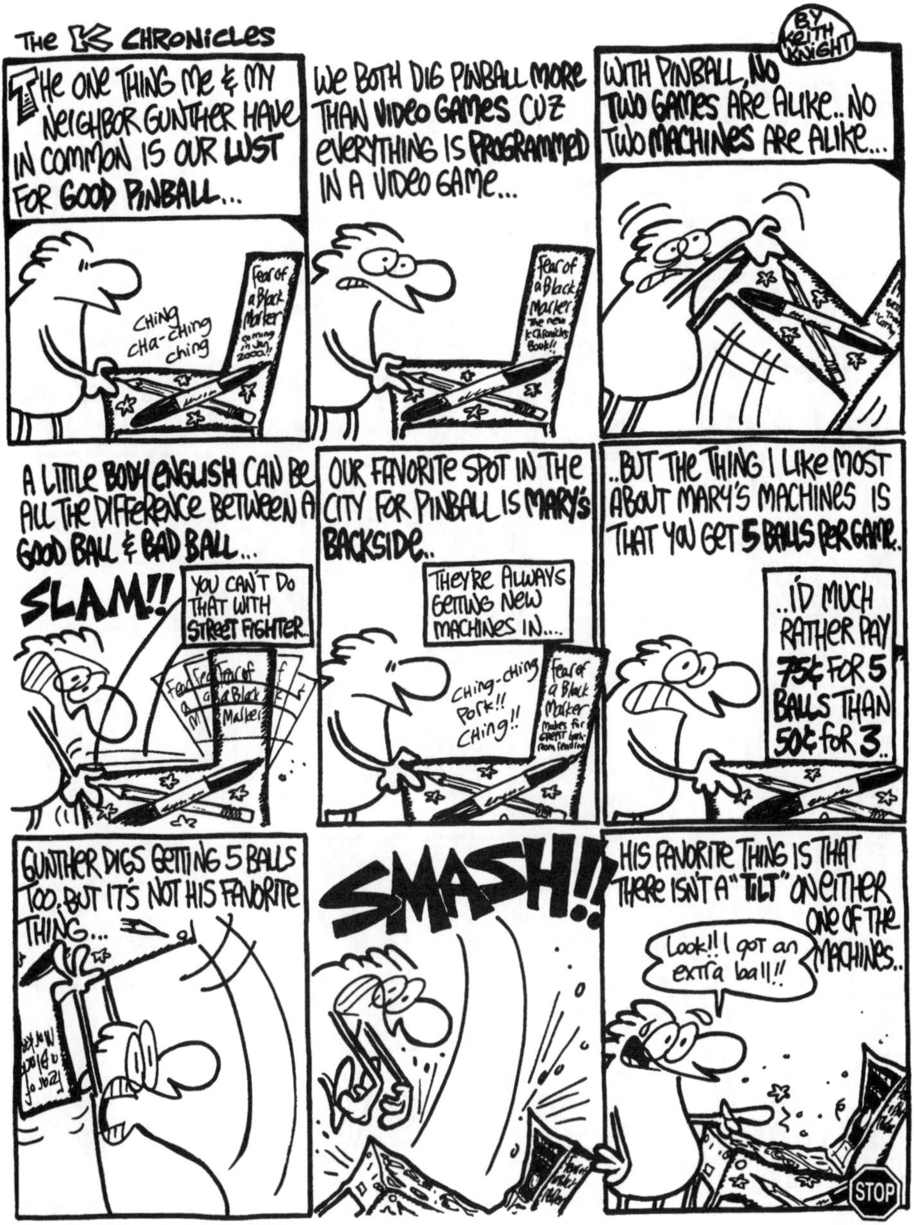
THE K CHRONICLES
BY KEITH KNIGHT
THE ONE THING ME & MY NEIGHBOR GUNTHER HAVE IN COMMON IS OUR LUST FOR GOOD PINBALL...
CHING CHA-CHING ching
Fear of a Black Marker coming in Jan. 2000!!
WE BOTH DIG PINBALL MORE THAN VIDEO GAMES CUZ EVERYTHING IS PROGRAMMED IN A VIDEO GAME...
Fear of a Black Marker The new K Chronicles Book!!
WITH PINBALL, NO TWO GAMES ARE ALIKE.. NO TWO MACHINES ARE ALIKE...
A LITTLE BODY ENGLISH CAN BE ALL THE DIFFERENCE BETWEEN A GOOD BALL & BAD BALL...
SLAM!!
YOU CAN'T DO THAT WITH STREET FIGHTER..
OUR FAVORITE SPOT IN THE CITY FOR PINBALL IS MARY'S BACKSIDE..
THEY'RE ALWAYS GETTING NEW MACHINES IN....
Ching-ching Pork!! Ching!!
Fear of a Black Marker Makes for GREAT bathroom reading
..BUT THE THING I LIKE MOST ABOUT MARY'S MACHINES IS THAT YOU GET 5 BALLS PER GAME..
..I'D MUCH RATHER PAY 75¢ FOR 5 BALLS THAN 50¢ FOR 3..
GUNTHER DIGS GETTING 5 BALLS TOO, BUT IT'S NOT HIS FAVORITE THING...
SMASH!!
HIS FAVORITE THING IS THAT THERE ISN'T A "TILT" ON EITHER ONE OF THE MACHINES..
Look!! I got an extra ball!!
STOP

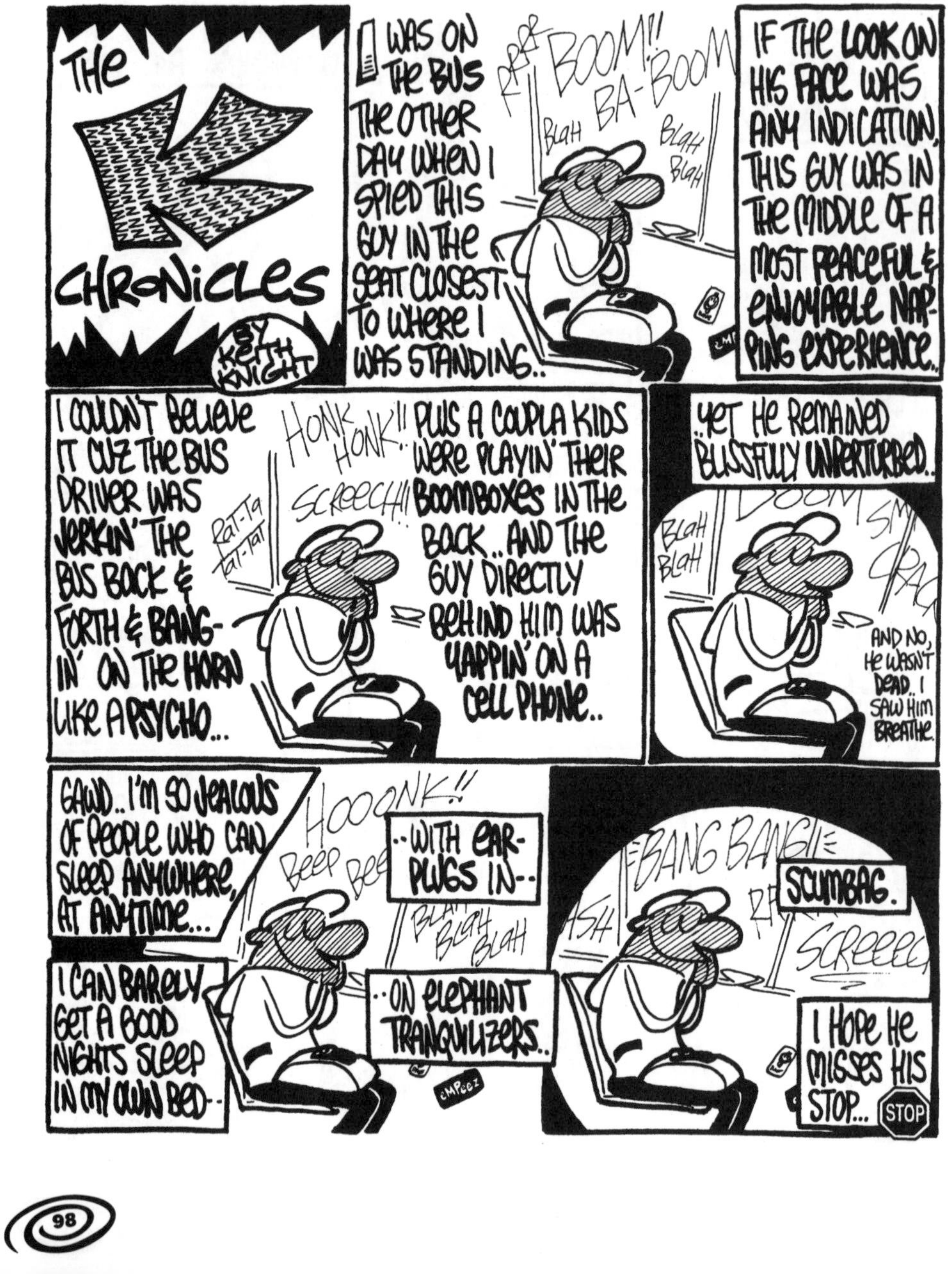
THE K CHRONICLES
BY KEITH KNIGHT
I WAS ON THE BUS THE OTHER DAY WHEN I SPIED THIS GUY IN THE SEAT CLOSEST TO WHERE I WAS STANDING..
RRRR
BOOM!!
BA-BOOM
BLAH
BLAH BLAH
IF THE LOOK ON HIS FACE WAS ANY INDICATION, THIS GUY WAS IN THE MIDDLE OF A MOST PEACEFUL & ENJOYABLE NAP-PING EXPERIENCE..
I COULDN'T BELIEVE IT CUZ THE BUS DRIVER WAS JERKIN' THE BUS BACK & FORTH & BANG-IN' ON THE HORN LIKE A PSYCHO...
HONK HONK!!
SCREECH!!
RAT-TA TAT-TAT
PLUS A COUPLA KIDS WERE PLAYIN' THEIR BOOMBOXES IN THE BACK.. AND THE GUY DIRECTLY BEHIND HIM WAS YAPPIN' ON A CELL PHONE..
..YET HE REMAINED BLISSFULLY UNPERTURBED..
BOOM
BLAH BLAH
CRACK
AND NO, HE WASN'T DEAD.. I SAW HIM BREATHE.
GAWD.. I'M SO JEALOUS OF PEOPLE WHO CAN SLEEP ANYWHERE, AT ANYTIME...
HOOOONK!!
BEEP
..WITH EAR-PLUGS IN--
BLAH BLAH BLAH
I CAN BARELY GET A GOOD NIGHTS SLEEP IN MY OWN BED--
..ON ELEPHANT TRANQUILIZERS..
BANG BANG!!
SCUMBAG.
SCREEECH
I HOPE HE MISSES HIS STOP...
STOP

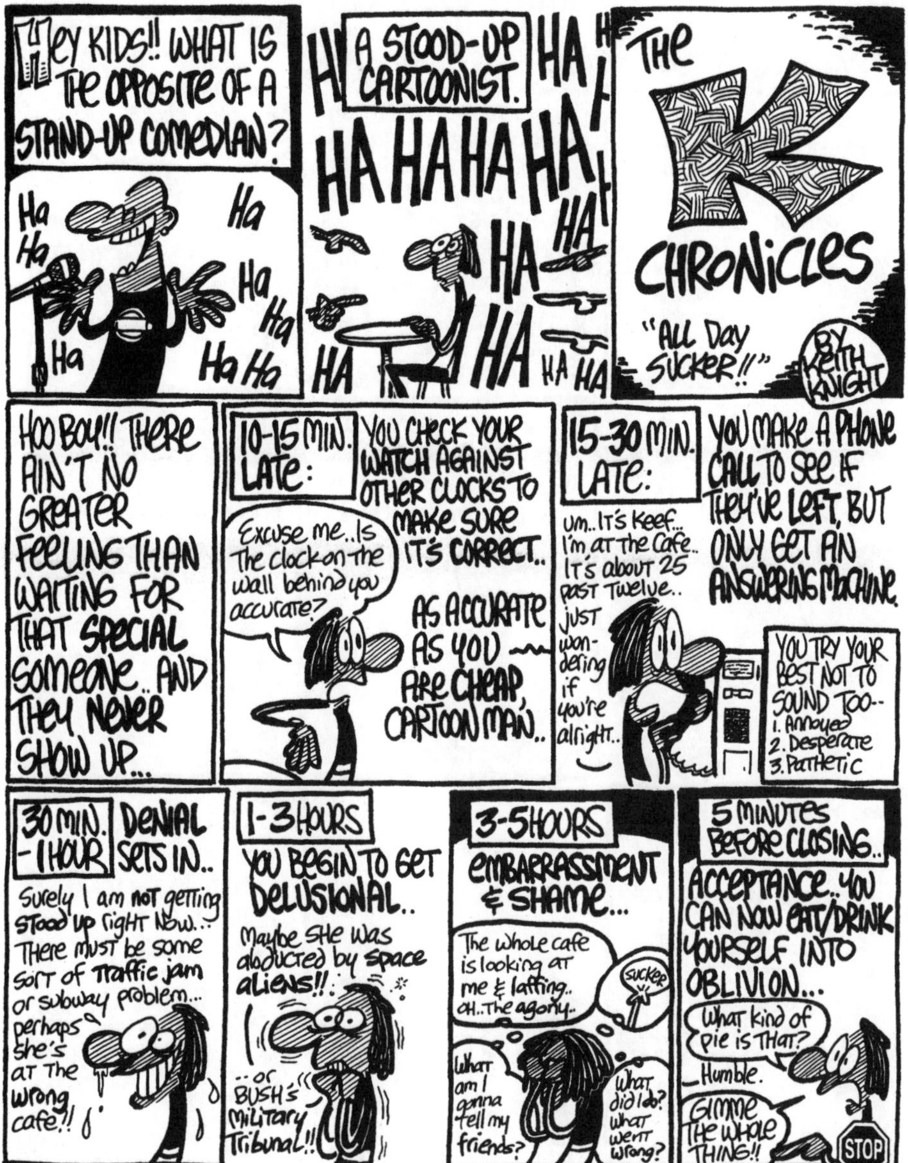
Hey kids!! What is the opposite of a stand-up comedian?
Ha Ha Ha Ha Ha Ha Ha Ha Ha
A stood-up cartoonist.
HA HA HA HA HA HA HA HA HA HA HA HA
The K Chronicles
"All day sucker!!"
By Keith Knight
Hoo boy!! There ain't no greater feeling than waiting for that special someone.. and they never show up...
10-15 min. late:
You check your watch against other clocks to make sure it's correct..
Excuse me..Is the clock on the wall behind you accurate?
As accurate as you are cheap, cartoon man..
15-30 min. late:
You make a phone call to see if they've left, but only get an answering machine.
Um..It's Keef.. I'm at the cafe.. It's about 25 past twelve.. just wondering if you're alright..
You try your best not to sound too--
1. Annoyed
2. Desperate
3. Pathetic
30 min. - 1 hour
Denial sets in..
Surely I am not getting stood up right now.. There must be some sort of traffic jam or subway problem... perhaps she's at the wrong cafe!!
1-3 hours
You begin to get delusional..
Maybe she was abducted by space aliens!!
..or Bush's military tribunal!!
3-5 hours
Embarrassment & shame...
The whole cafe is looking at me & laffing.. oh..the agony..
Sucker
What am I gonna tell my friends?
What did I do? What went wrong?
5 minutes before closing..
Acceptance.. you can now eat/drink yourself into oblivion...
What kind of pie is that?
—Humble.
Gimme the whole thing!!
STOP

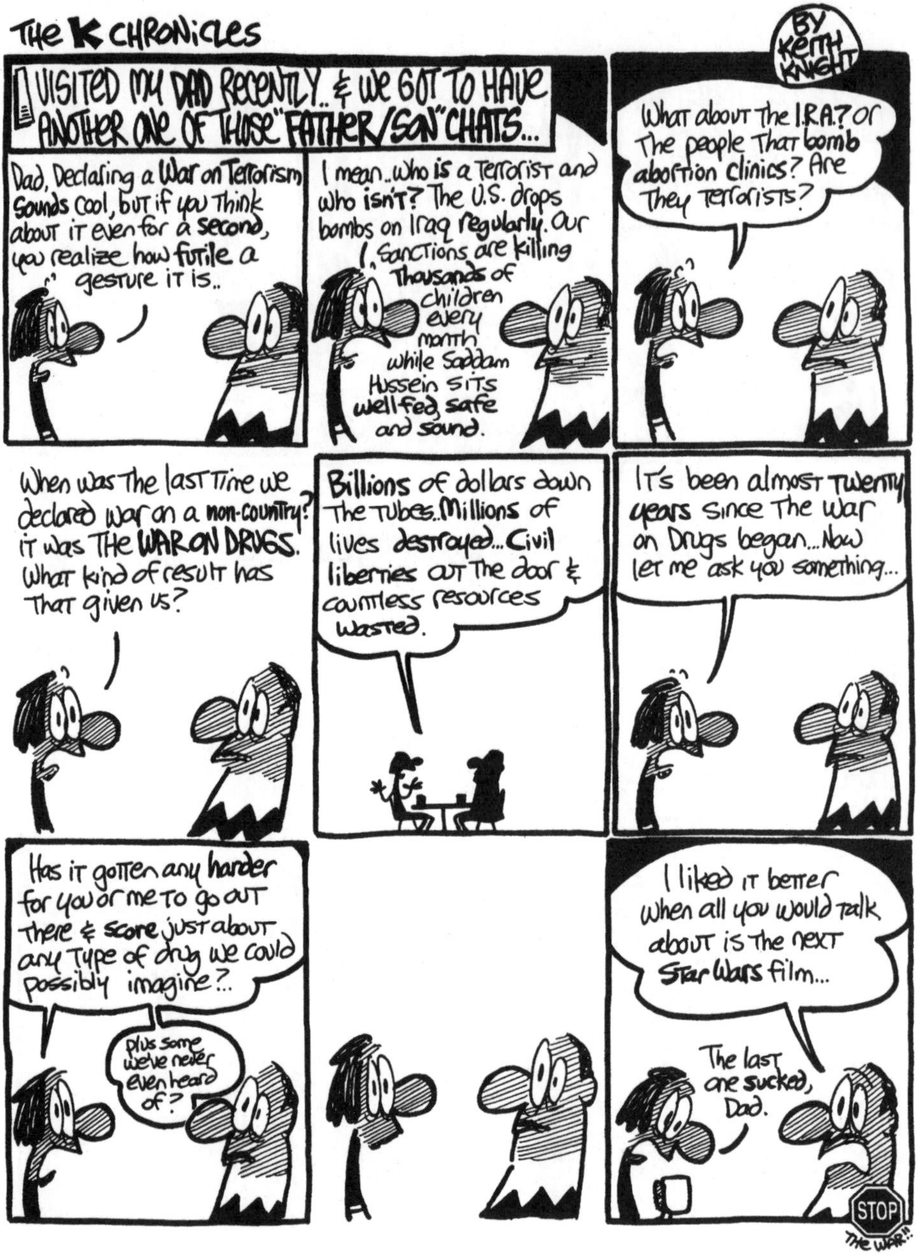
THE K CHRONICLES
BY KEITH KNIGHT
I VISITED MY DAD RECENTLY.. & WE GOT TO HAVE ANOTHER ONE OF THOSE "FATHER/SON" CHATS...
Dad, Declaring a War on Terrorism sounds cool, but if you think about it even for a second, you realize how futile a gesture it is..
I mean..who is a terrorist and who isn't? The U.S. drops bombs on Iraq regularly. Our sanctions are killing thousands of children every month while Saddam Hussein sits well fed, safe and sound.
What about the I.R.A.? or The people that bomb abortion clinics? Are they terrorists?
When was the last time we declared war on a non-country? It was THE WAR ON DRUGS. What kind of result has that given us?
Billions of dollars down the tubes..Millions of lives destroyed...Civil liberties out the door & countless resources wasted.
It's been almost twenty years since the war on Drugs began...Now let me ask you something...
Has it gotten any harder for you or me to go out there & score just about any type of drug we could possibly imagine?..
plus some we've never even heard of?
I liked it better when all you would talk about is the next Star Wars film...
The last one sucked, Dad.
STOP THE WAR!!

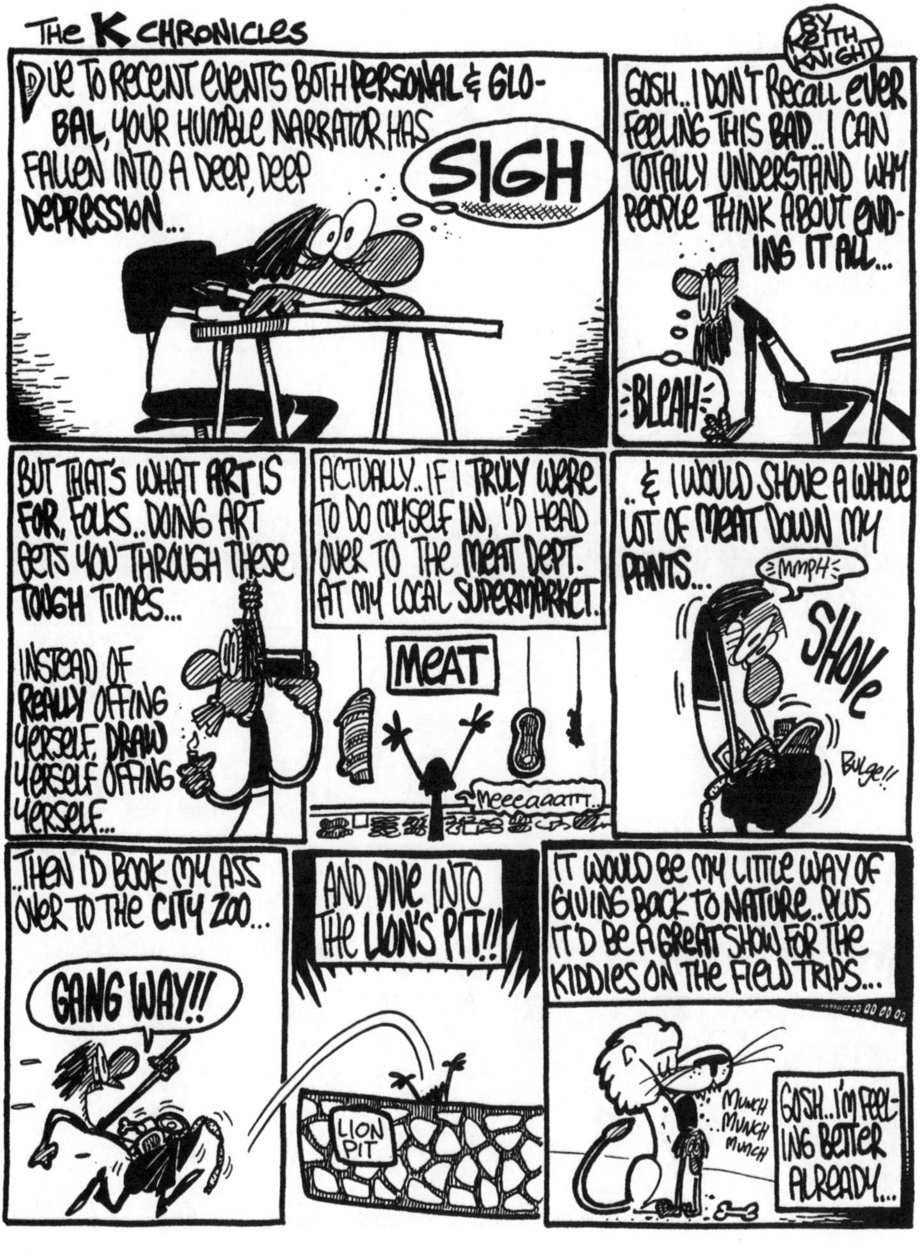
THE K CHRONICLES
BY KEITH KNIGHT
DUE TO RECENT EVENTS BOTH PERSONAL & GLOBAL, YOUR HUMBLE NARRATOR HAS FALLEN INTO A DEEP, DEEP DEPRESSION...
SIGH
GOSH.. I DON'T RECALL EVER FEELING THIS BAD.. I CAN TOTALLY UNDERSTAND WHY PEOPLE THINK ABOUT ENDING IT ALL...
BLEAH
BUT THAT'S WHAT ART IS FOR, FOLKS.. DOING ART GETS YOU THROUGH THESE TOUGH TIMES...
INSTEAD OF REALLY OFFING YERSELF, DRAW YERSELF OFFING YERSELF...
ACTUALLY.. IF I TRULY WERE TO DO MYSELF IN, I'D HEAD OVER TO THE MEAT DEPT. AT MY LOCAL SUPERMARKET.
MEAT
MEEEAAATTT..
..& I WOULD SHOVE A WHOLE LOT OF MEAT DOWN MY PANTS...
MMPH
SHOVE
BULGE!!
..THEN I'D BOOK MY ASS OVER TO THE CITY ZOO...
GANG WAY!!
AND DIVE INTO THE LION'S PIT!!
LION PIT
IT WOULD BE MY LITTLE WAY OF GIVING BACK TO NATURE.. PLUS IT'D BE A GREAT SHOW FOR THE KIDDIES ON THE FIELD TRIPS...
MUNCH ..MUNCH MUNCH
GOSH.. I'M FEELING BETTER ALREADY...

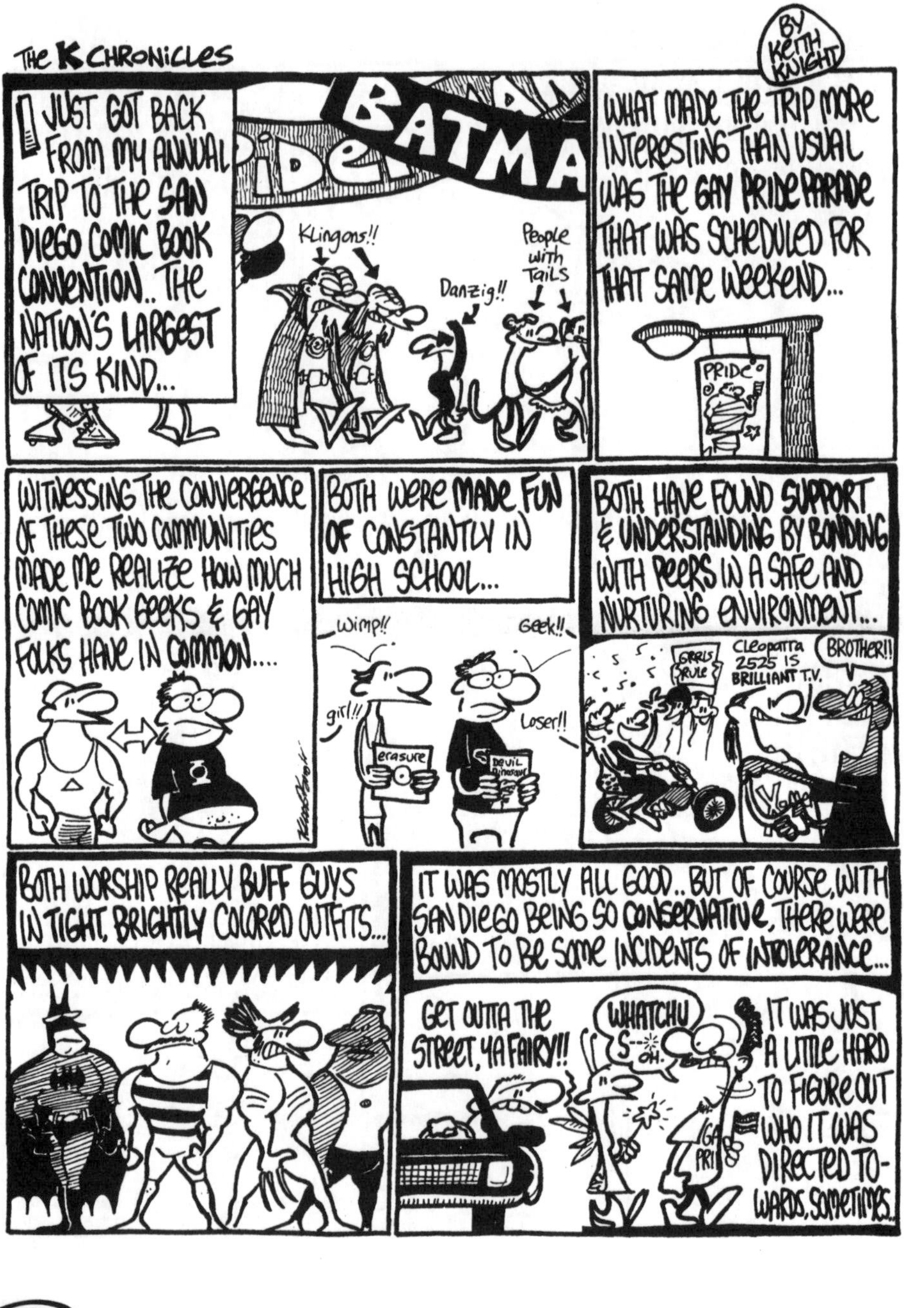
THE K CHRONICLES
BY KEITH KNIGHT
I JUST GOT BACK FROM MY ANNUAL TRIP TO THE SAN DIEGO COMIC BOOK CONVENTION.. THE NATION'S LARGEST OF ITS KIND...
PRIDE
BATMA
Klingons!!
Danzig!!
People with Tails
WHAT MADE THE TRIP MORE INTERESTING THAN USUAL WAS THE GAY PRIDE PARADE THAT WAS SCHEDULED FOR THAT SAME WEEKEND...
PRIDE
WITNESSING THE CONVERGENCE OF THESE TWO COMMUNITIES MADE ME REALIZE HOW MUCH COMIC BOOK GEEKS & GAY FOLKS HAVE IN COMMON....
BOTH WERE MADE FUN OF CONSTANTLY IN HIGH SCHOOL...
Wimp!!
Geek!!
girl!!!
Loser!!
erasure
Devil Dinosaur
BOTH HAVE FOUND SUPPORT & UNDERSTANDING BY BONDING WITH PEERS IN A SAFE AND NURTURING ENVIRONMENT...
GRRLS RULE
Cleopatra 2525 IS BRILLIANT T.V.
BROTHER!!
BOTH WORSHIP REALLY BUFF GUYS IN TIGHT, BRIGHTLY COLORED OUTFITS...
IT WAS MOSTLY ALL GOOD.. BUT OF COURSE, WITH SAN DIEGO BEING SO CONSERVATIVE, THERE WERE BOUND TO BE SOME INCIDENTS OF INTOLERANCE...
GET OUTTA THE STREET, YA FAIRY!!
WHATCHU S-- OH.
IT WAS JUST A LITTLE HARD TO FIGURE OUT WHO IT WAS DIRECTED TOWARDS, SOMETIMES...

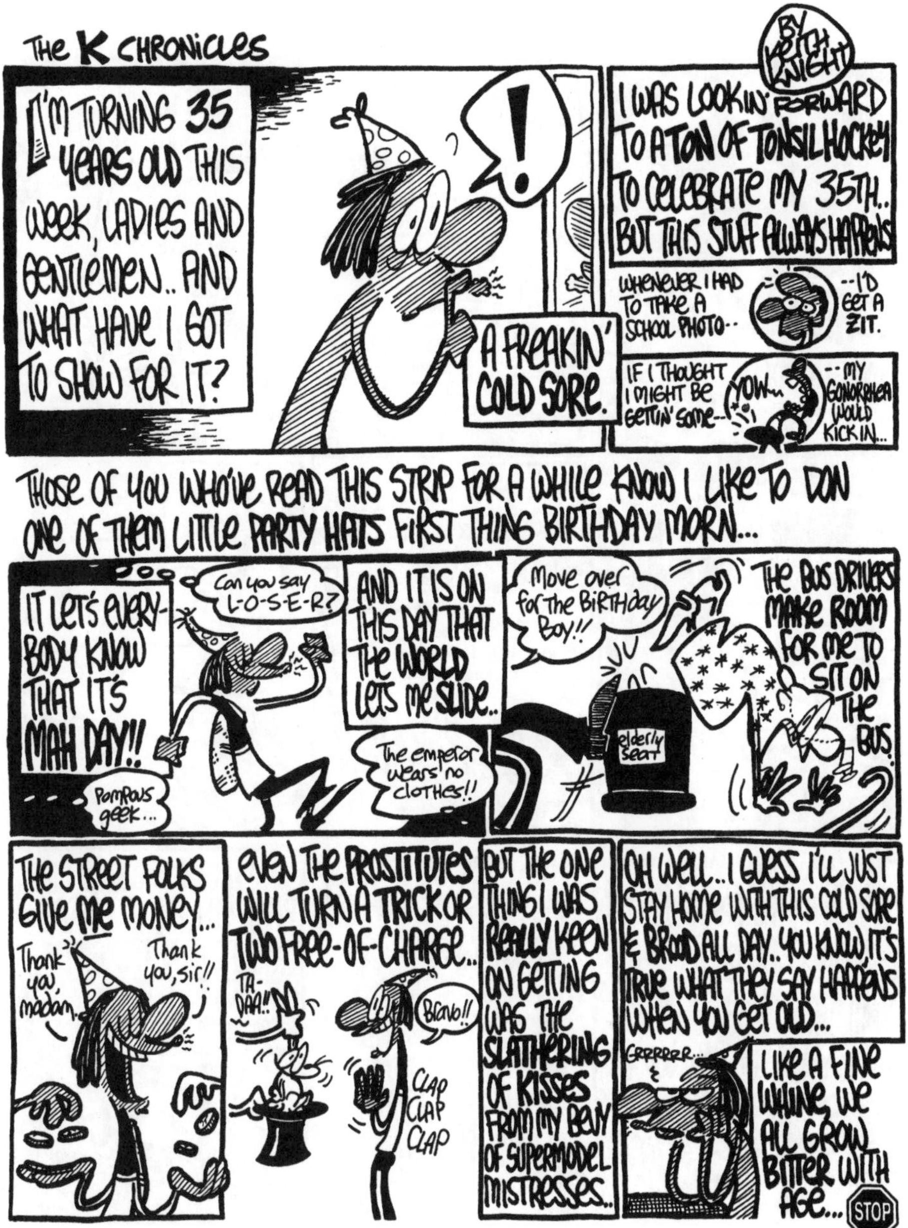
THE K CHRONICLES
BY KEITH KNIGHT
I'M TURNING 35 YEARS OLD THIS WEEK, LADIES AND GENTLEMEN.. AND WHAT HAVE I GOT TO SHOW FOR IT?
!
A FREAKIN' COLD SORE.
I WAS LOOKIN' FORWARD TO A TON OF TONSIL HOCKEY TO CELEBRATE MY 35TH.. BUT THIS STUFF ALWAYS HAPPENS
WHENEVER I HAD TO TAKE A SCHOOL PHOTO--
--I'D GET A ZIT.
IF I THOUGHT I MIGHT BE GETTIN' SOME--
YOW..
--MY GONORRHEA WOULD KICK IN...
THOSE OF YOU WHO'VE READ THIS STRIP FOR A WHILE KNOW I LIKE TO DON ONE OF THEM LITTLE PARTY HATS FIRST THING BIRTHDAY MORN...
IT LET'S EVERYBODY KNOW THAT IT'S MAH DAY!!
Can you say L-O-S-E-R?
Pompous geek...
AND IT IS ON THIS DAY THAT THE WORLD LETS ME SLIDE..
The emperor wears no clothes!!
Move over for the Birthday Boy!!
elderly seat
THE BUS DRIVERS MAKE ROOM FOR ME TO SIT ON THE BUS.
THE STREET FOLKS GIVE ME MONEY...
Thank you, madam.
Thank you, sir!!
EVEN THE PROSTITUTES WILL TURN A TRICK OR TWO FREE-OF-CHARGE...
TA-DAA!!
Bravo!!
CLAP CLAP CLAP
BUT THE ONE THING I WAS REALLY KEEN ON GETTING WAS THE SLATHERING OF KISSES FROM MY BEVY OF SUPERMODEL MISTRESSES..
OH WELL.. I GUESS I'LL JUST STAY HOME WITH THIS COLD SORE & BROOD ALL DAY.. YOU KNOW, IT'S TRUE WHAT THEY SAY HAPPENS WHEN YOU GET OLD...
GRRRRRR...
LIKE A FINE WHINE, WE ALL GROW BITTER WITH AGE...
STOP

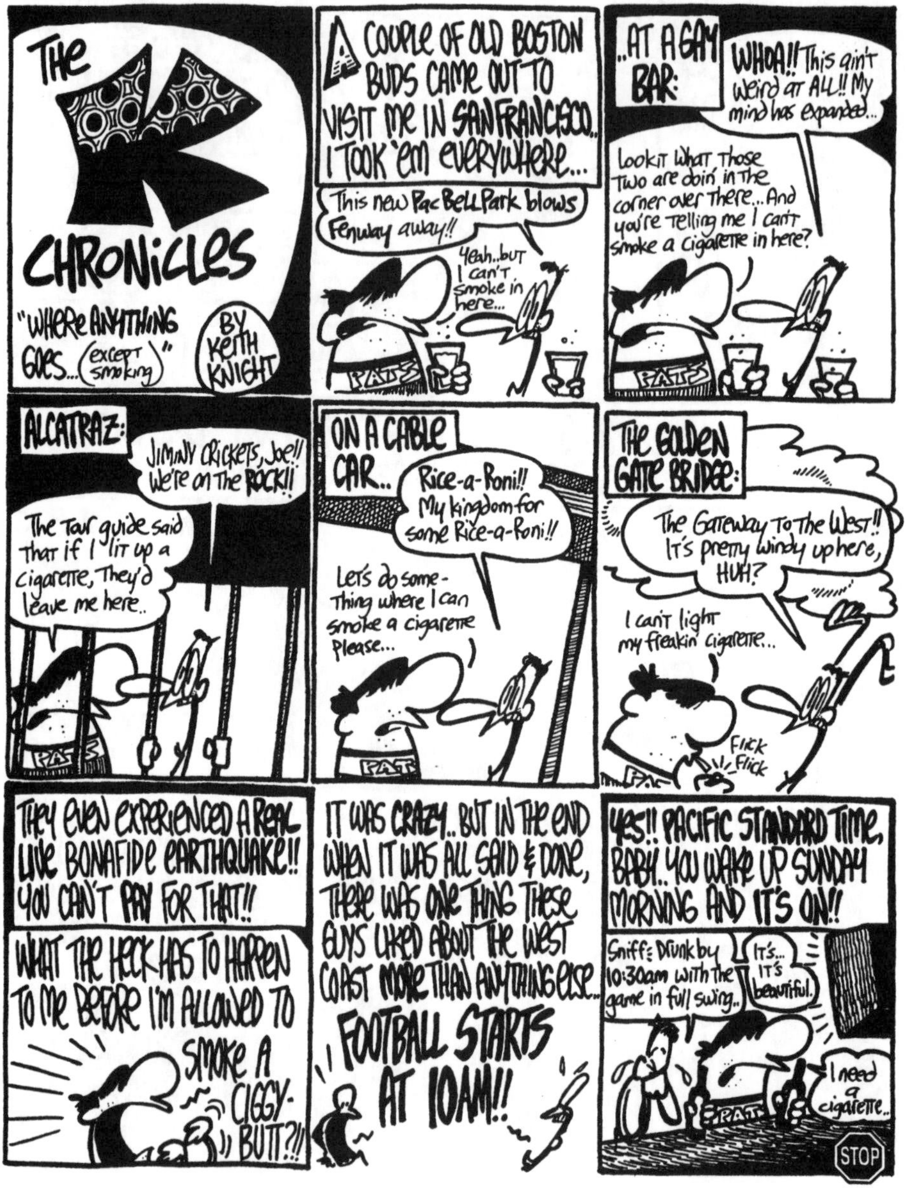
THE K CHRONICLES
"WHERE ANYTHING GOES... (EXCEPT SMOKING)"
BY KEITH KNIGHT
A COUPLE OF OLD BOSTON BUDS CAME OUT TO VISIT ME IN SAN FRANCISCO.. I TOOK 'EM EVERYWHERE...
This new PacBell Park blows Fenway away!!
Yeah..but I can't smoke in here...
..AT A GAY BAR:
WHOA!! This ain't weird at ALL!! My mind has expanded...
Lookit what those two are doin' in the corner over there... And you're telling me I can't smoke a cigarette in here?
ALCATRAZ:
JIMINY CRICKETS, JOE!! We're on the ROCK!!
The tour guide said that if I lit up a cigarette, they'd leave me here..
ON A CABLE CAR..
Rice-a-Roni!! My kingdom for some Rice-a-Roni!!
Let's do some-thing where I can smoke a cigarette please...
THE GOLDEN GATE BRIDGE:
The Gateway to the West!! It's pretty windy up here, HUH?
I can't light my freakin' cigarette...
Flick Flick
THEY EVEN EXPERIENCED A REAL LIVE BONAFIDE EARTHQUAKE!! YOU CAN'T PAY FOR THAT!!
WHAT THE HECK HAS TO HAPPEN TO ME BEFORE I'M ALLOWED TO SMOKE A CIGGY-BUTT?!!
IT WAS CRAZY.. BUT IN THE END WHEN IT WAS ALL SAID & DONE, THERE WAS ONE THING THESE GUYS LIKED ABOUT THE WEST COAST MORE THAN ANYTHING ELSE...
FOOTBALL STARTS AT 10AM!!
YES!! PACIFIC STANDARD TIME, BABY.. YOU WAKE UP SUNDAY MORNING AND IT'S ON!!
Sniff: Drunk by 10:30am with the game in full swing..
It's... it's beautiful.
I need a cigarette..
STOP

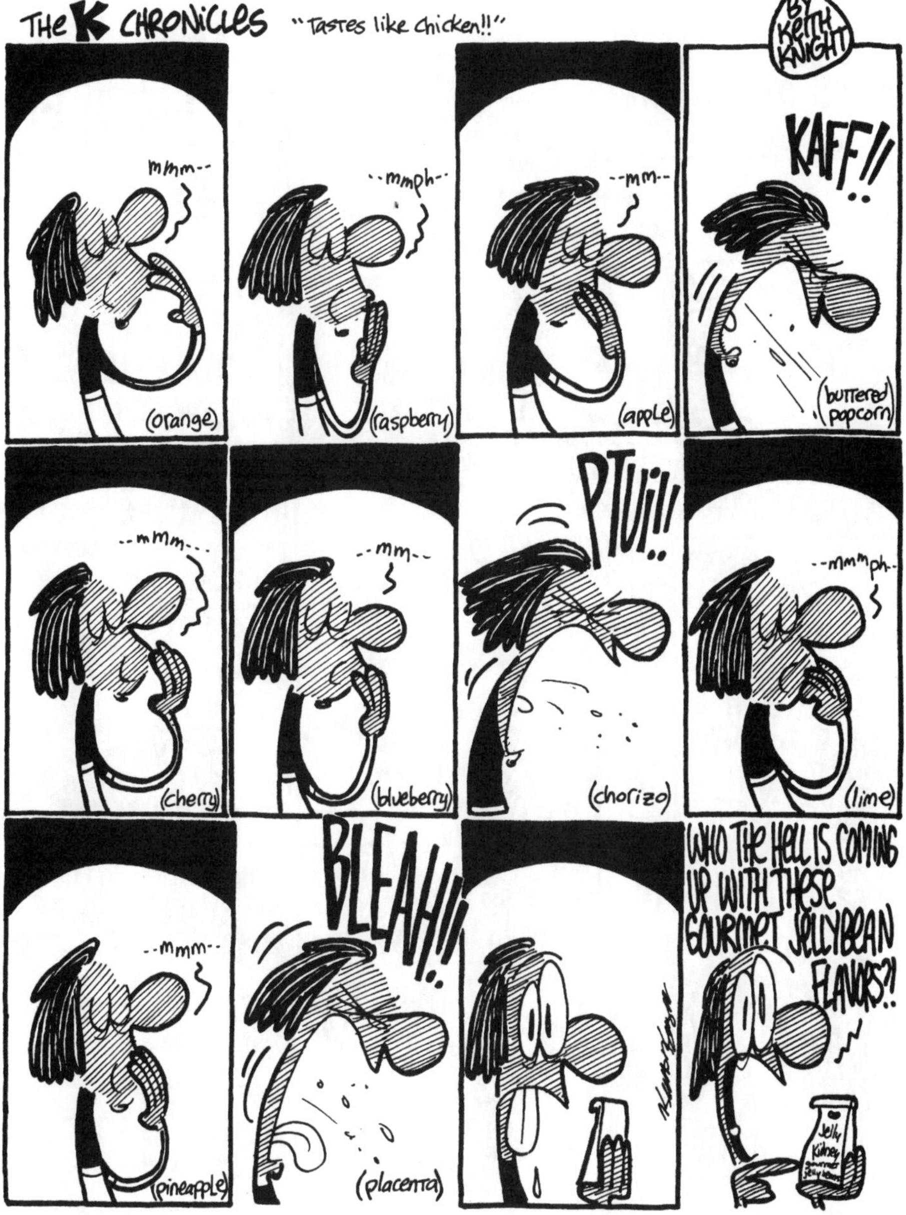
THE K CHRONICLES
"Tastes like chicken!!"
BY KEITH KNIGHT
mmm--
(orange)
--mmph--
(raspberry)
--mm--
(apple)
KAFF!!..
(buttered popcorn)
--mmm---
(cherry)
--mm--
(blueberry)
PTUI!!..
(chorizo)
--mmmph--
(lime)
--mmm--
(pineapple)
BLEAH!!!..
(placenta)
WHO THE HELL IS COMING UP WITH THESE GOURMET JELLYBEAN FLAVORS?!..
Jelly Kidney gourmet jelly beans

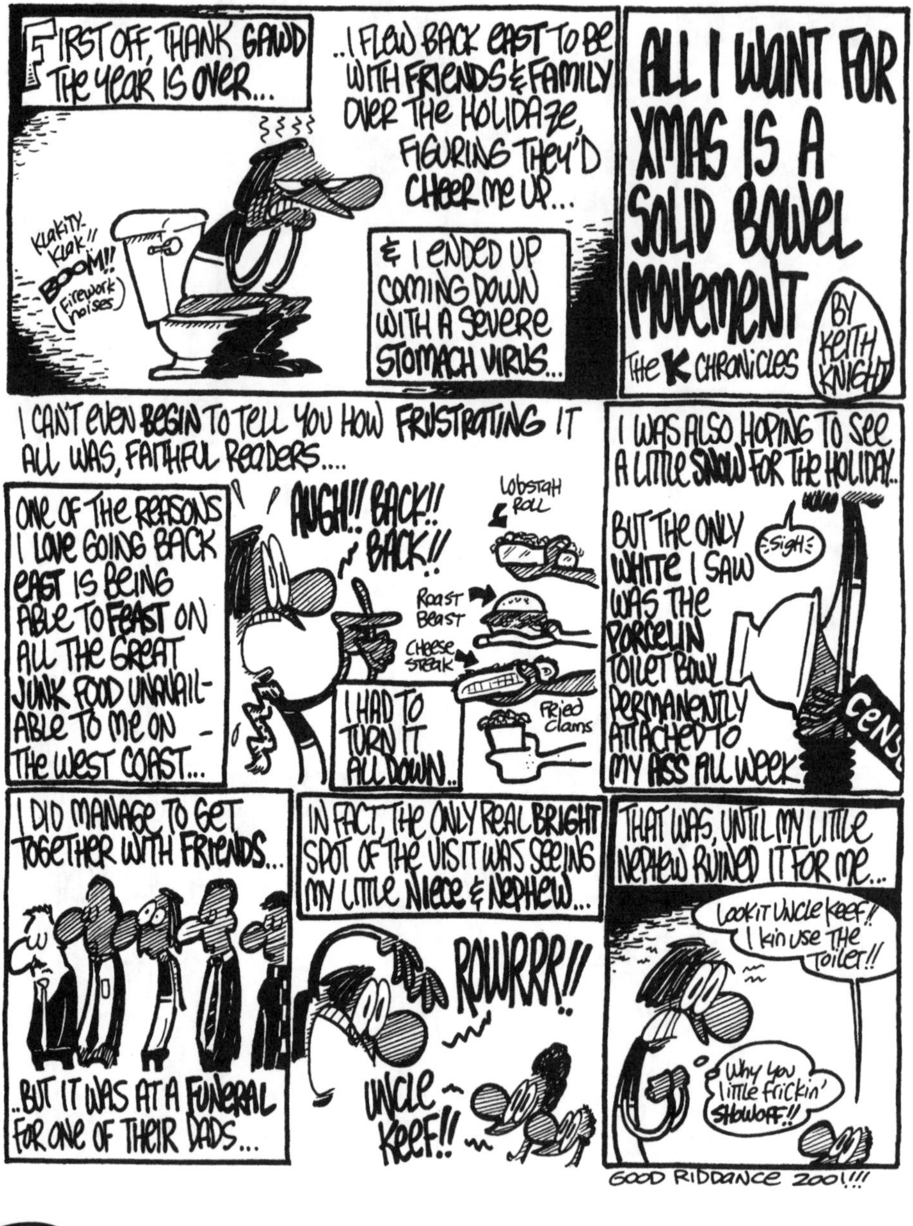
FIRST OFF, THANK GAWD THE YEAR IS OVER...
...I FLEW BACK EAST TO BE WITH FRIENDS & FAMILY OVER THE HOLIDAZE, FIGURING THEY'D CHEER ME UP...
KLAKITY-KLAK!!
BOOM!!
(Firework noises)
& I ENDED UP COMING DOWN WITH A SEVERE STOMACH VIRUS...
ALL I WANT FOR XMAS IS A SOLID BOWEL MOVEMENT
THE K CHRONICLES
BY KEITH KNIGHT
I CAN'T EVEN BEGIN TO TELL YOU HOW FRUSTRATING IT ALL WAS, FAITHFUL READERS....
ONE OF THE REASONS I LOVE GOING BACK EAST IS BEING ABLE TO FEAST ON ALL THE GREAT JUNK FOOD UNAVAILABLE TO ME ON THE WEST COAST...
AUGH!! BACK!! BACK!!
Lobstah Roll
Roast Beast
Cheese Steak
Fried Clams
I HAD TO TURN IT ALL DOWN..
I WAS ALSO HOPING TO SEE A LITTLE SNOW FOR THE HOLIDAY..
BUT THE ONLY WHITE I SAW WAS THE PORCELIN TOILET BOWL PERMANENTLY ATTACHED TO MY ASS ALL WEEK
Sigh
I DID MANAGE TO GET TOGETHER WITH FRIENDS...
..BUT IT WAS AT A FUNERAL FOR ONE OF THEIR DADS...
IN FACT, THE ONLY REAL BRIGHT SPOT OF THE VISIT WAS SEEING MY LITTLE NIECE & NEPHEW...
ROWRRR!!
UNCLE KEEF!!
THAT WAS, UNTIL MY LITTLE NEPHEW RUINED IT FOR ME...
Lookit Uncle Keef!! I kin use the Toilet!!
Why you little frickin' SHOWOFF!!
GOOD RIDDANCE 2001!!!

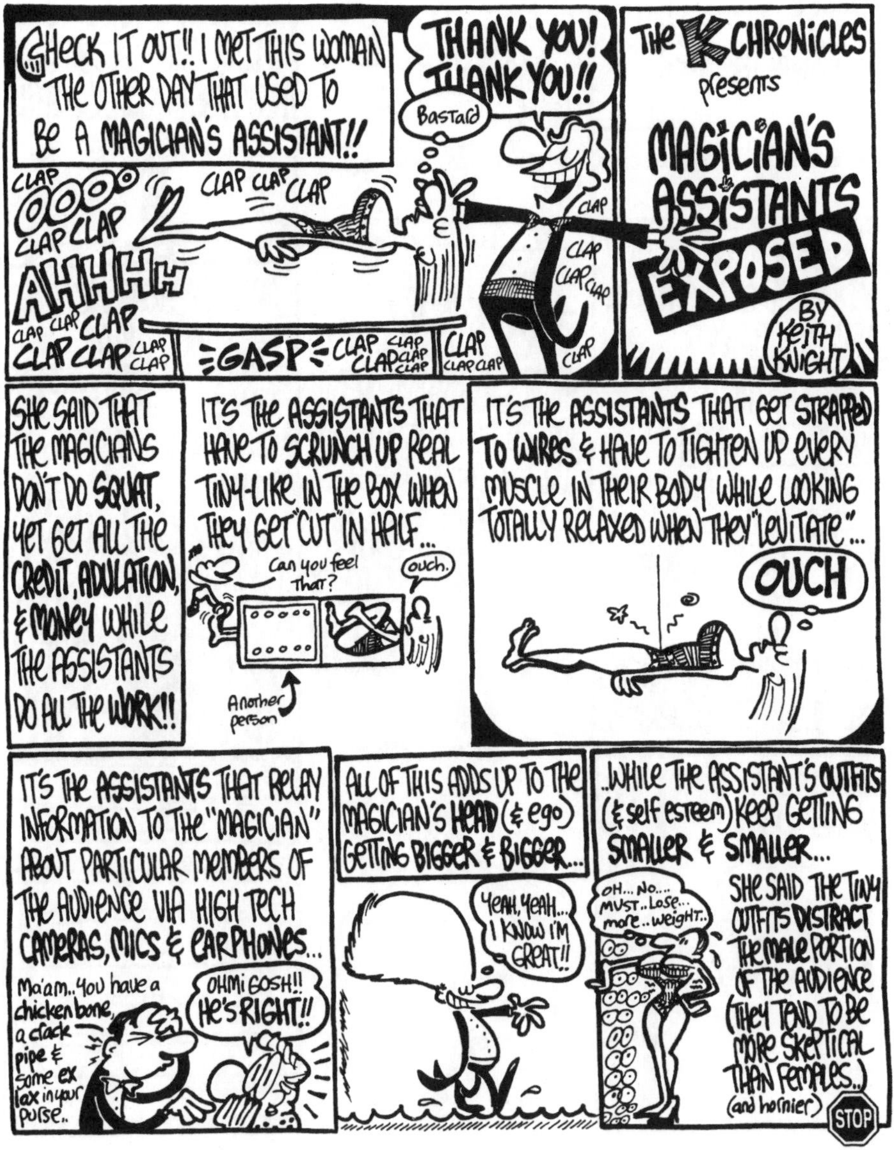

CHECK IT OUT!! I MET THIS WOMAN THE OTHER DAY THAT USED TO BE A MAGICIAN'S ASSISTANT!!
CLAP OOOO CLAP CLAP
AHHHH
CLAP CLAP CLAP CLAP
CLAP CLAP CLAP CLAP
GASP
CLAP CLAP CLAP CLAP
THANK YOU! THANK YOU!!
Bastard
CLAP
CLAP CLAP CLAP
CLAP
The K CHRONICLES presents
MAGICIAN'S ASSISTANTS EXPOSED
BY KEITH KNIGHT
SHE SAID THAT THE MAGICIANS DON'T DO SQUAT, YET GET ALL THE CREDIT, ADULATION, & MONEY WHILE THE ASSISTANTS DO ALL THE WORK!!
IT'S THE ASSISTANTS THAT HAVE TO SCRUNCH UP REAL TINY-LIKE IN THE BOX WHEN THEY GET "CUT" IN HALF...
Can you feel that?
ouch.
Another person
IT'S THE ASSISTANTS THAT GET STRAPPED TO WIRES & HAVE TO TIGHTEN UP EVERY MUSCLE IN THEIR BODY WHILE LOOKING TOTALLY RELAXED WHEN THEY "LEVITATE"...
OUCH
IT'S THE ASSISTANTS THAT RELAY INFORMATION TO THE "MAGICIAN" ABOUT PARTICULAR MEMBERS OF THE AUDIENCE VIA HIGH TECH CAMERAS, MICS & EARPHONES...
Ma'am.. You have a chicken bone, a crack pipe & some ex lax in your purse..
OH MY GOSH!! HE'S RIGHT!!
ALL OF THIS ADDS UP TO THE MAGICIAN'S HEAD (& ego) GETTING BIGGER & BIGGER...
YEAH, YEAH... I KNOW I'M GREAT!!
..WHILE THE ASSISTANT'S OUTFITS (& self esteem) KEEP GETTING SMALLER & SMALLER...
OH... NO... MUST.. LOSE.. more.. WEIGHT..
SHE SAID THE TINY OUTFITS DISTRACT THE MALE PORTION OF THE AUDIENCE (THEY TEND TO BE MORE SKEPTICAL THAN FEMALES..)
(and hornier)
STOP

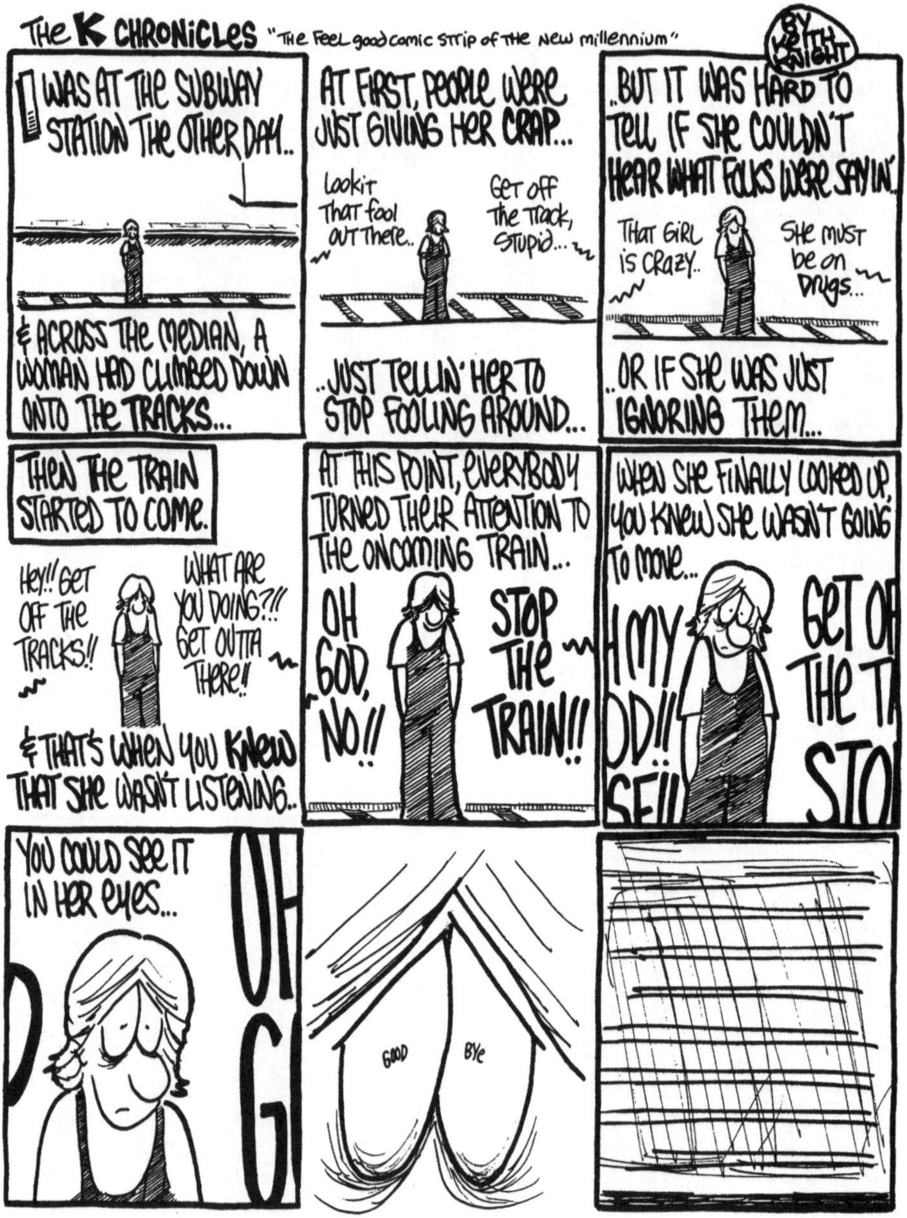
THE K CHRONICLES
"THE FEEL GOOD COMIC STRIP OF THE NEW MILLENNIUM"
BY KEITH KNIGHT
I WAS AT THE SUBWAY STATION THE OTHER DAY..
& ACROSS THE MEDIAN, A WOMAN HAD CLIMBED DOWN ONTO THE TRACKS...
AT FIRST, PEOPLE WERE JUST GIVING HER CRAP...
Lookit That fool out There..
Get off The Track, Stupid...
..JUST TELLIN' HER TO STOP FOOLING AROUND...
..BUT IT WAS HARD TO TELL IF SHE COULDN'T HEAR WHAT FOLKS WERE SAYIN'..
THAT GIRL IS CRAZY..
SHE MUST be on Drugs...
..OR IF SHE WAS JUST IGNORING THEM...
THEN THE TRAIN STARTED TO COME.
HEY!! GET OFF THE TRACKS!!
WHAT ARE YOU DOING?!! GET OUTTA THERE!!
& THAT'S WHEN YOU KNEW THAT SHE WASN'T LISTENING..
AT THIS POINT, EVERYBODY TURNED THEIR ATTENTION TO THE ONCOMING TRAIN...
OH GOD, NO!!
STOP THE TRAIN!!
WHEN SHE FINALLY LOOKED UP, YOU KNEW SHE WASN'T GOING TO MOVE...
YOU COULD SEE IT IN HER EYES...
GOOD
BYE

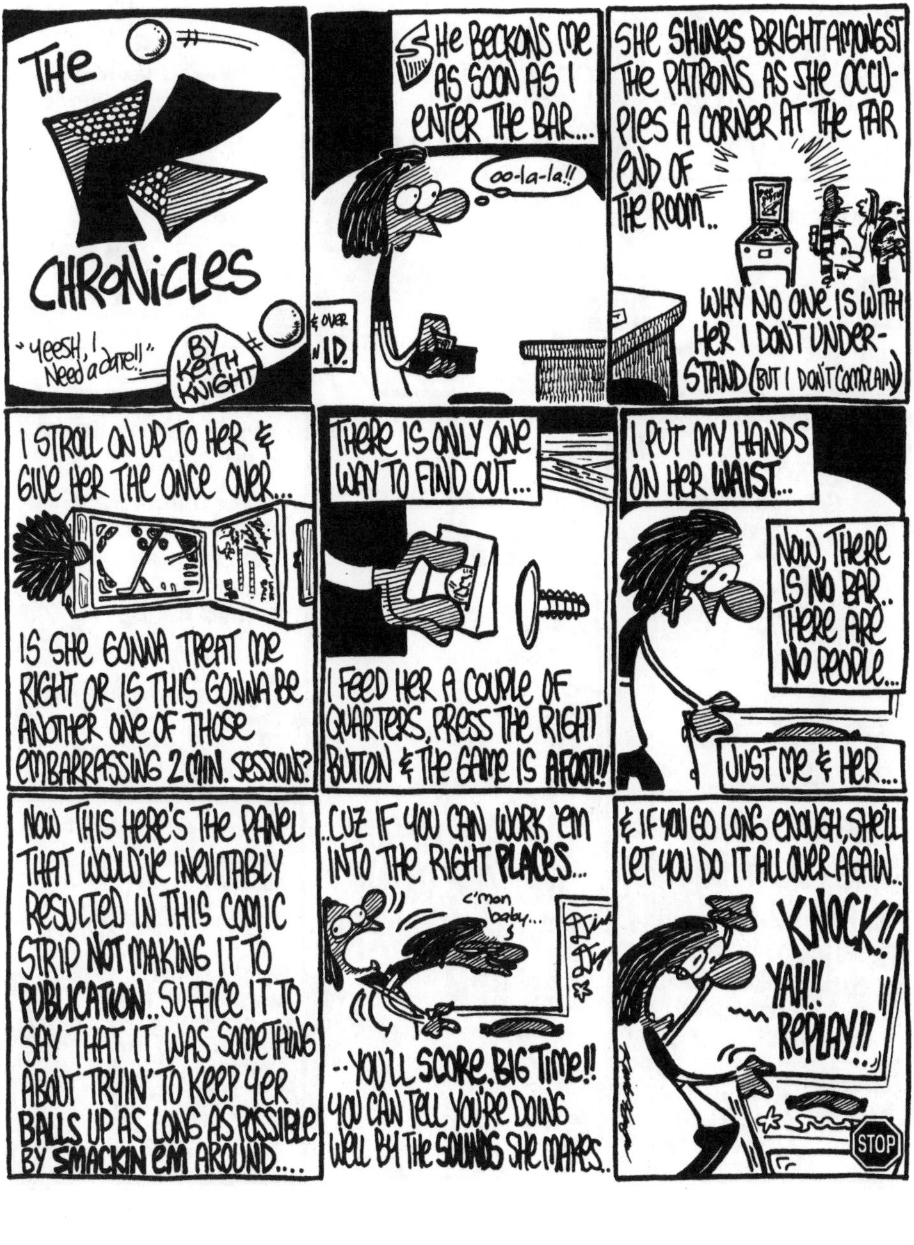
THE K CHRONICLES
"YEESH, I NEED A DAME!!"
BY KEITH KNIGHT
SHE BECKONS ME AS SOON AS I ENTER THE BAR...
OO-LA-LA!!
& OVER W/ I.D.
SHE SHINES BRIGHT AMONGST THE PATRONS AS SHE OCCUPIES A CORNER AT THE FAR END OF THE ROOM..
WHY NO ONE IS WITH HER I DON'T UNDERSTAND (BUT I DON'T COMPLAIN)
I STROLL ON UP TO HER & GIVE HER THE ONCE OVER...
IS SHE GONNA TREAT ME RIGHT OR IS THIS GONNA BE ANOTHER ONE OF THOSE EMBARRASSING 2 MIN. SESSIONS?
THERE IS ONLY ONE WAY TO FIND OUT...
I FEED HER A COUPLE OF QUARTERS, PRESS THE RIGHT BUTTON & THE GAME IS AFOOT!!
I PUT MY HANDS ON HER WAIST...
NOW, THERE IS NO BAR... THERE ARE NO PEOPLE...
JUST ME & HER...
NOW THIS HERE'S THE PANEL THAT WOULD'VE INEVITABLY RESULTED IN THIS COMIC STRIP NOT MAKING IT TO PUBLICATION.. SUFFICE IT TO SAY THAT IT WAS SOMETHING ABOUT TRYIN' TO KEEP YER BALLS UP AS LONG AS POSSIBLE BY SMACKIN EM AROUND....
..CUZ IF YOU CAN WORK 'EM INTO THE RIGHT PLACES...
C'MON BABY...
..YOU'LL SCORE BIG TIME!! YOU CAN TELL YOU'RE DOING WELL BY THE SOUNDS SHE MAKES..
& IF YOU GO LONG ENOUGH, SHE'LL LET YOU DO IT ALL OVER AGAIN..
KNOCK!!
YAH!!
REPLAY!!
STOP

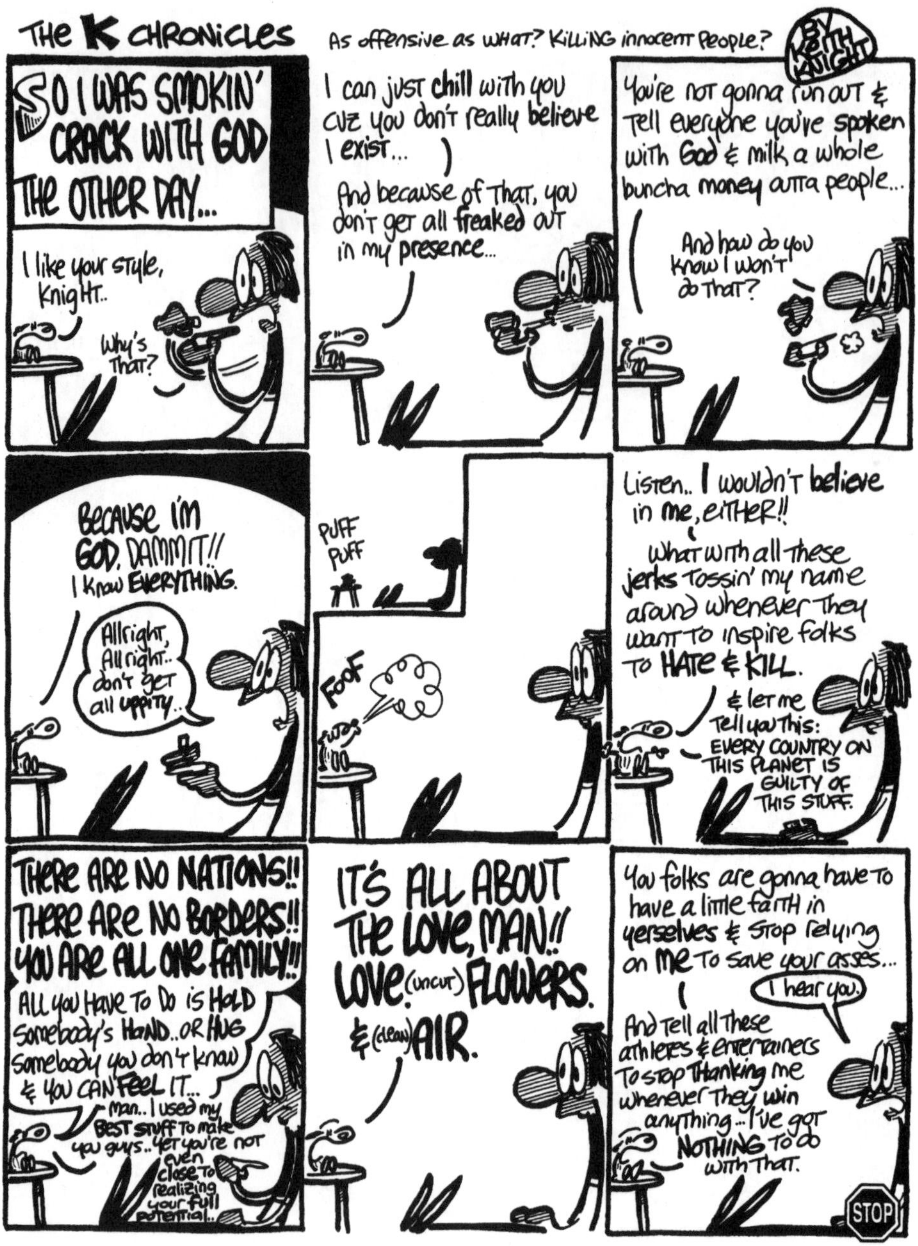
THE K CHRONICLES
As offensive as WHAT? KILLING innocent People?
BY KEITH KNIGHT
SO I WAS SMOKIN' CRACK WITH GOD THE OTHER DAY...
I like your style, Knight..
Why's That?
I can just chill with you cuz you don't really believe I exist...
And because of That, you don't get all freaked out in my presence...
You're not gonna run out & Tell everyone you've spoken with God & milk a whole buncha money outta people...
And how do you know I won't do That?
Because I'm GOD, DAMMIT!! I know EVERYTHING.
Allright, All right.. don't get all uppity..
PUFF PUFF
FOOF
Listen.. I wouldn't believe in me, eiTHER!!
What with all these jerks Tossin' my name around whenever They want To inspire folks To HATE & KILL.
& let me Tell you This: EVERY COUNTRY ON THIS PLANET IS GUILTY OF THIS STUFF.
THERE ARE NO NATIONS!! THERE ARE NO BORDERS!! YOU ARE ALL ONE FAMILY!!
ALL you Have To Do is HOLD Somebody's HAND..OR HUG Somebody you don't know & You CAN FEEL IT...
Man.. I used my BEST STUFF To make you guys.. yet you're not even close To realizing your full potential..
IT'S ALL ABOUT THE LOVE, MAN!! LOVE. (uncut) FLOWERS. & (clean) AIR.
You folks are gonna have To have a little faith in yerselves & Stop relying on ME To save your asses...
I hear you.
And Tell all These athletes & entertainers To stop Thanking me whenever They win anything... I've got NOTHING To do with That.
STOP

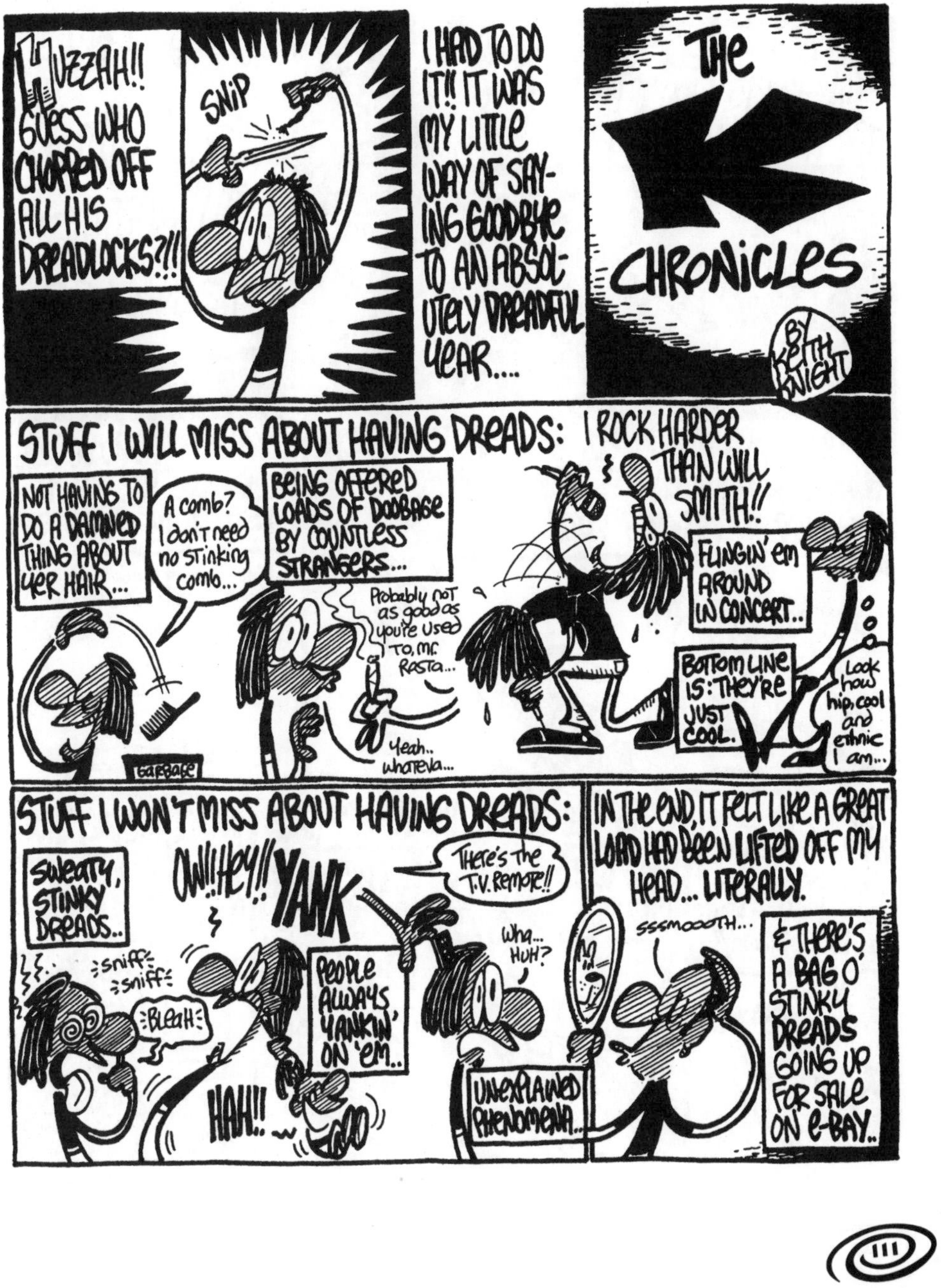
HUZZAH!! GUESS WHO CHOPPED OFF ALL HIS DREADLOCKS?!!
SNIP
I HAD TO DO IT!! IT WAS MY LITTLE WAY OF SAYING GOODBYE TO AN ABSOLUTELY DREADFUL YEAR....
THE K CHRONICLES
BY KEITH KNIGHT
STUFF I WILL MISS ABOUT HAVING DREADS:
NOT HAVING TO DO A DAMNED THING ABOUT YER HAIR...
A comb? I don't need no stinking comb...
GARBAGE
BEING OFFERED LOADS OF DOOBAGE BY COUNTLESS STRANGERS...
Probably not as good as you're used to, mr. Rasta...
Yeah.. whateva...
I ROCK HARDER THAN WILL SMITH!!
FLINGIN' 'EM AROUND IN CONCERT..
BOTTOM LINE IS: THEY'RE JUST COOL.
Look how hip, cool and ethnic I am...
STUFF I WON'T MISS ABOUT HAVING DREADS:
SWEATY, STINKY DREADS..
sniff sniff
BLEAH
OW!! HEY!!
YANK
PEOPLE ALWAYS YANKIN' ON 'EM..
HAH!!
There's the T.V. Remote!!
Wha... HUH?
UNEXPLAINED PHENOMENA..
IN THE END, IT FELT LIKE A GREAT LOAD HAD BEEN LIFTED OFF MY HEAD... LITERALLY.
SSSMOOOTH...
& THERE'S A BAG O' STINKY DREADS GOING UP FOR SALE ON E-BAY..

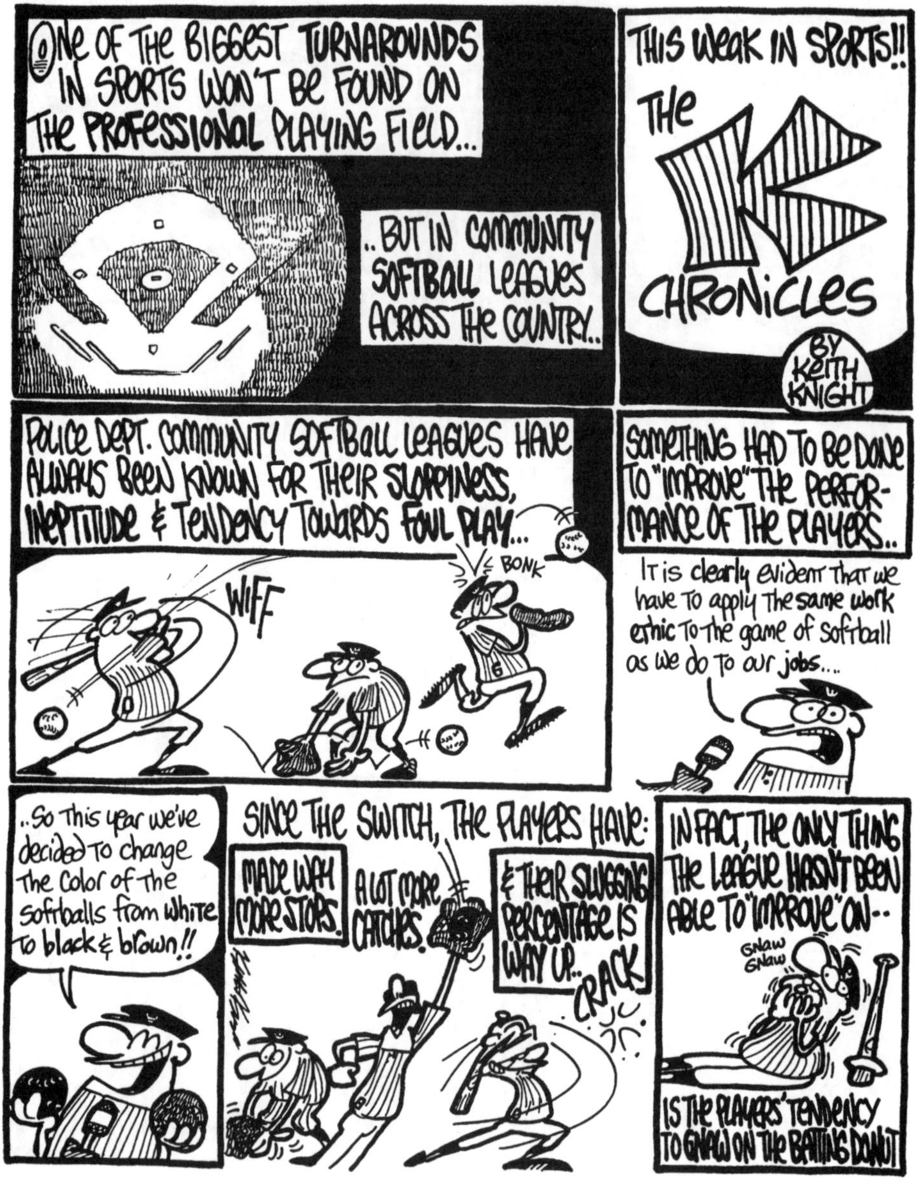
ONE OF THE BIGGEST TURNAROUNDS IN SPORTS WON'T BE FOUND ON THE PROFESSIONAL PLAYING FIELD...
..BUT IN COMMUNITY SOFTBALL LEAGUES ACROSS THE COUNTRY..
THIS WEAK IN SPORTS!!
THE K CHRONICLES
BY KEITH KNIGHT
POLICE DEPT. COMMUNITY SOFTBALL LEAGUES HAVE ALWAYS BEEN KNOWN FOR THEIR SLOPPINESS, INEPTITUDE & TENDENCY TOWARDS FOUL PLAY...
WIFF
BONK
SOMETHING HAD TO BE DONE TO "IMPROVE" THE PERFORMANCE OF THE PLAYERS..
It is clearly evident that we have to apply the same work ethic to the game of softball as we do to our jobs....
..So this year we've decided to change the color of the softballs from white to black & brown!!
SINCE THE SWITCH, THE PLAYERS HAVE:
MADE WAY MORE STOPS.
A LOT MORE CATCHES.
& THEIR SLUGGING PERCENTAGE IS WAY UP..
CRACK
IN FACT, THE ONLY THING THE LEAGUE HASN'T BEEN ABLE TO "IMPROVE" ON--
GNAW GNAW
IS THE PLAYERS' TENDENCY TO GNAW ON THE BATTING DONUT

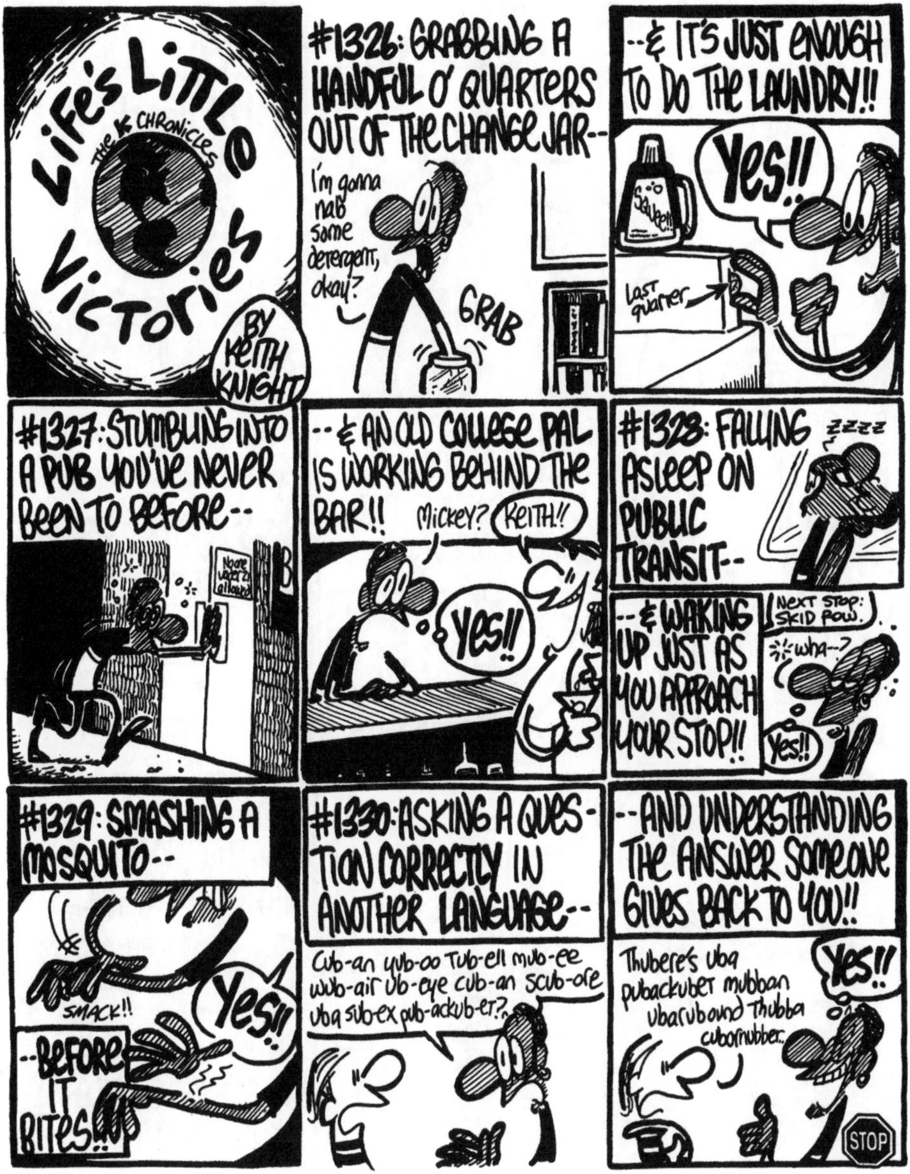
Life's Little Victories
The K Chronicles
By Keith Knight
#1326: Grabbing a handful o' quarters out of the change jar--
I'm gonna nab some detergent, okay?
GRAB
--& it's just enough to do the laundry!!
Yes!!
Squeez!!
Last quarter
#1327: Stumbling into a pub you've never been to before--
--& an old college pal is working behind the bar!!
Mickey?
Keith!!
Yes!!
#1328: Falling asleep on public transit--
zzzz
--& waking up just as you approach your stop!!
Next stop: Skid Row.
wha--?
Yes!!
#1329: Smashing a mosquito--
SMACK!!
Yes!!
--Before it bites!!
#1330: Asking a question correctly in another language--
Cub-an yub-oo Tub-ell mub-ee wub-air ub-eye cub-an scub-ore uba sub-ex pub-ackub-et?
--And understanding the answer someone gives back to you!!
Thubere's uba pubackubet mubban ubarubound thubba cubornubber..
Yes!!
STOP

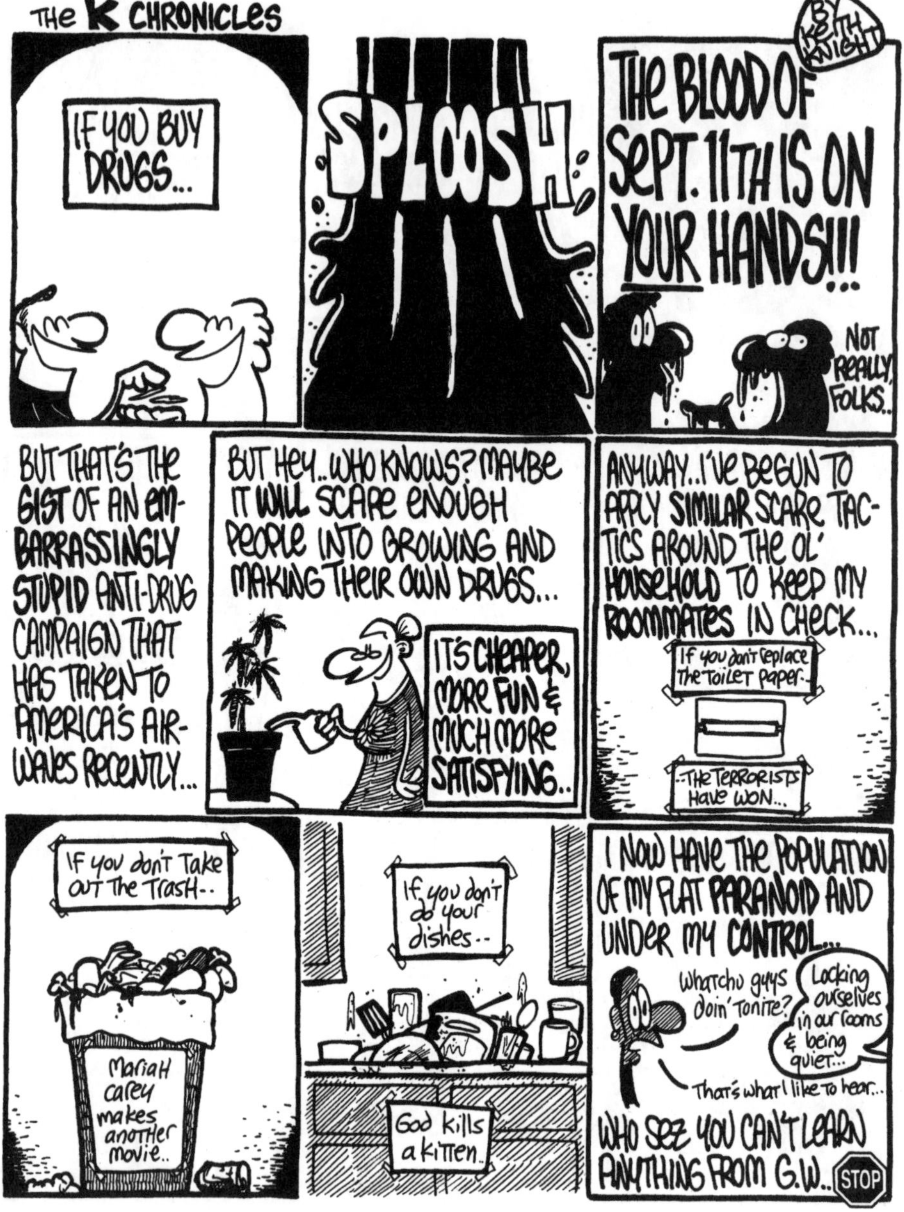
THE K CHRONICLES
BY KEITH KNIGHT
IF YOU BUY DRUGS...
SPLOOSH
THE BLOOD OF SEPT. 11TH IS ON YOUR HANDS!!!...
NOT REALLY, FOLKS..
BUT THAT'S THE GIST OF AN EMBARRASSINGLY STUPID ANTI-DRUG CAMPAIGN THAT HAS TAKEN TO AMERICA'S AIRWAVES RECENTLY...
BUT HEY.. WHO KNOWS? MAYBE IT WILL SCARE ENOUGH PEOPLE INTO GROWING AND MAKING THEIR OWN DRUGS...
IT'S CHEAPER, MORE FUN & MUCH MORE SATISFYING..
ANYWAY.. I'VE BEGUN TO APPLY SIMILAR SCARE TACTICS AROUND THE OL' HOUSEHOLD TO KEEP MY ROOMMATES IN CHECK...
If you don't replace the Toilet paper..
..The Terrorists have won...
If you don't Take out The Trash..
Mariah Carey makes another movie..
If you don't do your dishes..
God kills a kitten..
I NOW HAVE THE POPULATION OF MY FLAT PARANOID AND UNDER MY CONTROL...
Whatchu guys doin' Tonite?
Locking ourselves in our rooms & being quiet...
That's what I like to hear...
WHO SEZ YOU CAN'T LEARN ANYTHING FROM G.W..
STOP

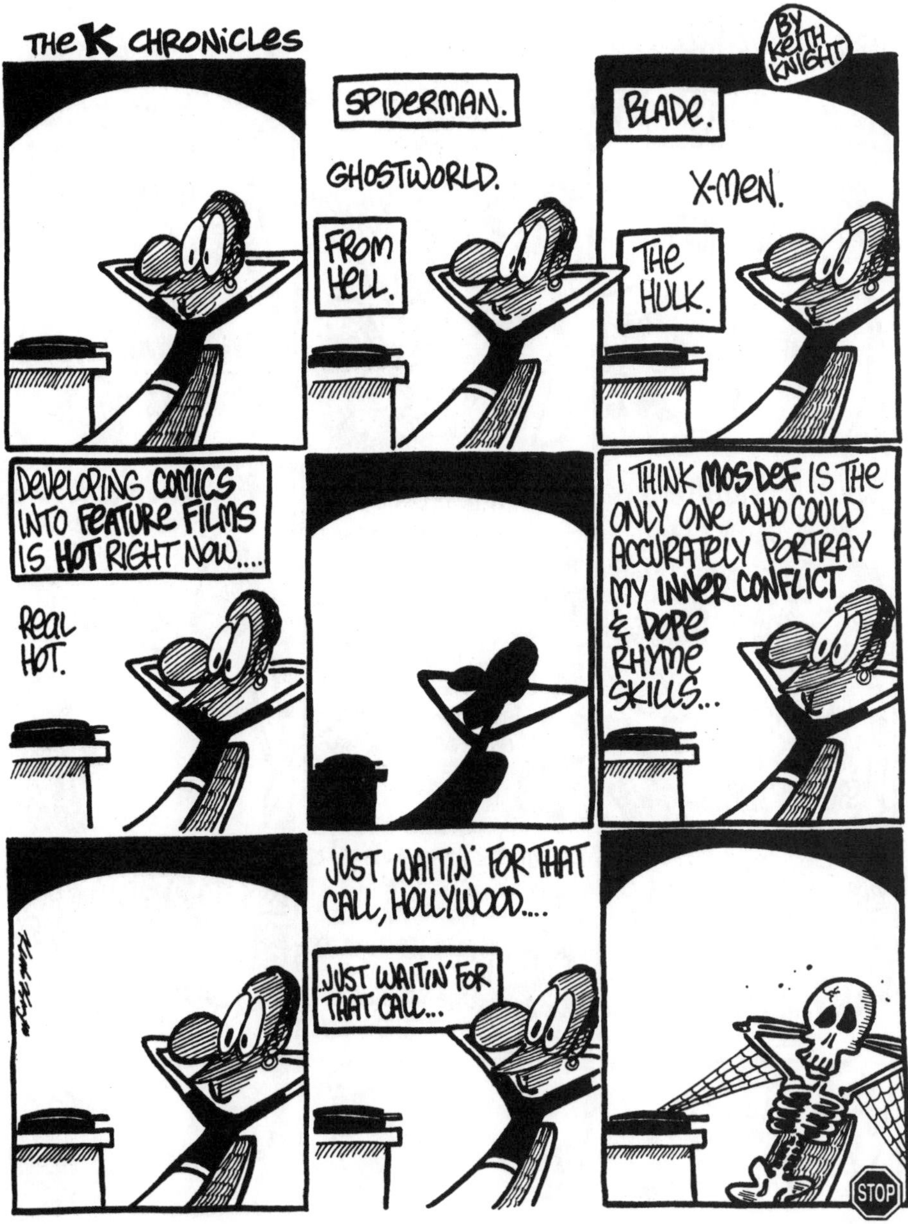
THE K CHRONICLES
BY KEITH KNIGHT
SPIDERMAN.
GHOSTWORLD.
FROM HELL.
BLADE.
X-MEN.
THE HULK.
DEVELOPING COMICS INTO FEATURE FILMS IS HOT RIGHT NOW....
REAL HOT.
I THINK MOS DEF IS THE ONLY ONE WHO COULD ACCURATELY PORTRAY MY INNER CONFLICT & DOPE RHYME SKILLS...
JUST WAITIN' FOR THAT CALL, HOLLYWOOD....
..JUST WAITIN' FOR THAT CALL...
STOP

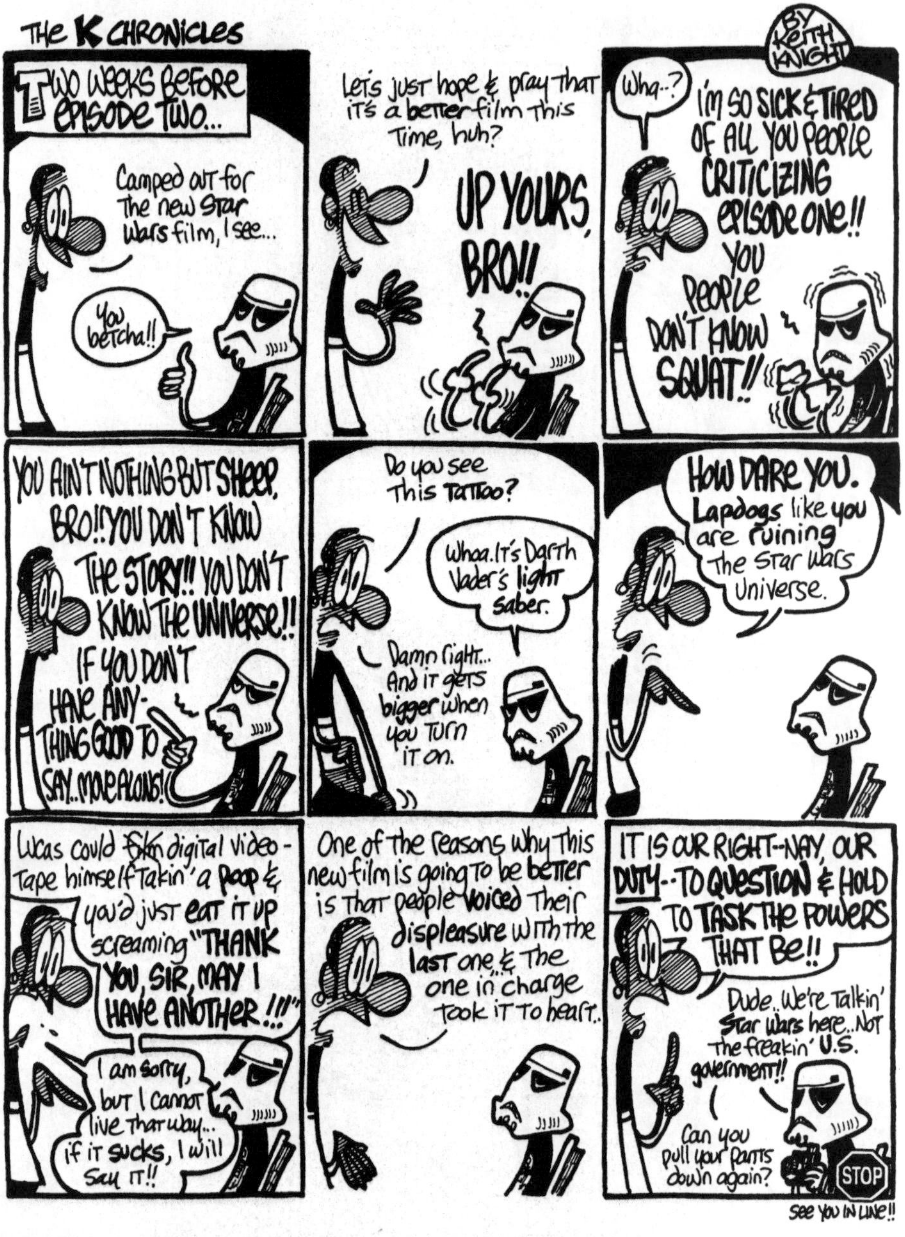
THE K CHRONICLES
BY KEITH KNIGHT
TWO WEEKS BEFORE EPISODE TWO...
Camped out for the new Star Wars film, I see...
You betcha!!
Let's just hope & pray that it's a better film this time, huh?
UP YOURS, BRO!!
Whq..?
I'M SO SICK & TIRED OF ALL YOU PEOPLE CRITICIZING EPISODE ONE!! YOU PEOPLE DON'T KNOW SQUAT!!
YOU AIN'T NOTHING BUT SHEEP, BRO!! YOU DON'T KNOW THE STORY!! YOU DON'T KNOW THE UNIVERSE!! IF YOU DON'T HAVE ANYTHING GOOD TO SAY.. MOVE ALONG!
Do you see this tattoo?
Whoa. It's Darth Vader's light saber.
Damn right... And it gets bigger when you turn it on.
HOW DARE YOU. Lapdogs like you are ruining the Star Wars universe.
Lucas could film digital video-tape himself takin' a poop & you'd just eat it up screaming "THANK YOU, SIR, MAY I HAVE ANOTHER!!!"
I am sorry, but I cannot live that way... if it sucks, I will say it!!
One of the reasons why this new film is going to be better is that people voiced their displeasure with the last one, & the one in charge took it to heart..
IT IS OUR RIGHT--NAY, OUR DUTY--TO QUESTION & HOLD TO TASK THE POWERS THAT BE!!
Dude.. We're talkin' Star Wars here.. Not the freakin' U.S. government!!
Can you pull your pants down again?
STOP
SEE YOU IN LINE!!

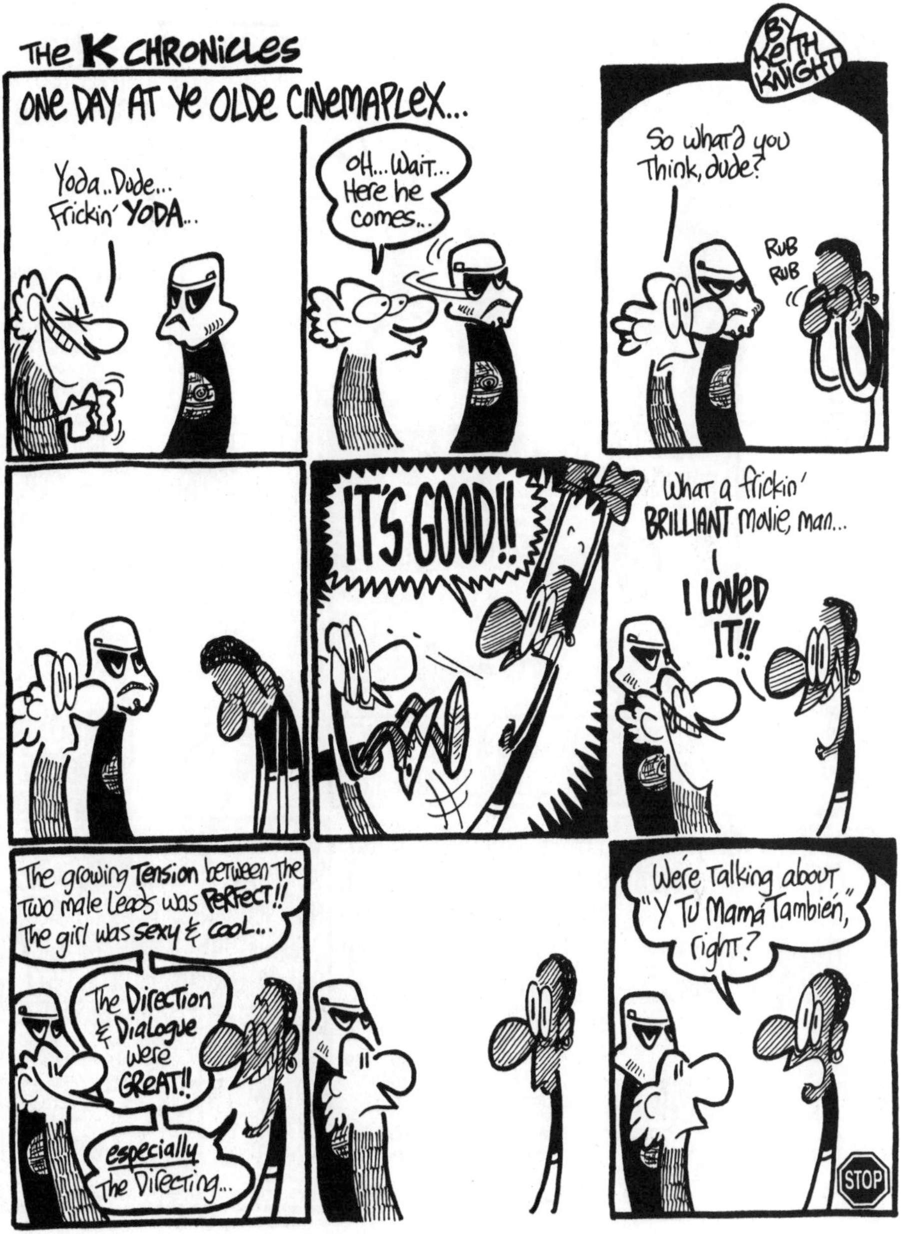
THE K CHRONICLES
BY KEITH KNIGHT
ONE DAY AT YE OLDE CINEMAPLEX...
Yoda..Dude... Frickin' YODA...
OH... Wait... Here he comes...
So what'd you Think, dude?
RUB RUB
IT'S GOOD!!
What a frickin' BRILLIANT movie, man...
I LOVED IT!!
The growing Tension between the two male leads was PERFECT!! The girl was sexy & cool...
The Direction & Dialogue were GREAT!!
especially the Directing...
We're Talking about "Y Tu Mamá También," right?
STOP

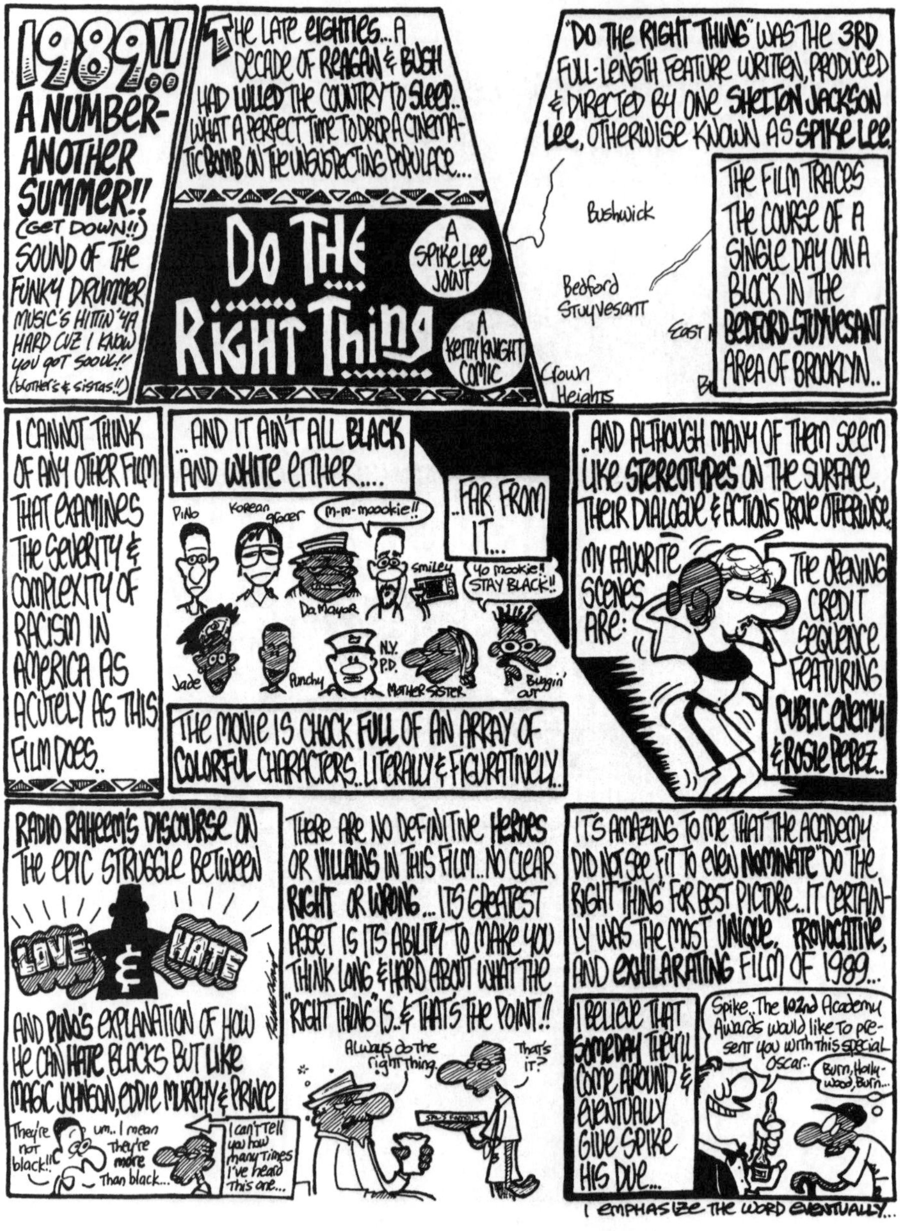
1989!!
A NUMBER-ANOTHER SUMMER!!
(GET DOWN!!)
SOUND OF THE FUNKY DRUMMER
MUSIC'S HITTIN' YA HARD CUZ I KNOW YOU GOT SOUL!!
(brother's & sistas!!)
THE LATE EIGHTIES... A DECADE OF REAGAN & BUSH HAD LULLED THE COUNTRY TO SLEEP.. WHAT A PERFECT TIME TO DROP A CINEMATIC BOMB ON THE UNSUSPECTING POPULACE...
DO THE RIGHT THING
A SPIKE LEE JOINT
A KEITH KNIGHT COMIC
"DO THE RIGHT THING" WAS THE 3RD FULL-LENGTH FEATURE WRITTEN, PRODUCED & DIRECTED BY ONE SHELTON JACKSON LEE, OTHERWISE KNOWN AS SPIKE LEE.
Bushwick
Bedford Stuyvesant
East N
Crown Heights
THE FILM TRACES THE COURSE OF A SINGLE DAY ON A BLOCK IN THE BEDFORD-STUYVESANT AREA OF BROOKLYN..
I CANNOT THINK OF ANY OTHER FILM THAT EXAMINES THE SEVERITY & COMPLEXITY OF RACISM IN AMERICA AS ACUTELY AS THIS FILM DOES..
...AND IT AIN'T ALL BLACK AND WHITE EITHER....
..FAR FROM IT...
Pino
Korean grocer
m-m-moookie!!
Da Mayor
Smiley
Yo Mookie!! STAY BLACK!!
Jade
Punchy
N.Y. P.D.
Mother Sister
Buggin' out
THE MOVIE IS CHOCK FULL OF AN ARRAY OF COLORFUL CHARACTERS.. LITERALLY & FIGURATIVELY..
..AND ALTHOUGH MANY OF THEM SEEM LIKE STEREOTYPES ON THE SURFACE, THEIR DIALOGUE & ACTIONS PROVE OTHERWISE.
MY FAVORITE SCENES ARE:
THE OPENING CREDIT SEQUENCE FEATURING PUBLIC ENEMY & ROSIE PEREZ..
RADIO RAHEEM'S DISCOURSE ON THE EPIC STRUGGLE BETWEEN
LOVE & HATE
AND PINO'S EXPLANATION OF HOW HE CAN HATE BLACKS BUT LIKE MAGIC JOHNSON, EDDIE MURPHY & PRINCE
They're not black!!
um.. I mean they're more than black...
I can't tell you how many times I've heard this one...
THERE ARE NO DEFINITIVE HEROES OR VILLAINS IN THIS FILM.. NO CLEAR RIGHT OR WRONG... ITS GREATEST ASSET IS ITS ABILITY TO MAKE YOU THINK LONG & HARD ABOUT WHAT THE "RIGHT THING" IS.. & THAT'S THE POINT!!
Always do the right thing.
That's it?
IT'S AMAZING TO ME THAT THE ACADEMY DID NOT SEE FIT TO EVEN NOMINATE "DO THE RIGHT THING" FOR BEST PICTURE.. IT CERTAINLY WAS THE MOST UNIQUE, PROVOCATIVE, AND EXHILARATING FILM OF 1989...
I BELIEVE THAT SOMEDAY THEY'LL COME AROUND & EVENTUALLY GIVE SPIKE HIS DUE...
Spike.. The 102nd Academy Awards would like to present you with this special Oscar..
Burn, Hollywood, Burn...
I EMPHASIZE THE WORD EVENTUALLY...

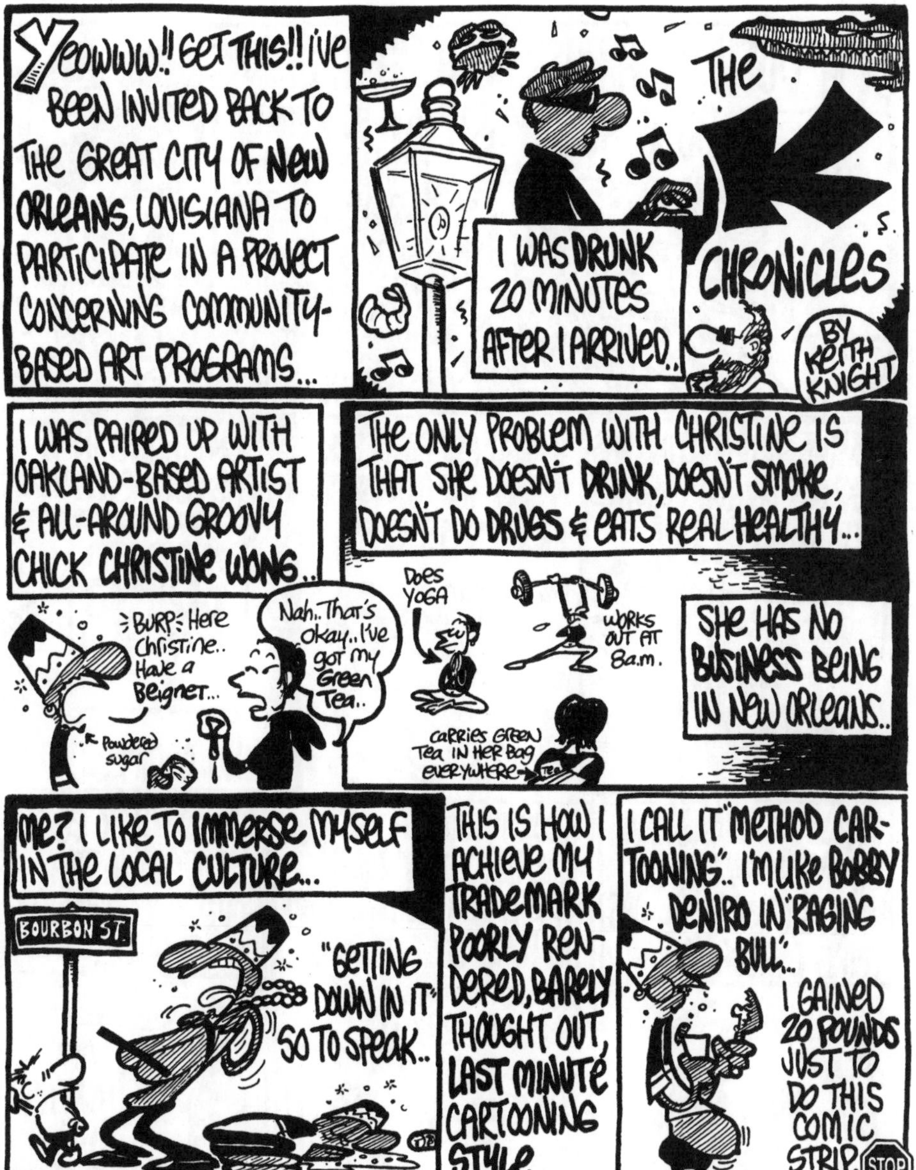
YEOWWW!! GET THIS!! I'VE BEEN INVITED BACK TO THE GREAT CITY OF NEW ORLEANS, LOUISIANA TO PARTICIPATE IN A PROJECT CONCERNING COMMUNITY-BASED ART PROGRAMS...
THE K CHRONICLES
BY KEITH KNIGHT
I WAS DRUNK 20 MINUTES AFTER I ARRIVED..
I WAS PAIRED UP WITH OAKLAND-BASED ARTIST & ALL-AROUND GROOVY CHICK CHRISTINE WONG...
BURP Here Christine.. Have a Beignet...
Powdered sugar
Nah.. That's okay.. I've got my Green Tea..
THE ONLY PROBLEM WITH CHRISTINE IS THAT SHE DOESN'T DRINK, DOESN'T SMOKE, DOESN'T DO DRUGS & EATS REAL HEALTHY...
DOES YOGA
WORKS OUT AT 8a.m.
CARRIES GREEN TEA IN HER BAG EVERYWHERE
TEA
SHE HAS NO BUSINESS BEING IN NEW ORLEANS..
ME? I LIKE TO IMMERSE MYSELF IN THE LOCAL CULTURE...
BOURBON ST.
"GETTING DOWN IN IT" SO TO SPEAK...
THIS IS HOW I ACHIEVE MY TRADEMARK POORLY RENDERED, BARELY THOUGHT OUT, LAST MINUTE CARTOONING STYLE...
I CALL IT "METHOD CARTOONING".. I'M LIKE BOBBY DENIRO IN "RAGING BULL"...
I GAINED 20 POUNDS JUST TO DO THIS COMIC STRIP.
STOP

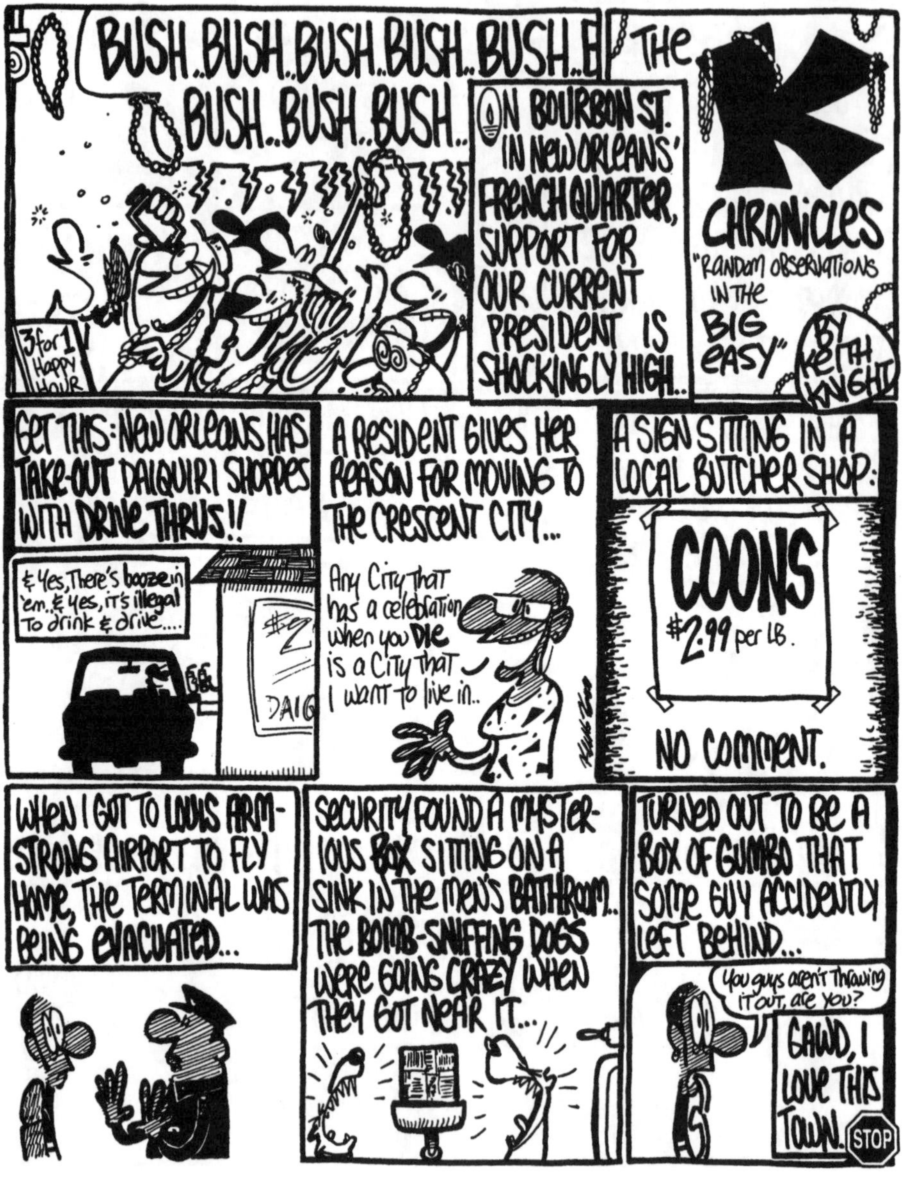
BUSH..BUSH..BUSH..BUSH..BUSH..B BUSH..BUSH..BUSH..
3 for 1 Happy Hour
ON BOURBON ST. IN NEW ORLEANS' FRENCH QUARTER, SUPPORT FOR OUR CURRENT PRESIDENT IS SHOCKINGLY HIGH..
THE K CHRONICLES
"RANDOM OBSERVATIONS IN THE BIG EASY"
BY KEITH KNIGHT
GET THIS: NEW ORLEANS HAS TAKE-OUT DAIQUIRI SHOPPES WITH DRIVE THRUS!!
& Yes, There's booze in 'em.. & yes, it's illegal to drink & drive....
DAIQ
A RESIDENT GIVES HER REASON FOR MOVING TO THE CRESCENT CITY...
Any City that has a celebration when you DIE is a City that I want to live in..
A SIGN SITTING IN A LOCAL BUTCHER SHOP:
COONS
$2.99 per LB.
NO COMMENT.
WHEN I GOT TO LOUIS ARMSTRONG AIRPORT TO FLY HOME, THE TERMINAL WAS BEING EVACUATED...
SECURITY FOUND A MYSTERIOUS BOX SITTING ON A SINK IN THE MEN'S BATHROOM.. THE BOMB-SNIFFING DOGS WERE GOING CRAZY WHEN THEY GOT NEAR IT...
TURNED OUT TO BE A BOX OF GUMBO THAT SOME GUY ACCIDENTLY LEFT BEHIND...
You guys aren't Throwing it out, are you?
GAWD, I LOVE THIS TOWN.
STOP

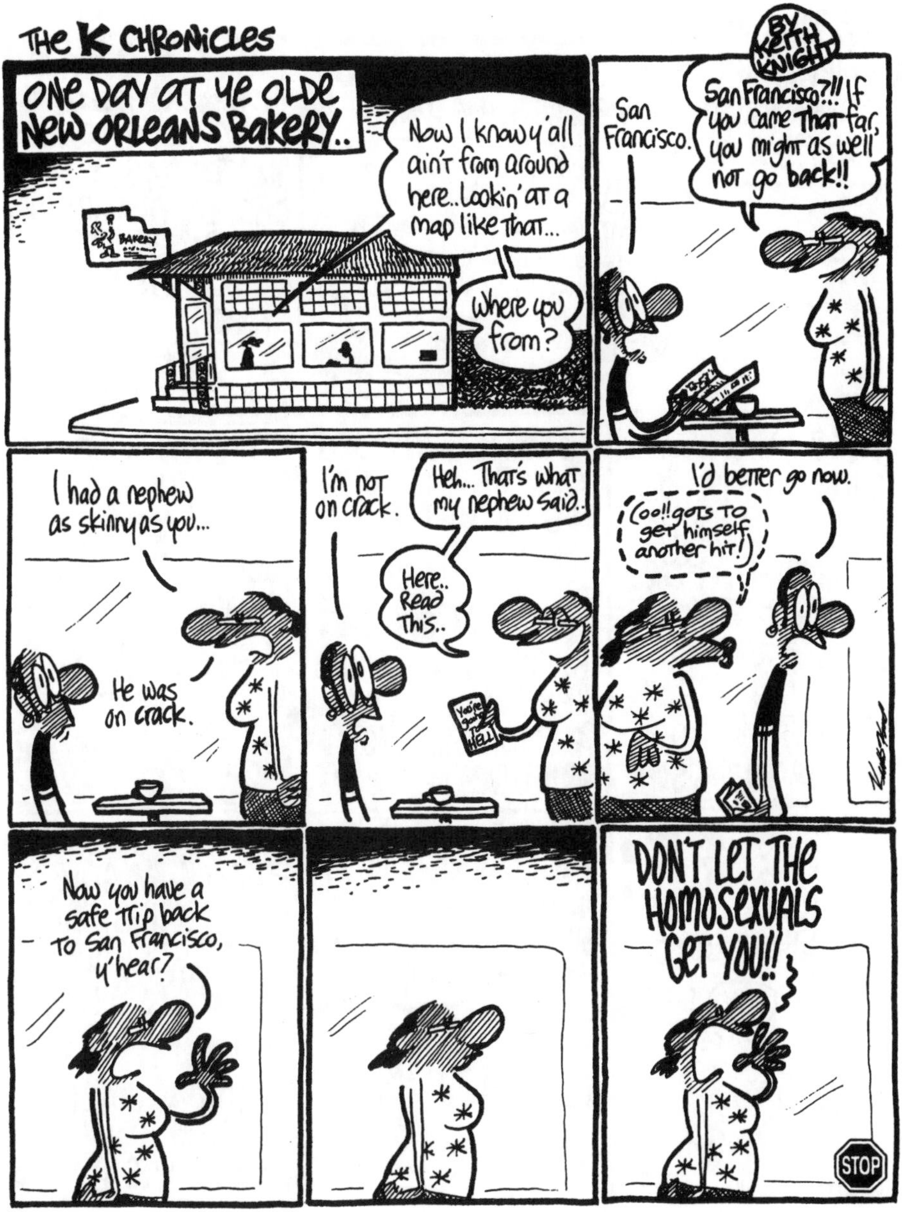
THE K CHRONICLES
BY KEITH KNIGHT
ONE DAY AT YE OLDE NEW ORLEANS BAKERY..
Now I know y'all ain't from around here..Lookin' at a map like that...
Where you from?
San Francisco.
San Francisco?!! If you came that far, you might as well not go back!!
I had a nephew as skinny as you...
He was on crack.
I'm not on crack.
Heh... That's what my nephew said.
Here.. Read This..
I'd better go now.
(oo!! gots to get himself another hit!)
Now you have a safe trip back to San Francisco, y'hear?
DON'T LET THE HOMOSEXUALS GET YOU!!
STOP

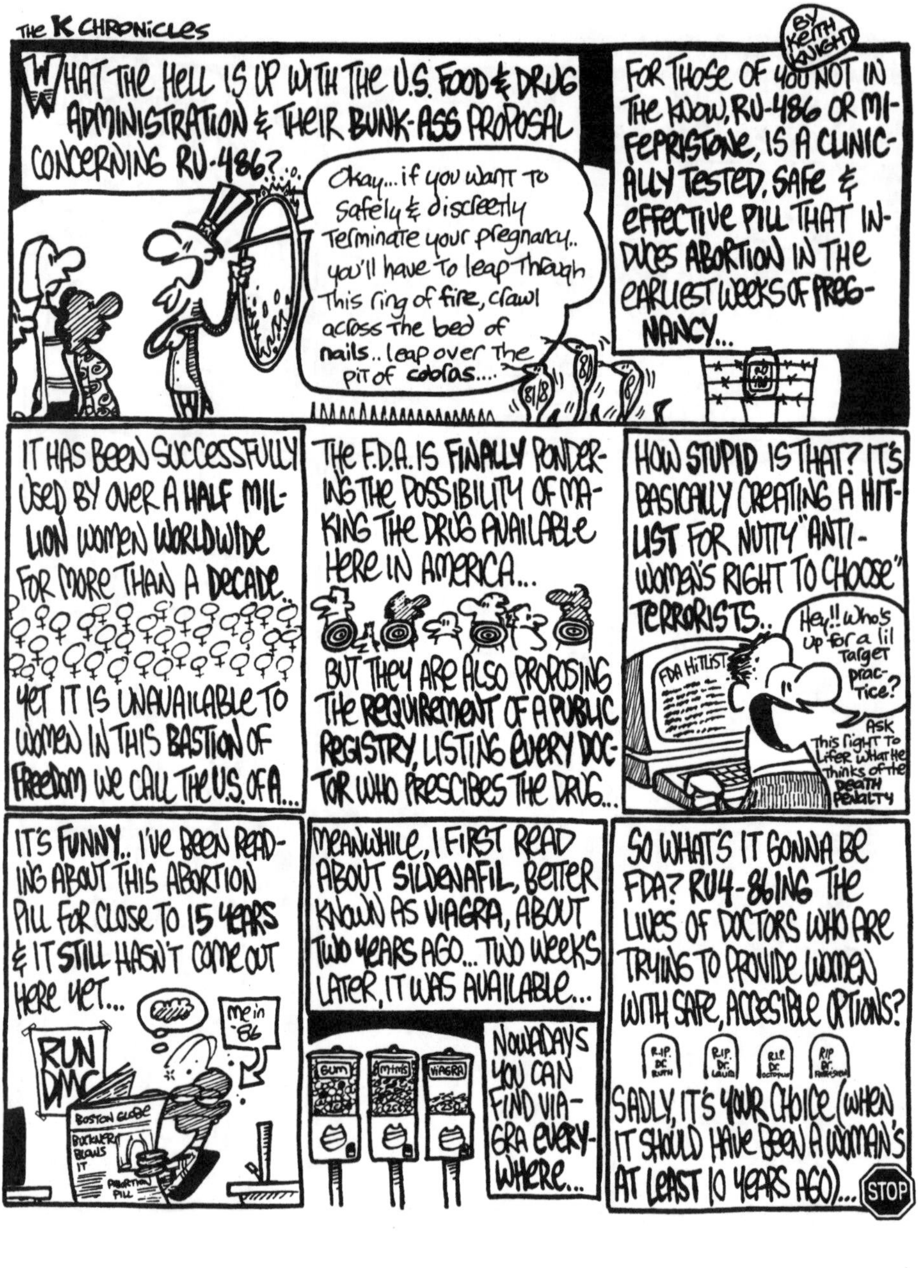
THE K CHRONICLES
BY KEITH KNIGHT
WHAT THE HELL IS UP WITH THE U.S. FOOD & DRUG ADMINISTRATION & THEIR BUNK-ASS PROPOSAL CONCERNING RU-486?
Okay... if you want to safely & discreetly terminate your pregnancy.. you'll have to leap through this ring of fire, crawl across the bed of nails.. leap over the pit of cobras....
FOR THOSE OF YOU NOT IN THE KNOW, RU-486 OR MIFEPRISTONE, IS A CLINICALLY TESTED, SAFE & EFFECTIVE PILL THAT INDUCES ABORTION IN THE EARLIEST WEEKS OF PREGNANCY...
IT HAS BEEN SUCCESSFULLY USED BY OVER A HALF MILLION WOMEN WORLDWIDE FOR MORE THAN A DECADE...
YET IT IS UNAVAILABLE TO WOMEN IN THIS BASTION OF FREEDOM WE CALL THE U.S. OF A...
THE F.D.A. IS FINALLY PONDERING THE POSSIBILITY OF MAKING THE DRUG AVAILABLE HERE IN AMERICA...
BUT THEY ARE ALSO PROPOSING THE REQUIREMENT OF A PUBLIC REGISTRY, LISTING EVERY DOCTOR WHO PRESCIBES THE DRUG...
HOW STUPID IS THAT? IT'S BASICALLY CREATING A HIT-LIST FOR NUTTY "ANTI-WOMEN'S RIGHT TO CHOOSE" TERRORISTS..
FDA HITLIST
Hey!! Who's up for a lil target practice?
ASK this right to lifer what he thinks of the DEATH PENALTY
IT'S FUNNY.. I'VE BEEN READING ABOUT THIS ABORTION PILL FOR CLOSE TO 15 YEARS & IT STILL HASN'T COME OUT HERE YET...
me in '86
RUN DMC
BOSTON GLOBE
BUCKNER BLOWS IT
ABORTION PILL
MEANWHILE, I FIRST READ ABOUT SILDENAFIL, BETTER KNOWN AS VIAGRA, ABOUT TWO YEARS AGO... TWO WEEKS LATER, IT WAS AVAILABLE...
GUM
MINTS
VIAGRA
NOWADAYS YOU CAN FIND VIAGRA EVERYWHERE...
SO WHAT'S IT GONNA BE FDA? RU4-86ING THE LIVES OF DOCTORS WHO ARE TRYING TO PROVIDE WOMEN WITH SAFE, ACCESIBLE OPTIONS?
SADLY, IT'S YOUR CHOICE (WHEN IT SHOULD HAVE BEEN A WOMAN'S AT LEAST 10 YEARS AGO)...
STOP

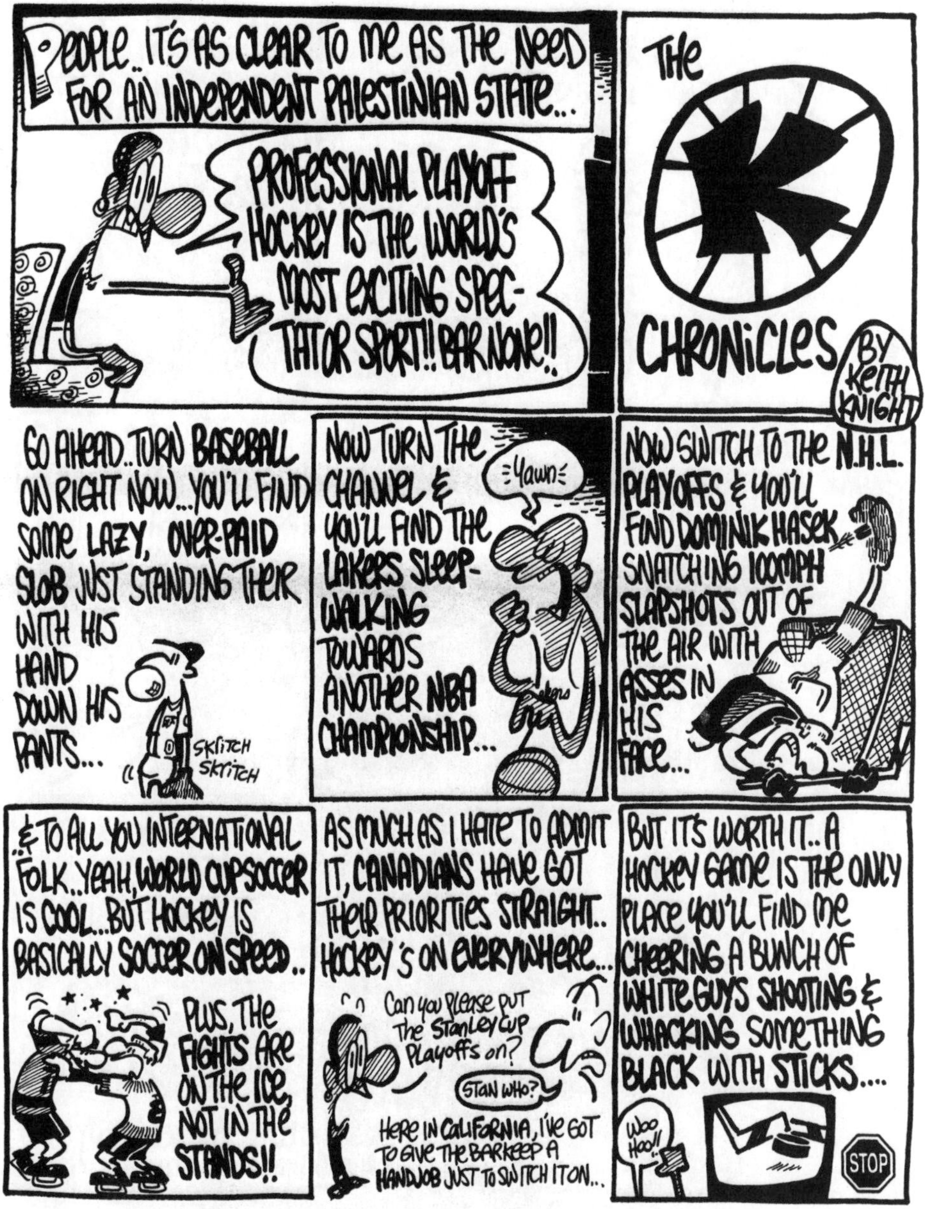
PEOPLE.. IT'S AS CLEAR TO ME AS THE NEED FOR AN INDEPENDENT PALESTINIAN STATE...
PROFESSIONAL PLAYOFF HOCKEY IS THE WORLD'S MOST EXCITING SPECTATOR SPORT!! BAR NONE!!
THE K CHRONICLES
BY KEITH KNIGHT
GO AHEAD..TURN BASEBALL ON RIGHT NOW...YOU'LL FIND SOME LAZY, OVER-PAID SLOB JUST STANDING THEIR WITH HIS HAND DOWN HIS PANTS...
SKRITCH SKRITCH
NOW TURN THE CHANNEL & YOU'LL FIND THE LAKERS SLEEP-WALKING TOWARDS ANOTHER NBA CHAMPIONSHIP...
Yawn
NOW SWITCH TO THE N.H.L. PLAYOFFS & YOU'LL FIND DOMINIK HASEK SNATCHING 100MPH SLAPSHOTS OUT OF THE AIR WITH ASSES IN HIS FACE...
..& TO ALL YOU INTERNATIONAL FOLK..YEAH, WORLD CUP SOCCER IS COOL...BUT HOCKEY IS BASICALLY SOCCER ON SPEED..
PLUS, THE FIGHTS ARE ON THE ICE, NOT IN THE STANDS!!
AS MUCH AS I HATE TO ADMIT IT, CANADIANS HAVE GOT THEIR PRIORITIES STRAIGHT.. HOCKEY'S ON EVERYWHERE...
Can you please put the Stanley Cup Playoffs on?
STAN WHO?
HERE IN CALIFORNIA, I'VE GOT TO GIVE THE BARKEEP A HANDJOB JUST TO SWITCH IT ON...
BUT IT'S WORTH IT.. A HOCKEY GAME IS THE ONLY PLACE YOU'LL FIND ME CHEERING A BUNCH OF WHITE GUYS SHOOTING & WHACKING SOMETHING BLACK WITH STICKS....
Woo Hoo!!
STOP

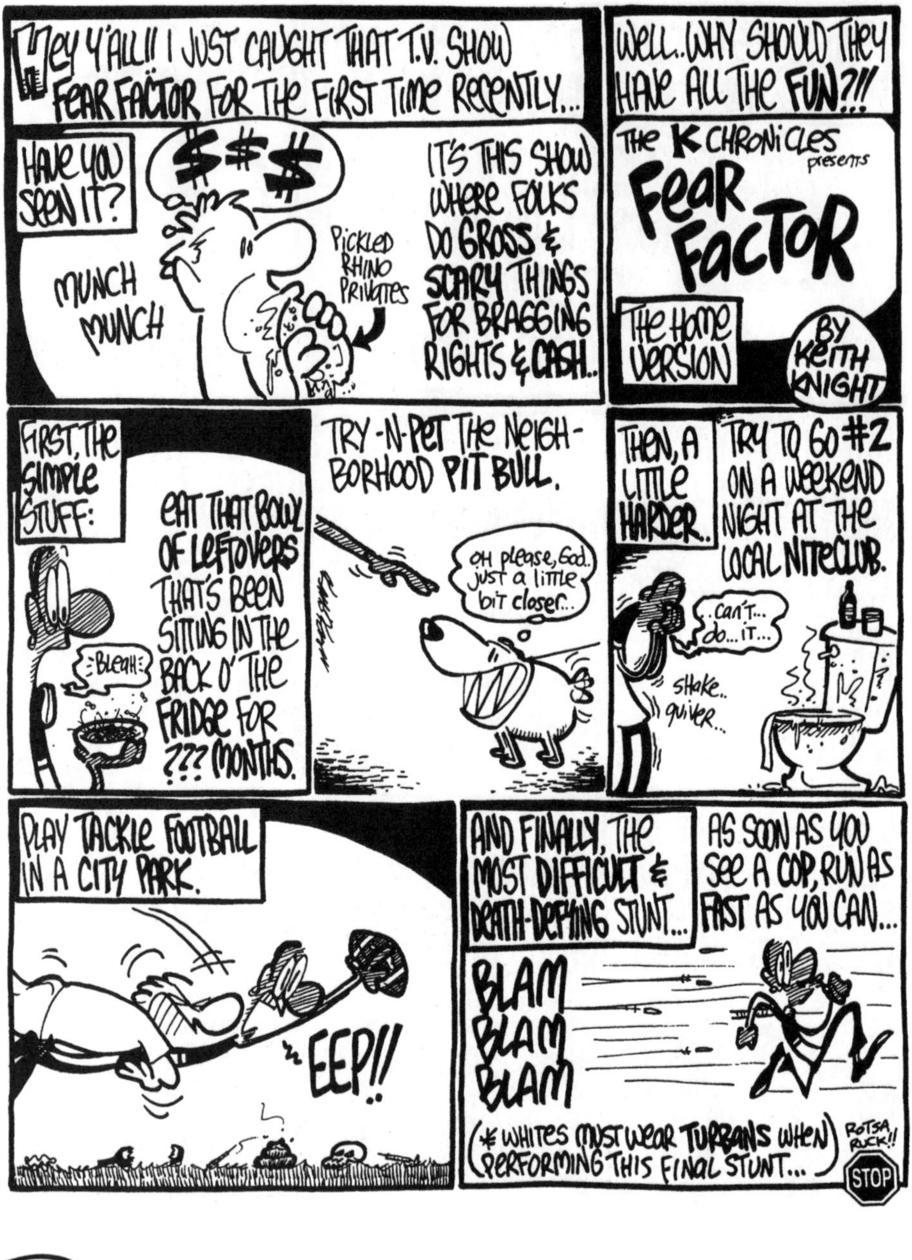

HEY Y'ALL!! I JUST CAUGHT THAT T.V. SHOW FEAR FACTOR FOR THE FIRST TIME RECENTLY...
HAVE YOU SEEN IT?
$$$
MUNCH MUNCH
PICKLED RHINO PRIVATES
IT'S THIS SHOW WHERE FOLKS DO GROSS & SCARY THINGS FOR BRAGGING RIGHTS & CASH..
WELL..WHY SHOULD THEY HAVE ALL THE FUN?!!
THE K CHRONICLES presents
FEAR FACTOR
THE HOME VERSION
BY KEITH KNIGHT
FIRST, THE SIMPLE STUFF:
EAT THAT BOWL OF LEFTOVERS THAT'S BEEN SITTING IN THE BACK O' THE FRIDGE FOR ??? MONTHS.
BLEAH
TRY-N-PET THE NEIGHBORHOOD PIT BULL.
OH please, God.. just a little bit closer...
THEN, A LITTLE HARDER..
TRY TO GO #2 ON A WEEKEND NIGHT AT THE LOCAL NITECLUB.
..can't... do...IT...
shake.. quiver...
PLAY TACKLE FOOTBALL IN A CITY PARK.
EEP!!
AND FINALLY, THE MOST DIFFICULT & DEATH-DEFYING STUNT...
AS SOON AS YOU SEE A COP, RUN AS FAST AS YOU CAN...
BLAM BLAM BLAM BLAM
(* WHITES MUST WEAR TURBANS WHEN PERFORMING THIS FINAL STUNT...)
ROTSA RUCK!!
STOP

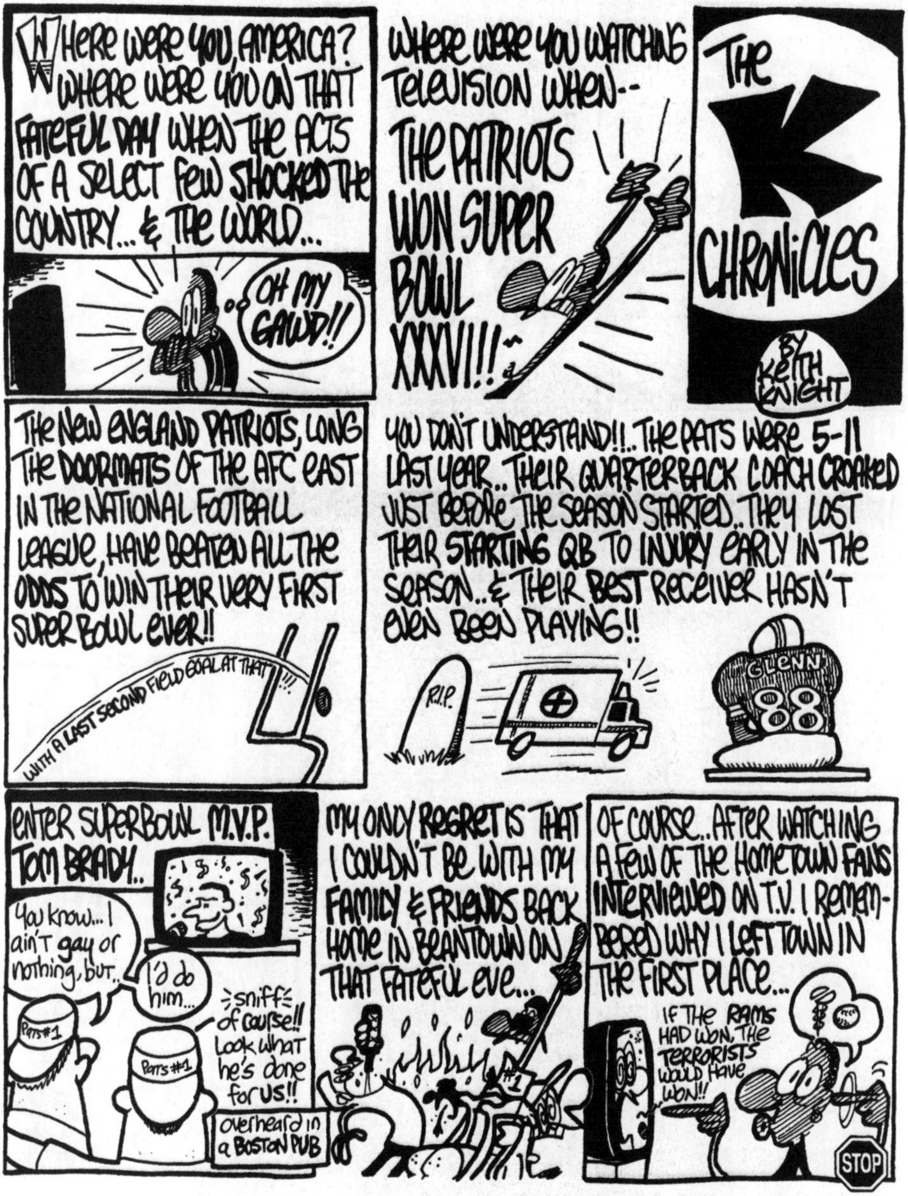
WHERE WERE YOU, AMERICA? WHERE WERE YOU ON THAT FATEFUL DAY WHEN THE ACTS OF A SELECT FEW SHOCKED THE COUNTRY... & THE WORLD...
OH MY GAWD!!
WHERE WERE YOU WATCHING TELEVISION WHEN--
THE PATRIOTS WON SUPER BOWL XXXVI!!!
THE K CHRONICLES
BY KEITH KNIGHT
THE NEW ENGLAND PATRIOTS, LONG THE DOORMATS OF THE AFC EAST IN THE NATIONAL FOOTBALL LEAGUE, HAVE BEATEN ALL THE ODDS TO WIN THEIR VERY FIRST SUPER BOWL EVER!!
WITH A LAST SECOND FIELD GOAL AT THAT!!!
YOU DON'T UNDERSTAND!!.. THE PATS WERE 5-11 LAST YEAR.. THEIR QUARTERBACK COACH CROAKED JUST BEFORE THE SEASON STARTED.. THEY LOST THEIR STARTING QB TO INJURY EARLY IN THE SEASON.. & THEIR BEST RECEIVER HASN'T EVEN BEEN PLAYING!!
R.I.P.
GLENN
88
ENTER SUPERBOWL M.V.P. TOM BRADY..
You know... I ain't gay or nothing, but...
I'd do him...
sniff!! of course!! Look what he's done for US!!
PATS #1
PATS #1
overheard in a BOSTON PUB
MY ONLY REGRET IS THAT I COULDN'T BE WITH MY FAMILY & FRIENDS BACK HOME IN BEANTOWN ON THAT FATEFUL EVE...
#1
OF COURSE.. AFTER WATCHING A FEW OF THE HOMETOWN FANS INTERVIEWED ON T.V. I REMEMBERED WHY I LEFT TOWN IN THE FIRST PLACE...
IF THE RAMS HAD WON, THE TERRORISTS WOULD HAVE WON!!
STOP

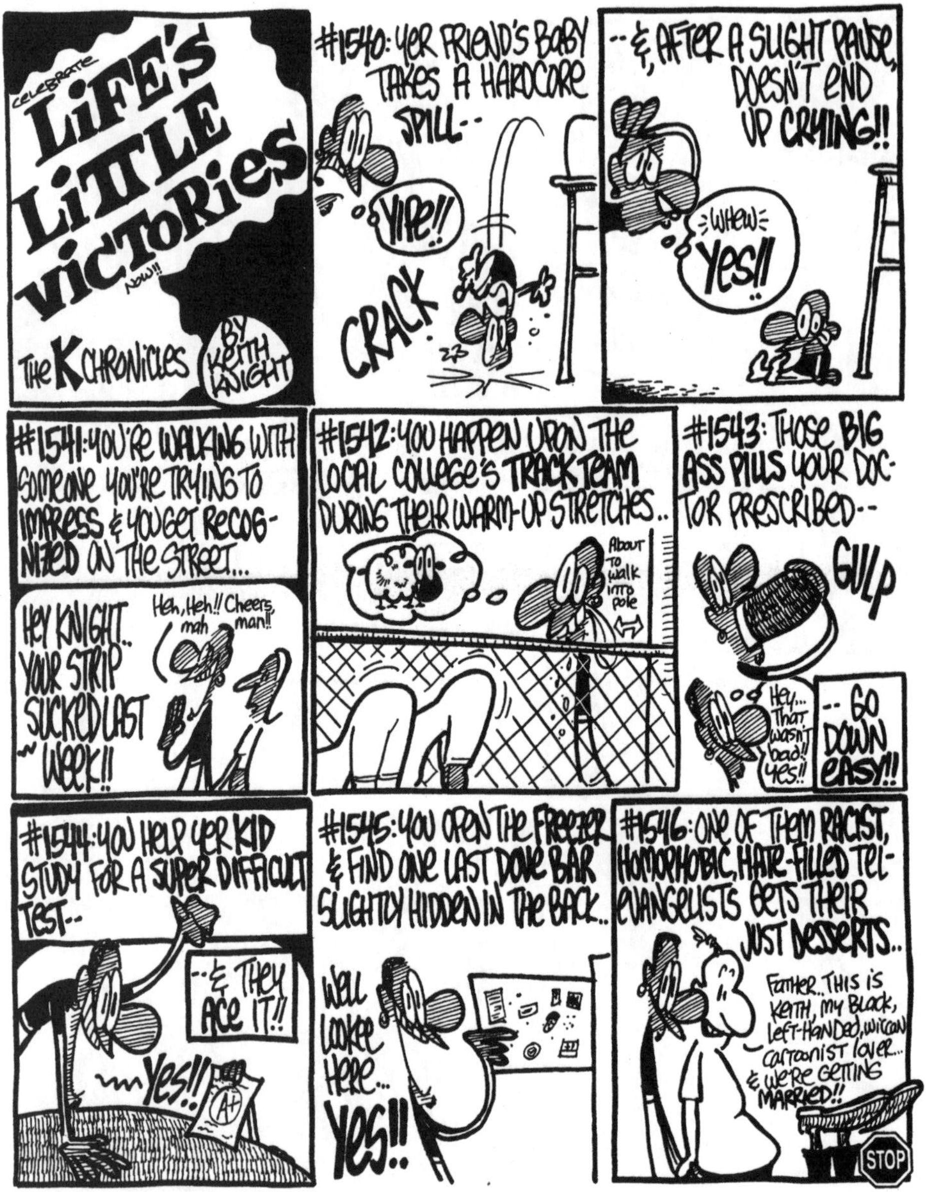

Celebrate LIFE'S LITTLE VICTORIES Now!!
THE K CHRONICLES
BY KEITH KNIGHT
#1540: YER FRIEND'S BABY TAKES A HARDCORE SPILL--
YIPE!!
CRACK
--& AFTER A SLIGHT PAUSE, DOESN'T END UP CRYING!!
WHEW
YES!!
#1541: YOU'RE WALKING WITH SOMEONE YOU'RE TRYING TO IMPRESS & YOU GET RECOGNIZED ON THE STREET...
HEY KNIGHT.. YOUR STRIP SUCKED LAST WEEK!!
Heh, Heh!! Cheers, mah man!!
#1542: YOU HAPPEN UPON THE LOCAL COLLEGE'S TRACK TEAM DURING THEIR WARM-UP STRETCHES...
About to walk into pole
#1543: THOSE BIG ASS PILLS YOUR DOCTOR PRESCRIBED--
GULP
Hey... That wasn't bad!! Yes!!
-- GO DOWN EASY!!
#1544: YOU HELP YER KID STUDY FOR A SUPER DIFFICULT TEST--
--& THEY ACE IT!!
YES!!
A+
#1545: YOU OPEN THE FREEZER & FIND ONE LAST DOVE BAR SLIGHTLY HIDDEN IN THE BACK...
WELL LOOKEE HERE...
YES!!
#1546: ONE OF THEM RACIST, HOMOPHOBIC, HATE-FILLED TELEVANGELISTS GETS THEIR JUST DESSERTS..
FATHER.. THIS IS KEITH, MY BLACK, LEFT-HANDED, WICCAN CARTOONIST LOVER... & WE'RE GETTING MARRIED!!
STOP

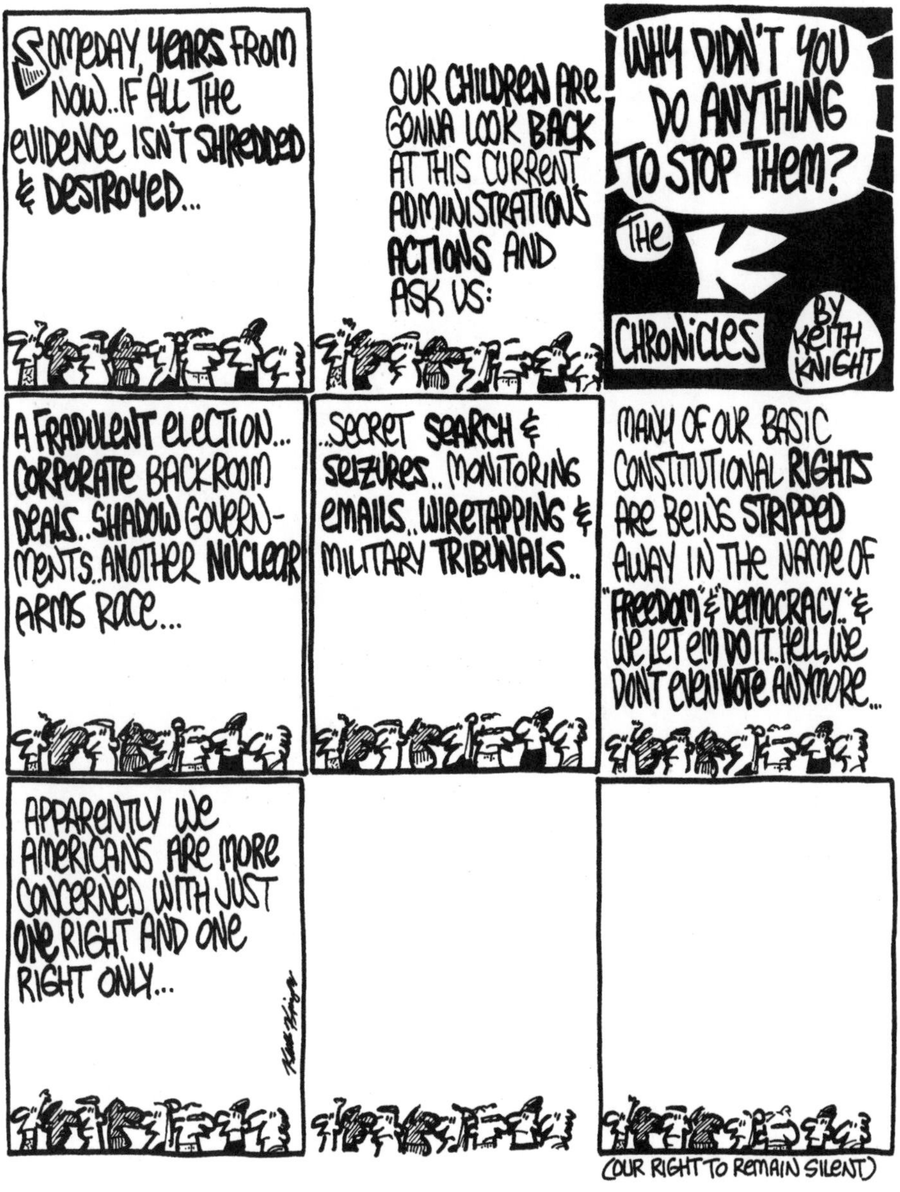
SOMEDAY, YEARS FROM NOW.. IF ALL THE EVIDENCE ISN'T SHREDDED & DESTROYED...
OUR CHILDREN ARE GONNA LOOK BACK AT THIS CURRENT ADMINISTRATION'S ACTIONS AND ASK US:
WHY DIDN'T YOU DO ANYTHING TO STOP THEM?
THE K CHRONICLES
BY KEITH KNIGHT
A FRADULENT ELECTION... CORPORATE BACKROOM DEALS.. SHADOW GOVERN-MENTS.. ANOTHER NUCLEAR ARMS RACE...
...SECRET SEARCH & SEIZURES.. MONITORING EMAILS.. WIRETAPPING & MILITARY TRIBUNALS..
MANY OF OUR BASIC CONSTITUTIONAL RIGHTS ARE BEING STRIPPED AWAY IN THE NAME OF "FREEDOM" & "DEMOCRACY.." & WE LET EM DO IT.. HELL, WE DON'T EVEN VOTE ANYMORE...
APPARENTLY WE AMERICANS ARE MORE CONCERNED WITH JUST ONE RIGHT AND ONE RIGHT ONLY...
(OUR RIGHT TO REMAIN SILENT)